Flying Wisdom:
The Proficient Pilot

Volume 3

Also by Barry Schiff

Flight 902 is Down!*

The Vatican Target*

Golden Science Guide to Flying

The Boeing 707

All About Flying

Basic Meteorology

The Pilot's Digest

The Proficient Pilot, Volume 1

The Proficient Pilot, Volume 2

Air Navigation**

*in collaboration
**in progress

Flying Wisdom

The Proficient Pilot Volume 3

Barry Schiff

Foreword by R.A. "Bob" Hoover

Aviation Supplies & Academics, Inc.
Newcastle, Washington

Flying Wisdom: The Proficient Pilot, Volume 3
by Barry Schiff

Aviation Supplies & Academics, Inc.
7005 132nd Place SE
Newcastle, Washington 98059-3153

Many of the tables and illustrations in this book appear courtesy of *AOPA Pilot*.

Published 1997 by Aviation Supplies & Academics, Inc.

Printed in the United States of America

9   8   7   6   5   4   3   2

ASA-PP3
ISBN 1-56027-283-X

Library of Congress Catalog Card Number: 94-14249

Dedication

For Kathy,
My wife, the pilgrim soul...
Next year in Jerusalem,
Where it all began.

Contents

Section 3　Turbine Operations

Section 4　Personal Observations

Acknowledgments

People acquire most of their knowledge from others. In this respect, no man is an island. Similarly, what has been written on these pages consists primarily of a distillation of flying wisdom gleaned from others during my aviation career. Crediting each of these individuals is not possible because I would need to include everyone with whom I have shared a cockpit. In one way or another, each has contributed to my aeronautical education. And for this I am genuinely grateful.

My deepest appreciation is extended to those directly involved with the creation of this book: Paul Blackman, Art Davis, Bart Everett, Hal Fishman, Eleanor Friede, Jack Norris, Wally Roberts, Rob Sacks, Perry Schreffler, Stephen Singleton, and Norman Schuyler. Their efforts on my behalf have been invaluable.

Barry Schiff
Los Angeles, California

Foreword

Captain Barry Schiff has some invaluable experience that he'd like to share with you.

This third volume in his *Proficient Pilot* series goes beyond the captivating and outpouring of flying knowledge and expert tips packed into Barry's first two volumes. This time around, he gets personal; you'll learn about a veteran flier's thought processes as well as his gut reactions.

And the combination can do you a world of good.

Barry's *Flying Wisdom* is a combination of straightforward, no-nonsense advice about how to fly the airplane proficiently. He employs such simple logic that you'll easily absorb each lesson and retain it for future use. It's a deep contemplation of both the conscious and subconscious decisions made during flight.

Some of the wisdom contained in these pages has evolved from a lifetime habit of considering principles, mechanics, and—most significantly— human factors. Barry is an extraordinary teacher, because he plants himself squarely in your place as he writes about what he knows so well. He combines his experience as a veteran airline captain with his equally vast experience as a general aviation pilot and flight instructor to share the trade secrets he has learned along the way. Great communicators know how to get under your skin, how to get the facts to stick to your ribs. This is some of the most effective pilot-to-pilot talk you'll find in a book. It ought to be required reading for all pilots.

Barry's insights bring life to the subjects we studied in ground school by teaching how to take advantage of these lessons during our everyday flights. Imagine what it would be like if Ben Franklin—who was a great teacher— could talk about electricity to electricians. Barry is also one of those who possess a deep understanding of his subject and knows how to get it across to others.

I can't wait for you to begin reading, so take a look at some of what's covered: Those interested in advanced material will find Barry's section on flying jet airplanes so comprehensive that it is virtually an independent course of study, which includes enlightening discussions about Mach airspeed, high-altitude meteorology and operational considerations, all in his inimitable and entertaining style.

Learn the anatomy and hazards of a skidding turn, the myth of the downwind turn, and how (and how not) to cope with an open door in flight. Black-hole approaches at night is a misunderstood subject that is illuminated under Barry's advice, and to gain invaluable lessons about pilot error (and our susceptibility to it), read Chapter 9 very carefully. Learn about what causes deep stalls and how to avoid getting that far into trouble.

So much of this book is just plain common sense, especially Barry's section dealing with his personal observations. In this section you're *really* in there, flying *with* him, thinking about issues, questioning what you're doing, weighing every experience. The challenge offered here is this: to use every bit of your own personal resources, through reading the wisdom of Barry's experience, to deal with "destinationitis," complacency, poor judgment, expectations vs. reality, fatigue, pilot errors, survival, and how to escape the grip of a killer downdraft.

And these are a few of the highlights. Just take a look at the table of contents to see what a wide spectrum is covered in this book.

Barry saves some of my favorite subjects for last, interesting chapters that discuss how to build flying time by towing gliders, towing banners, and flying on skis. And then, as a special bonus, he describes some of his most memorable and heartwarming flights.

Read on and benefit from the wisdom of a veteran aviator who wants to share his thoughts, his feelings, and even his cockpit. You'll be thankful for the opportunity.

R.A. "Bob" Hoover

Section 1

Pilot Proficiency

A proficient pilot earns an advanced degree of competence mainly through practice and experience. But a depth of knowledge and an understanding of how to operate an aircraft can originate from a variety of sources. This book is one such source, a distillation of much of what I have learned during a lifetime of diligent study and more than 25,000 hours in the air.

Chapter 1 **The Danger of Skidding Turns**

My first instructor was somewhat of a sadist. Sitting in the back seat of the Aeronca Champ, he would take great delight in swatting me on the back of the head with a rolled-up sectional. I could expect to get clobbered whenever I failed to maintain glide speed during a landing approach and whenever I allowed the slip-skid ball to wander off-center, which seemingly was every time I entered or recovered from a turn. Mike taught me how to make coordinated turns all right, but he never did teach me why it was so important.

Most slips and skids are unnoticeable indiscretions. At other times, they are minor annoyances. But every once in a while, they kill people.

One of the most dangerous and insidious forms of uncoordinated flight is the inadvertent low-altitude skidding turn. It occurs most often in the traffic pattern, when turning from a close-in base leg to a relatively short final approach.

The scenario typically begins when a pilot incorrectly perceives an excess of airspeed while on base leg, a sensation most often caused by a tailwind that increases groundspeed while on base. A similar groundspeed increase also occurs while in the traffic pattern at high density altitudes and is the result of true airspeed being significantly greater than indicated airspeed.

In either event, or perhaps as a result of both, the pilot peripherally senses the increased groundspeed and subconsciously interprets this as excessive airspeed. Without so much as a glance at his airspeed indicator, he responds by applying back-pressure to the control wheel and raising the nose. Airspeed begins to wane. A similar speed bleed occurs when a pilot low on altitude misguidedly attempts to stretch his glide by raising the nose.

The second factor of the low-altitude skidding turn is introduced while turning from base leg to final approach. If the aircraft is being pushed along base leg by a tailwind, the turn onto final will take more room and consequently must be started sooner than usual.

A close-in base leg also necessitates turning earlier onto final approach. A pilot might ordinarily begin turning final when viewing the approach end of the runway at his 10 o'clock position, for example. But when flying a tight pattern, the same turn must begin sooner, when the runway is at the 11 o'clock position.

Often, however, the pilot is unaware of the need to begin turning so soon. As a result, the aircraft overshoots final. But if final approach is relatively short, the turn must be much steeper than usual to align the aircraft on final while there still is enough time, distance, and altitude to do so. Many pilots, however, are ground shy; they are apprehensive about making steep turns near the ground, an ordinarily healthy attitude. As a result, the turn onto final approach may be too shallow.

Shallow bank angles, however, result in low turn rates. If the aircraft does not turn rapidly enough to become aligned with the runway, a pilot reluctant to steepen the bank might instead and unwittingly apply bottom rudder to help the nose come around. Applying bottom rudder causes the bank to steepen, which is what the pilot wanted to avoid in the first place. Overbanking due to rudder input is a result of the outer wing being given more airspeed, and hence more lift, than the inner wing. To counter the increasing bank angle, the pilot then applies opposite aileron, which places the aircraft in a skidding, cross-controlled turn. (The most extreme skidding turn is called a flat turn; yaw is induced with rudder while opposite aileron is applied to maintain a wings-level attitude.) Because bottom rudder also causes the nose to drop somewhat, the pilot may offset this by pulling back on the control wheel, which causes a further erosion of airspeed.

An interesting aspect of a skidding turn is that the nose always points inside the turn. (During a slipping turn, the nose points outside the turn.) As a result, a pilot may perceive that the airplane is turning faster than it really is. The rate of turn, however, is less. This is because a rudder usually is not powerful enough to turn an airplane rapidly. High turn rates are best accomplished in a conventional manner using the horizontal component of lift from a banked wing.

Assume that the pilot is in a skidding left turn and, therefore, is applying left rudder and right aileron. Applying right aileron creates adverse yaw effect that causes the nose to yaw left even further. Every pilot knows that adverse yaw effect causes the airplane to yaw opposite to the direction in which the airplane is being rolled. But is there such a thing as *proverse* yaw, a force that yaws the airplane in the same direction as the roll? Yes, some sophisticated aircraft have exhibited this tendency. Fighter pilots claim that proverse yaw is beneficial while dogfighting because the nose moves a bit more rapidly in the direction of the roll and makes sighting a target a bit easier.

All of this skidding means that the airplane is flying somewhat sideways, which adds substantial drag. This reduces glide performance and may cause the pilot—in another misguided attempt to stretch the glide—to raise the nose and decrease airspeed even further.

Moving the control wheel or stick to the right while in a left skidding turn means that the left aileron is deflected downward. And this has the effect of increasing the angle of attack of the left, or inside, wing. Conversely, the right aileron is deflected upward, which decreases the angle of attack of the outside wing. The lowered aileron increases the lift coefficient of that wing, but it also reduces the angle of attack at which the wing will stall. The raised aileron on the outside wing decreases the lift coefficient of that wing but increases its critical angle of attack.

In other words, if the nose is raised sufficiently during a cross-controlled, skidding turn, the inside wing will stall well ahead of the outside wing.

Such an asymmetric stall most often occurs with the nose below the horizon. Unfortunately, modern training methods do not adequately prepare a pilot to anticipate stalling in such a nose-low attitude. Instead, stalls normally are associated only with an exaggerated nose-high attitude. And because the airplane is skidding, the nature of the stall is going to be somewhat different than is ordinarily expected. During conventional stalls in a typical general aviation aircraft, the stall usually begins at the trailing edge of the wing root and spreads, or propagates, forward and outboard (spanwise) as the stall deepens. As a result, the outboard wing panels often do not stall at all. This provides a measure of stability to the stall and explains why airplanes usually tend not to roll right or left during power-off stalls.

But during skidding flight, the stall tends to begin in the vicinity of the wing tip of the inside wing, a characteristic similar to that of a swept wing. The result is a loss of roll stability, an increase in stall speed, and a more abrupt stall. (The inside wing behaves like a swept wing because the relative wind during a skidding turn does not come from straight ahead. Instead, it comes from the right during a left skidding turn, and vice versa.) The airflow about the aircraft during skidding flight might also allow a stall to occur without warning. This is because one wing can stall without activating the stall warning indicator or causing the tail to buffet.

When the left wing does stall, the aircraft obviously rolls left. This occurs not only because of the loss of lift, but because the right wing is still flying and wants to rise. The combination of one wing stalling and the other lifting can produce an impressive roll rate. But as the left wing drops, its angle of attack increases even more because the relative wind is now coming more from beneath the wing. Conversely, the angle of attack of the right wing decreases during roll entry, which protects it against stalling. In other words, the roll rate increases further. Do not forget, however, that the pilot in this scenario is simultaneously holding left rudder. He also is holding right aileron, which results in adverse yaw effect that acts in the same direction as the rudder. These yaw forces combine to produce a powerful pro-spin force. A pilot could not enter a spin more perfectly if he had planned on it from the beginning. The rest of the spin generally continues unabated until the earth rises sufficiently to put an end to things.

Interestingly, adding power while in the left turn typical of most traffic patterns can compound the problem unless other corrective measures are taken. This is because the p-factor that occurs when the wing of a single-engine aircraft is at high angles of attack produces another yawing force that acts in the direction of spin entry.

Aircraft most likely to spin out of a skidding turn are those with significant elevator and rudder effectiveness and substantial adverse yaw effect.

Spins resulting from skidding turns in the traffic pattern usually begin at such low altitudes that the aircraft seldom has enough room within which to begin revolving in the classical manner of a fully developed spin. Instead, aircraft often crash during what test pilots refer to as the departure phase of spin entry. This is the uncommanded motion of an aircraft that occurs between a stall and the time that a spin becomes recognizable.

Those fortunate enough to have survived such an accident usually do not realize that they have been victims of an incipient spin. This is because impact often occurs before the development of significant rotation. Instead, the aircraft seems to have simply mushed into the ground. Inspection of the wreckage and accident site, however, often reveals that the accident was caused by spin entry.

Although low-altitude skidding turns can be lethal, they are easily avoidable. Avoid extremely tight traffic patterns and final approaches that are less than a quarter-mile long. Develop an awareness of cross-controlling. If you find yourself applying rudder one way and aileron the other, release the controls and recover using a coordinated effort, particularly at low altitude. Never force the issue. If unusual measures are required to complete an approach, consider going around.

The next time you plan to practice stalls, hire a competent instructor to demonstrate how an airplane can be made to stall with the nose on or below the horizon. Only then can you fully appreciate how lethal and insidious a low-altitude skidding turn can be.

Chapter 2 **Coping With an Open Door in Flight**

A door popping open at liftoff can be a startling, unnerving experience. The takeoff sequence is interrupted by what can sound like a small explosion followed by a loud, steady onslaught of air and engine noise. Although an open door rarely is critical—most airplanes fly sufficiently well even if a door blows off—a pilot's reaction to it often is.

Even experienced pilots fall victim to the distraction caused by an open door, resulting in numerous fatal accidents every year. Most of these occur because the pilots involved become more concerned with the open door than maintaining control of the airplane, classic examples of how distraction leads to disaster.

A pilot usually can cope with the problem by focusing his attention on maintaining control of the aircraft irrespective of distractive noises and passenger reaction. This is best summarized by the expression, "aviate, navigate, communicate." During any emergency, a pilot's first obligation is to aviate, to concentrate on flying the aircraft in a safe, professional manner despite any distractions that may exist.

A door popping open during takeoff most often occurs because of improper latching. On rare occasions, it is the result of a failed latch. As the aircraft gathers speed, air flowing past the door creates a low-pressure area that attempts to pull the door open. This is particularly true of curved doors, which behave like cambered airfoils. Everything else being equal, therefore, curved doors pop open at lower speeds than do flat doors. Additionally, doors situated above a low wing are influenced by low pressure above the wing and tend to get "sucked" open at lower speeds than doors situated beneath a high wing.

Regardless of door shape and location, doors that open usually do so as the aircraft is rotated during liftoff. In the case of low-wing aircraft, this is partially due to a sudden increase in wing lift that occurs as the angle of attack is increased. More significantly, when the angle of attack is increased, airflow pushes underneath the overhanging bottom edge of an unsecured door.

When a door pops open, a pilot has two options. The first is to abort the takeoff, but only if sufficient runway remains to do so safely. The other option is to continue the takeoff and climb to a safe altitude. At such a time, the pilot must concentrate on flying the airplane. Aviate first; everything else can wait. Ignore the open door and maintain control as if nothing had happened. (This, of course, may be easier said than done, especially at night or during an IFR departure.)

In most cases, an open door is like a dog that is all bark and no bite. There are, however, some effects that should be anticipated:

- The substantial air noise creates the illusion of excess airspeed. Do not raise the nose unnecessarily.
- Increased airflow in the cabin can raise dust. Aeronautical charts and other important items might get sucked out.
- Although the door usually trails open only a few inches, passengers might be anxious about it opening further. Some may fear falling or being sucked out of the aircraft. Allay fears by advising that the door will not open further because of the blast of air pushing against it and that leaving the aircraft would be difficult even if they tried to do so. (This, of course, would not necessarily be true at the moment a door pops open during pressurized flight at altitude.)

The aerodynamic effects of an open door are not always predictable because airframe manufacturers are not required to flight-test their aircraft with doors ajar. Nevertheless, experience has taught that certain effects may be expected:

- An open door frequently results in some loss of climb performance due to an increase in drag. This usually is not significant unless the aircraft is underpowered to begin with (such as when operating at a high density altitude or in a twin with a failed engine). An open airstair door, however, can result in substantial loss of performance.
- If the door is situated above a wing, this could result in some loss of lift on that wing, resulting in a further decrease in climb performance and a possible tendency to roll or yaw toward the affected wing.
- If the open door is ahead of the horizontal stabilizer, this can interrupt air flowing toward the tail and result in some buffeting. This flow interruption across the stabilizer also reduces the aerodynamic downloading normally produced by the tail and could result in some tendency of the nose to pitch down. These effects are lessened or imperceptible when the door is below the tail, such as when flying aircraft with T-, cruciform-, or V-tail configurations.
- Although the combined aerodynamic effects usually are minimal (and sometimes unnoticeable), there are rare instances when an open door

results in an almost uncontrollable rolling moment and significant nose-down pitching. This has been known to occur on such aircraft as the Piper Apache and Piper Aztec. At such a time, increasing airspeed helps to improve controllability.

- An open door can interrupt air flowing past a static-pressure port and result in erratic or inaccurate altimeter, airspeed, and rate-of-climb indications. If these instruments are adversely affected, it might be prudent to use the alternate static source, if available. If this is used, however, be alert for the effects that reduced cabin pressure (caused by the open door) has on pitot-static instruments: The altimeter indicates slightly higher than actual; the airspeed indicator shows faster than actual, and momentarily, upon opening the alternate-static source, the rate-of-climb indicator indicates an excess climb rate (or reduced sink rate).

Upon reaching a safe altitude, a pilot once again is confronted with two options: attempt to close the door while airborne or return to the airport and land with the door ajar. In some cases, such as in a Cessna 152 or 172, closing the door is simple. All a pilot has to do is open the window on that door, grab the windowsill, and pull the door closed. On other aircraft, such as a Cessna 310, closing the door is much more difficult, if not impossible. If the door cannot be closed easily, a pilot often is better off landing with the door open (unless weather conditions make such a choice impossible or impractical).

If the option is taken to close the door while airborne, remember that a pilot must not allow himself to become so preoccupied with the procedure that he loses control of the aircraft, allowing a minor annoyance to become a major emergency. Under no circumstances should an attempt be made to close an airstair door unless the person making the attempt can do so while seated with a seat belt fastened snugly around him.

The following steps might be helpful when attempting to close a cabin door:

- Trim the aircraft in level flight at a relatively low airspeed, but not so low as to jeopardize safety or controllability. The idea is to reduce power as much as is practicable. This is because propwash flowing past the door tends to "suck" the door open, making it more difficult to close. It usually is much easier to close a door while gliding (if practical) than during a high-power climb.

- Closing a door in flight can be like trying to shut the door of an airtight automobile. Substantial muscle is required to overcome the buildup of air pressure that occurs within the cabin as the door is brought toward the closed position. Consequently, open a window prior to closing the door to prevent such a pressure increase. Also, close the air vents, which tend to pressurize the cabin slightly.
- Finally, grip something on the door that maximizes leverage, push the door outward as far as is possible and safe, and then give a mighty pull.
- If the attempt is unsuccessful, momentarily slip the aircraft away from the open door (a left slip, for example, reduces airflow against a right door and allows that door to be opened further prior to its being pulled closed). Then transition into a slip toward the open door and simultaneously pull it closed. (Slipping toward the door causes the relative wind to help push the door shut.)

If the door cannot be closed in flight, it most often is because a pilot cannot apply the needed leverage or is not sufficiently strong. In some instances, aerodynamic forces temporarily warp a door and prevent it from fitting into its frame, no matter how strong the pilot.

Prior to landing with an open door, it might be wise to simulate an approach and landing at altitude to determine what nasty control problems—if any—might occur during an actual landing. It is best not to be taken by surprise during a landing flare. For example, if the aircraft tends to roll at low airspeed or if elevator effectiveness is impaired, consider landing on a long runway with some excess airspeed. But do not get carried away; too much of a good thing can be dangerous.

Also before landing, ask the person seated next to the affected door to hold the door closed as much as possible during the approach and landing. This will prevent the door from opening further during the landing flare, when the angle of attack is increased and controllability is most critical. (When flying alone, it might be possible to restrain the door with seat belts.)

Improperly latched baggage-compartment doors and cowlings also can open unexpectedly. Unfortunately, these usually are inaccessible during flight. Not much can be done when one of these opens except to maintain control and land as soon as practical. The aluminum may rattle, bang, and buffet quite a bit, but this usually is another case of all bark and no bite. Remaining calm, however, can be easier said than done.

In February 1986, an experienced and well-known pilot was taking off from Coronado Airport near Albuquerque when—according to witnesses—

the baggage door on the right side of the Cessna 421C's nose popped open. Apparently intending to return for landing, the pilot continued the climb-out and turned onto the downwind leg at what was estimated to be 700 feet above ground level. A moment or so later, the cabin-class twin was observed in a steep bank and descending rapidly. It crashed into a wooded area near the airport and was immediately engulfed in flame. The pilot and all five passengers perished.

Based on witnesses' statements and the positions of certain engine controls, investigators concluded later that the pilot had reduced power on the right engine. It seems as though he had intended to shut down the right engine to prevent damage that he apparently feared might have occurred had loose objects in the baggage compartment become dislodged and blown into the propeller disc. Instead of feathering the right propeller, however, the pilot feathered the left propeller at a time when the left engine was developing substantial power. This accident is particularly tragic because—according to Cessna—the 421C can be flown easily with the nose baggage door open, noise and vibration notwithstanding. At the risk of being repetitious, the first priority is to aviate: Maintain composure and fly the airplane.

In its handbook titled Pilot Safety and Warning Supplements, Cessna goes on to say that nose baggage doors tend to close at high speed and gently open again as speed is reduced for landing. The pilot, however, is advised to avoid abrupt maneuvers that could throw loose objects out of the nose compartment and into the propeller. Furthermore, the handbook adds, a top-hinged baggage door on the side of the aft fuselage of a high-wing airplane can sometimes be moved to a nearly closed position by fully extending the flaps so that wing down-wash will act upon the door. Also, front-hinged wing locker doors in the aft part of the engine nacelle of Cessna twins "will likely trail open a few inches if they become unlatched. Just prior to touchdown, an unlatched locker door may momentarily float to an extreme open position."

It should be obvious that most incidents and accidents caused by doors popping open could have been prevented by paying more attention to securing them before departure. Here are some additional considerations:

- Door latching mechanisms often are taken for granted. Be certain to learn their idiosyncrasies, especially when checking out in new aircraft.
- Do not allow passengers to secure cabin doors and baggage compartments. This is the responsibility of the pilot in command and should never be delegated to someone not properly trained and qualified.

- Passengers must be briefed before departure about how to operate door-latching mechanisms. In case of a crash landing, for example, an unconscious pilot would not be able to direct an evacuation.
- Do not lock baggage doors that could be used by ground personnel to rescue trapped or unconscious occupants. (Key-locking a door, by the way, does not increase the security of the latch.)

In the final analysis, there can be only one valid reason for the inadvertent opening of a cabin or baggage door: mechanical failure of the latch. If this is the case, it should be repaired before the next flight. The next person to fly the aircraft might not be as well prepared to cope with the problem.

There are occasions when a pilot might need to fly with a door completely removed, such as when conducting operations involving sport parachuting and aerial photography. In some cases, door removal is legal and safe; in other cases, it might be illegal and highly dangerous.

To determine if a specific aircraft type may be flown with one cabin door removed, consult the FAA's Advisory Circular, Sport Parachute Jumping, which contains a list of approved aircraft. (The AC is available at any Flight Standards or General Aviation District Office.) If the aircraft in question is listed in the circular, a pilot may not simply remove the door and fly away. Instead, he first must request FAA approval and obtain a list of operating limitations that must be observed when flying an aircraft with a door removed:

- Maximum speed must not exceed the maneuvering speed, 70 percent of the maximum level-flight speed, or 70 percent of the maximum structural cruising speed, whichever is most restrictive.
- Aerobatic flight is not permitted.
- Maximum allowable yaw and bank angles are 10 and 15 degrees, respectively.
- An approved safety belt shall be provided and worn by each occupant during takeoff and landing and at all other times when required by the pilot in command in the interest of safety.
- Smoking shall not be permitted.
- All loose articles shall be tied down or stowed.
- No baggage shall be carried.
- Operations shall be limited to VFR conditions.
- The aircraft shall not be operated in solo flight by the holder of a student pilot certificate.

- When operations other than intentional parachute jumping and skydiving are conducted, a suitable guardrail or equivalent safety device shall be provided for the doorway.

There are a few other limitations, but most of these are applicable only to skydiving activities. Also, some of the approved aircraft require the installation of airflow deflectors to reduce vibration while being operated with a door removed.

Some aircraft not included on the FAA's list of approved aircraft may be flown with a door removed if the manufacturer publishes the required operating limitations in the FAA-approved airplane flight manual (AFM) applicable to the aircraft in question. Beech, for example, allows its B36TC Bonanza to be flown with the aft utility doors removed. In such a case, a pilot need not apply to the FAA for permission to fly the B36TC in this configuration as long as he abides by the limitations published in the AFM.

Supplemental-type certificates (STCs) have been issued that allow a few other aircraft types to be flown with a door removed. A list of these also is available from an FAA Flight Standards or General Aviation District Office (FSDO or GADO). An aircraft not approved for flight with a door removed may not be flown in this configuration without first having an engineering analysis performed with a door removed to determine if the aircraft can be operated safely.

Chapter 3 **The Black-Hole Approach**

During the 1940s, the bible for student pilots was the Civil Pilot Training Manual, published by the Civil Aeronautics Administration (the predecessor of the FAA). For its day, it was an exceptional, no-nonsense book that pulled few punches. It stated, for example, that "night flights should not be made in single-engine airplanes unless all occupants are provided with parachutes." This controversial advice seems to imply that bailing out is the preferred method of coping with an engine failure at night. Consider, however, that this was written during an era when aircraft powerplants were notoriously unreliable. (Even today, however, it must be conceded that an off-airport forced landing at night often requires more luck than skill.)

Despite claims to the contrary, night operations are still more hazardous than daylight flying because the horizon often is not visible, it is easier to become lost, optical illusions are more prevalent, and fatigue often is more of a factor. Also, obstructions and clouds may be difficult or impossible to see. Regarding this last point, consider that hundreds—if not thousands—of pilots and their passengers have collided with terrain that they never saw, even though visibility was unlimited. This is because night visibility is determined by the greatest distance that prominent lighted objects can be seen and identified. Just because a pilot can see a distant light, however, does not mean that he can see rising terrain directly in front of him on a moonless, overcast night.

Flying at night over certain areas and under certain conditions is much like instrument flying and requires similar skills, especially with respect to flight planning and the determination of minimum safe altitudes. Although obvious, it should be stated for emphasis that it is a pilot's responsibility to ensure that he is always at a sufficiently high altitude to preclude the possibility of flying headlong into unseen obstructions. This, however, can be easier said than done, particularly in the case of a long, straight-in approach to an airport at night. A subtle danger associated with some night visual approaches can lead even experienced pilots to fly at dangerously (and sometimes fatally) low approach altitudes.

When descending toward an airport during the day, a pilot uses depth perception to estimate distance to and altitude above an airport. It is relatively easy for him to descend along an approximately 3-degree (normal) visual descent profile to a distant runway. On a moonless or overcast night, however, a pilot has little or no depth perception because the necessary visual cues (color variations, shadows, and topographical references) are absent. This lack of depth perception makes it difficult to estimate altitude and distance. For example, a pilot flying 6 miles from and 2,000 feet above a runway that is 5,000 feet long and 250 feet wide sees the same "picture" through his windshield as when he is only 3 miles from and 1,000 feet above a runway that is only 2,500 feet long and 125 feet wide.

The problem is exacerbated when straight-in approaches are made over water or dark, featureless terrain on an overcast or moonless night. The only visual stimuli are distant sources of light in the vicinity of the destination airport. Such situations are often referred to as "black-hole approaches." The black hole refers not to the airport, but to the featureless darkness over which the approach is being conducted.

Over the years, the black-hole approach has claimed many lives, but it was not until 1969 that two Boeing Company engineers, Dr. Conrad L. Kraft and Dr. Charles L. Elworth, conducted an extensive study of the problem. The research program involved a specially developed visual night-approach simulator flown under various conditions by a dozen of Boeing's senior pilot-instructors. The results were published in a Boeing report titled Flight Deck Workload and Night Visual Approach Performance. Their conclusions finally explained what might have caused so many general aviation, military, and airline pilots to fly excessively low during black-hole approaches.

During the project, Kraft and Elworth had hypothesized and then confirmed that pilots executing black-hole approaches tend not to vary their descent profiles according to runway perspective as they normally do during conventional straight-in approaches. Instead, they discovered that pilots descend during such approaches while unwittingly maintaining a constant visual angle. The visual angle is the angle occupied by the destination airport (and surrounding lighting) in a pilot's vertical field of vision.

Figure 1 shows an aircraft overflying an airport at a constant altitude. At position A, the pilot looks at the airport (and its surrounding lighting). Note that at such a time, the airport occupies 5 degrees of the pilot's vertical field of vision. As the aircraft proceeds to position B, the airport fills a larger and larger portion of the pilot's field of vision. At position B, it occupies 10 degrees of visual angle. All of this is a fancy way of saying that the airport seems to get bigger as the pilot gets closer.

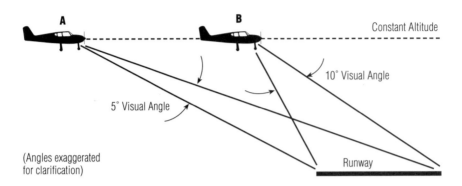

Figure 1. Overflying an airport at a constant altitude

Figure 2 shows what happens to the visual angle as an airplane descends vertically (assuming such a thing were possible) at some distance from the airport. At the higher altitude (position A), the airport occupies 10 degrees of a pilot's visual field, but as the aircraft descends, the visual angle becomes smaller. Finally, at position B, the visual is only 5 degrees. In other words, the visual angle decreases as the altitude decreases.

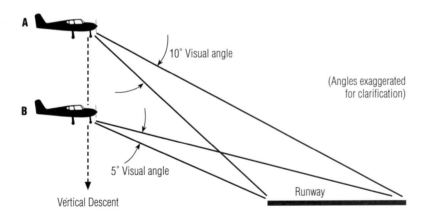

Figure 2. Approaching an airport in a vertical descent

Because the visual angle becomes larger as a pilot nears the airport and becomes smaller as he loses altitude, it should be obvious that it is possible to descend toward an airport in such a way that the resultant runway visual scene remains constant. It is not only possible to approach an airport while maintaining a constant visual angle, but this is what pilots tend to do—without realizing it—while executing black-hole approaches.

The problem is shown in Figure 3. The flight path during which the visual angle remains constant consists of the arc of a circle centered high above the light pattern toward which the pilot is descending. Note that flying such an arc places the aircraft well below the 3-degree descent profile normally used when a pilot has better depth perception. Also, the circumference of this arc is sufficiently large that the pilot has no way of detecting that he is flying along an arc instead of a straight line. The pilot actually makes a low approach to a point about 2 or 3 miles from the runway. Upon arriving at this point, the error starts to become apparent, and corrective action is taken (unless the aircraft first strikes terrain or obstructions).

Some may wonder how it is possible to crash during a straight-in approach without first losing sight of the airport. A pilot about to collide with terrain or obstructions does begin to lose sight of the airport, but this can occur after it is too late to effect a timely recovery.

The Boeing researchers also discovered that when an airport is at the edge of a small city, the additional lighting cues do not provide improved reference information as long as the approach is made over dark terrain or water. Curiously, their experiments suggested that the addition of lights around the airport can cause more dangerous approach deviations than when only the airport is visible in the distance. Their report notes also that "the

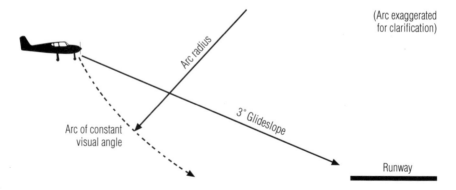

Figure 3. Descending along an arc

complex pattern of a city at night can replace to a large extent the normal daylight [visual] cues, and the experienced pilot can rely on them to get his bearings. However, an approach over water or unlighted terrain means that the visual reference points are at a distance where altitude and sink rate would be more difficult to judge."

Kraft and Elworth concluded that the problems associated with a black-hole approach appear to be aggravated by:

1. a long, straight-in approach to an airport located on the near side of a small city,
2. a runway length/width combination that is unfamiliar to a pilot,
3. an airport that is situated at a slightly lower elevation and on a different slope than the surrounding terrain,
4. substandard runway and airport lighting, and
5. a sprawling city with an irregular matrix of lights spread over various hillsides behind the airport.

There are, of course, other factors that mislead pilots during night visual approaches:

- Brightly lit runway lighting displays appear to be closer than they really are and cause pilots to descend prematurely. This is easily demonstrated by requesting a tower controller to vary runway lighting intensity during a lengthy, straight-in approach. As the lights dim, pilots tend to flatten out the approach; as they brighten, pilots tend to steepen the approach.
- Extremely clear air, such as that often found in the desert, also encourages early descents because lighted objects seem closer than they really are.
- When the horizon cannot be seen, scattered and distant ground lights can be mistaken for stars. These suggest to a pilot that he is maintaining a nose-high attitude, which results in a tendency to lower the nose and fly below the proper approach glidepath. A similar effect can be caused by the distant (upper) edge of city lights, which also can make the horizon seem lower than it is.
- Peering through a rain-soaked windshield can convince a pilot (because of refraction) that he is too high and can result in as much as a 200-foot altitude error per nautical mile from the runway. (Refraction bends the visual approach path in the same way that it "bends" the straw in a glass of water.)

- Viewing an airport through an intervening rainshower makes the runway lights seem bigger than they are, causing a pilot to believe he is too high.
- An upslope runway (and/or surrounding city lights) always—day or night—provides the illusion of being too high during a straight-in approach. This results in a strong tendency to descend prematurely. (Conversely, a downslope condition frequently leads to an overshoot.)

The best way to combat these often subtle and insidious factors is to avoid long, straight-in approaches at night, especially when overflying the infamous black hole. Instead, maintain a safe altitude until in the vicinity of the airport and descend in or near the traffic pattern. Pilots seldom are victim to illusions when their final approach legs are less than 2 or 3 miles long.

There are certain precautions a pilot can use to increase his altitude and distance awareness during long straight-in approaches at night. When available, use an electronic glideslope or VASI (visual approach slope indicator) for descent guidance. Consider, however, that although a VASI may be visible for up to 30 miles at night (3 to 5 miles during the day), safe obstruction clearance is guaranteed only when within 4 miles of the runway threshold.

DME (Distance Measuring Equipment) or GPS (Global Positioning System) can be used to establish a safe descent profile using the principle that a 3-degree glideslope is determined by maintaining 300 feet of altitude for each nautical mile from the runway (for example, an airplane 3 miles from the runway should be at 900 feet AGL). A 4-degree descent is established by maintaining 400 feet for each nautical mile from the airport, and so forth.

Always maintain a watchful eye on airspeed, altitude, and sink rate. An excessive sink rate for the airspeed being flown indicates either a strong tailwind or an abnormally steep descent profile. Remain alert.

Finally, be certain that you are descending toward an airport. Pilots have been deceived by highway lights or other parallel rows of lights that—from a distance—give the illusion of being runway lights. Maintain a safe altitude until the airport and its associated lighting are distinctly visible and identifiable.

Like most people, pilots usually believe what they see. In the case of a black-hole approach, however, there are compelling reasons not to.

Chapter 4 **Simulated Engine Failures**

An important part of every pilot's training involves preparing for a variety of emergencies. These include electrical malfunctions, cabin fires, landing with a flat tire, instrument failures, and so forth. Not surprisingly, more emphasis is placed on engine failure than on any other type of emergency. Unfortunately, the simulation of power failure leads occasionally to an actual emergency for which neither student nor instructor is prepared.

Consider, for example, the instructor who chopped the power of her Citabria 7GCAA and challenged her student to make a power-off approach to a forced landing. When the aircraft was 500 feet AGL, the instructor declared that the student had failed the exercise because he was not within gliding range of the selected field.

"Whaddya mean?" the student replied indignantly. "I can make that field."

So instead of adding power while at a safe altitude and climbing to an even safer one, the instructor allowed her student to continue. She apparently needed to prove to him that the aircraft was too low to glide to a safe landing.

But the instructor allowed the situation to go too far. When she finally advanced the throttle at 100 feet AGL, the engine did not respond because it had failed during the prolonged glide. The aircraft settled into a ditch and was damaged beyond repair. Neither occupant was seriously injured.

FAA records indicate that there were 43 accidents involving simulated emergencies during the past five years. The most common causes were:

1. improper use of systems and controls,
2. loss of control,
3. inadequate student supervision,
4. collision with an object or terrain,
5. poor judgment, and
6. loss of power.

An analysis of these training accidents by the Aviation Safety Institute of Worthington, Ohio, indicates that almost all were avoidable. The majority involved experienced instructors in airworthy aircraft, and five involved air carriers. Also, most of these accidents occurred while simulating powerplant failure in single- and multi-engine aircraft.

Although the accident causes listed above are apparently correct, they fail to describe what really went wrong. One can say, for example, that an accident occurred simply because a pilot lost control. But to learn from the mistakes of others, we need to know why they lost control.

A study of the accident reports (as well as some reading between the lines) reveals that most accidents related to simulated engine failure occur when an instructor misjudges his ability, his student's ability, or the performance capability of the aircraft.

Another common factor is that instructors often conduct the simulation at a time when an actual failure could not be tolerated. This is one reason, for example, why both the FAA and the aircraft manufacturers strongly discourage simulating an engine failure in a light, piston-powered twin immediately after liftoff. (Multi-engine instructors used to "fail" engines during initial climb, but this practice seemed almost as lethal as it was educational.)

Instructors also need to establish rules of conduct before departure. These help the student to recognize whether the emergency is actual or simulated and eliminates dangerous confusion. The instructor might say, for example, that he will not simulate an engine failure below 2,000 feet AGL and that any such indication of a failure should be regarded as a genuine emergency.

The two pilots also should determine before departure who is to be the pilot in command and responsible for managing any actual emergency that might occur. The failure to establish such an understanding has led to a number of accidents.

The method used to simulate an engine failure is somewhat controversial. An instructor has four choices. He can (1) close the throttle, (2) lean the mixture to idle cutoff, (3) turn off the magnetos, or (4) turn off the fuel supply. Which of these methods would you recommend?

As far as the engine is concerned, it is best to lean the mixture to idle cutoff while leaving the throttle open. This is because an open throttle permits the cylinders to fill with air and cushion engine deceleration, which reduces internal stresses during the simulation of a sudden engine failure.

Pulling the mixture control, however, actually shuts down the engine. Although this may be perfectly acceptable to the pistons, crankshaft counterweights, and other engine parts, it may not be in the best interest of those on board the aircraft. This is because the engine might not restart on demand, and the practice approach to a forced landing would suddenly become a genuine low-altitude emergency.

A practice power-off approach to a farmer's field usually is terminated by a full-power climb to a safe altitude. But if the engine has been genuinely shut down during descent, it will become quite cool. A quick restart and the application of full power at such a time is unhealthy for any engine. (Power-plant manufacturers also caution against conducting simulated engine failures during extremely cold weather because of the additional wear and tear this might create.)

For similar reasons, neither the magnetos nor the fuel-selector valve should be used to simulate an engine failure. (Turning off the fuel supply to fuel-injected engines is particularly hazardous because these engines can be difficult to restart following fuel starvation.)

Experts at both Teledyne Continental Motors and Textron Lycoming agree, therefore, that closing the throttle is the best way to simulate an engine failure in single-engine aircraft. (Simulating engine failure in a twin will be discussed later.)

During prolonged glides, be certain to "clear" the engine by applying power every 30 to 45 seconds. Many pilots believe that this prevents the spark plugs from fouling, but "clearing" usually does not do that because the power application is too short. The most important reason for applying occasional power is simply to confirm that the engine is still running. After all, an idling engine and a windmilling propeller are almost indistinguishable.

If an engine does fail during a prolonged glide, it is best to determine this at a relatively high altitude. A pilot cannot afford to wait until power is genuinely needed to discover that it is unavailable.

Applying power periodically during power-off descents also helps to keep the engine warm and provides a modicum of carburetor heat. (Carburetor ice can form during prolonged idling even when carburetor heat is applied because there often is not enough heat being generated by an idling engine to prevent ice from forming.)

During prolonged idling, fuel can condense and form small puddles in the induction lines of some carbureted engines, especially those using auto-gas. Adding power periodically also clears out this fuel before it can accrue sufficiently to cause the engine to falter.

When "clearing" the engine during a glide, do not jab the throttle or apply a large amount of power. Instead, move it gently, especially when operating engines with counterweighted crankshafts.

Although closing the throttle may be the best way to simulate an engine failure in a single-engine aircraft, this does not necessarily apply to twins. One reason is that a closed throttle signals to a student which engine has been failed. He is deprived of having to determine which engine failed and then confirming his discovery by retarding the appropriate throttle.

The preferred technique is to "fail" an engine using its mixture control. I usually make it a practice to hide the mixture controls from the student with a large piece of cardboard or a manila folder. In this way, he cannot determine which engine has failed by glancing at the mixture-control levers. This technique gives the student access to the throttles and propeller-pitch controls, and he is forced to go through the procedures just as if the engine had genuinely failed.

Once the student identifies the dead engine and retards the correct throttle, he then calls for "zero thrust," which simulates feathering the propeller. At this time—and with the throttle already retarded by the student—the instructor advances the mixture control, which restarts the engine. He then advances the throttle slightly, just enough so that the propeller produces as much thrust as it does drag (which explains why such a zero-thrust power setting closely simulates the effects of a feathered propeller).

This procedure incorporates the best of both worlds: using the mixture control to cushion the effects of engine shutdown and using the throttle to subsequently keep the engine running smoothly.

Simulating the failure of a turbocharged engine in either a single or a twin introduces the problem of shock cooling. This occurs when an engine operating at relatively warm temperatures is subjected to the rapid cooling that results from sudden power reduction. Although this can be tolerated on occasion without harmful effects, doing so frequently can cause cracked cylinders and other damaging effects. This explains why training aircraft ordinarily are not equipped with turbochargers. (Powerplant engineers concede that some normally aspirated, or nonturbocharged, engines also can be subjected to the long-term effects of shock cooling, but not to the extent of turbocharged engines.)

Finally, it might be interesting to discuss shutting down an engine at the end of a flight. Is there anything wrong with simply turning off the ignition? After all, this is how we turn off automobile engines.

According to powerplant engineers, there is absolutely nothing wrong with turning off the magnetos to shut down an engine. The practice of using the mixture control is to protect people, not engines. When an engine is shut down by turning off the ignition, some fuel remains in one or more cylinders. Someone moving the propeller at such a time (and while the engine is still hot) could cause one or more cylinders to fire and wind up losing a limb in the process. Shutting down the engine with the mixture control reduces this possibility by starving the cylinders of fuel. In any event, a stationary propeller must always be regarded as a potential weapon.

Chapter 5 **Flap Malfunctions**

The multi-engine student and his instructor were making a touch-and-go landing after simulating an engine-out approach. The airplane was observed making what appeared to be a normal liftoff, followed by an immediate and apparently uncontrollable roll to the right. The airplane hit the ground in an inverted, nose-down attitude, and both occupants were fatally injured.

The accident initially was thought to have been caused by a problem relating to an asymmetric power condition, but a National Transportation Safety Board investigation quickly revealed that the control loss had resulted from asymmetrically deployed flaps: The left flap was fully extended and the right flap was fully retracted.

Although pilots receive substantial emergency training, they receive little advice on how to cope with flap irregularities. Perhaps this is because flap systems generally are so reliable that we take them for granted. But flap system failures do occur, and it is worthwhile to consider the possible consequences.

The most startling flap abnormality occurs when one flap deploys or retracts while the other remains in position. The problem is immediately noticeable as a pronounced roll toward the wing with the least flap deflection and can result in the kind of tragedy described above. This strong rolling moment, however, usually is controllable. Regulations dealing with airplane certification requirements state that an airplane must exhibit safe flight characteristics with the flaps retracted on one wing and fully extended on the other. If an airplane cannot be flown safely in this configuration, then flap movement must be synchronized by a mechanical interconnection such as a torque tube. It is possible that an interconnect could fail and produce an uncontrollable situation, but this is rare.

Flap asymmetry usually catches a pilot off-guard and makes him wonder what in the world has occurred. A glance at the flaps will confirm the nature of the problem, but a pilot flying an airplane with split flaps—such as most twin-engine Cessnas—cannot see the flaps from the cockpit.

The problem obviously requires countering the roll with opposite aileron—lots of it. Also be prepared to cross-control and apply substantial opposite rudder. This usually is required to counter what might be a noticeable yaw caused by the additional drag created by the extended flap. Maintaining straight and level flight in an airplane with a deployed left flap, for example, requires applying left aileron and right rudder.

Almost full aileron may be required to maintain a wings-level attitude during an approach at reduced airspeed. Consequently, do not attempt to land with a crosswind blowing from the same side of the airplane as the deployed flap. The additional roll control required to compensate for the crosswind may not be available. Although controlling roll can be challenging during a split flap condition, the difference in stall speeds between one wing and the other has the potential to create a different kind of thrill. Consider, for example, that the flaps-down stall speed of an early model Cessna Skylane is 48 knots (calibrated airspeed), or 48 KCAS, while the flaps-up stall speed is 56 KCAS. If a Skylane with an asymmetric flap condition were flown too slowly, the wing with the retracted flap would stall 8 knots earlier than the wing with the deployed flap. This asymmetric stall is likely to result in an uncontrollable roll resembling a snap roll in the direction of the stalled wing and, altitude permitting, undoubtedly would evolve into a low-altitude spin from which recovery might not be possible.

This explains why an approach to landing with asymmetric flaps should be made at a higher-than-normal approach speed. Conduct the approach at least 30 percent faster than the flaps-up (clean) stall speed (represented by the lower limit of the green arc on the airspeed indicator). Additional airspeed, however, might be needed to maintain a comfortable level of roll control.

An approach with asymmetric flaps obviously is somewhat faster than a normal flaps-down approach. Also, deceleration during the flare will be less than usual because only partial flap is available to help slow down the airplane. Consequently, be aware that additional runway length will be required. Be particularly careful not to risk an asymmetric stall and loss of control by flaring excessively. Instead, fly the airplane onto the runway so the touchdown occurs at an airspeed that is safely in excess of the flaps-up stall speed.

Although most light airplanes can be handled safely during flap asymmetry, many turbine airplanes cannot. Some years ago, the pilots of a prototype business jet had to bail out when an asymmetric flap condition could not be corrected. Most jetliners are provided with systems that detect and prevent flap asymmetry by interrupting power to the flap actuating system as soon as a split-flap condition begins to develop.

Although a split-flap condition is the most dramatic type of flap malfunction, total flap failure is the most common. The notion of having to make a flaps-up approach and landing is not nearly as intimidating as having to cope with split flaps. Many pilots learned in airplanes that did not even have flaps, such as the Aeronca Champion, Bellanca Citabria, and Piper J-3 Cub. Others at least practiced slipping and making no-flap landings in training airplanes, such as the Cessna 152 and Piper Warrior. The problem is that many of these pilots have graduated into heavier and faster airplanes. Landing these with the flaps retracted is rarely contemplated, much less practiced. (A no-flap landing may be required of a candidate for an airline transport pilot certificate, depending upon the airplane.) How often do you see the pilot of a Beech Bonanza or Cessna 421 making a no-flap landing?

Although landing with the flaps retracted is not necessarily difficult, there are some critical factors worthy of review. For starters, consider that a no-flap landing requires substantially more runway. Unfortunately, the pilot's operating handbook rarely mentions the problem. When selecting a runway, therefore, consider that the landing distance could be as much as 50 percent longer than usual.

When flying flapless in the traffic pattern at reduced airspeed, a pilot will notice that the airplane must be flown in a relatively nose-high attitude to maintain altitude. Consequently, it will be more difficult to see traffic directly ahead. This makes us appreciate how effectively partial flap deployment lowers the nose and improves forward visibility in the pattern. On final approach, a nose-high attitude can make it difficult to see the runway. In this case, consider approaching the runway from the right side of the extended centerline so that the runway can be viewed to the left of the nose, or make a continuous turn from base to short final. (Those flying from the right seat should approach from the left side of the centerline.) This technique is used routinely by many pilots who fly airplanes with poor over-the-nose visibility (as when flying from the rear seat of a North American T-6).

Approaching the runway in a relatively nose-high attitude causes some pilots to perceive that the airplane is in danger of stalling. For this reason (and perhaps also to obtain a better view of the runway), some pilots lower the nose and accept an abnormally high approach speed. Although more comfortable, this might require more landing distance than is available. When executing a no-flap approach, use the same speed recommended earlier for an approach with split flaps: 1.3 times the flaps-up stall speed. This speed provides the usual 30 percent margin above stall and should allay a pilot's fear of stalling, even when holding a relatively nose-high attitude.

Losing altitude also can be more of a problem without the benefit of the drag normally provided by flaps. A pilot can avoid the temptation to dive (increasing airspeed unnecessarily) to lose altitude by flying a wider, longer traffic pattern than usual and giving himself plenty of room.

Flight characteristics during a no-flap approach usually offer no surprises, except that you might notice that the airplane is slightly less stable in pitch and roll with flaps up and power reduced.

Once the airplane has crossed the runway boundary, retard the throttle and begin the landing flare. Without flaps, the airplane will tend to float for what seems like an eternity. If approaching the far end of the runway too rapidly, consider going around and diverting to an airport with a longer runway. Do not be tempted to push the airplane onto the ground at high speed; this can lead to a loss of control. But neither should you flare excessively or aggressively; this might cause the tail to strike the runway, something much more likely when landing without flaps than with them. Instead, flare the airplane until it is in a comfortable, but not excessive, nose-high attitude and fly it onto the ground.

Although flaps failing to extend can be serious, their failure to retract can be much more so. Consider the pilot who begins to execute a go-around and discovers that the flaps remain stubbornly and fully deployed. Depending on airplane weight, power available, and density altitude, climb performance will either be lethargic or nonexistent. In this case, it usually is more important to maintain a safe airspeed than to attempt climbing much above obstacles. Gingerly fly the airplane to a safe landing, on or off the airport.

The possibility of flaps failing in the extended position is one reason many pilots prefer not to extend flaps fully until willing to commit to a landing. This is particularly applicable during instrument approaches because of the greater possibility of a missed approach.

Also, do not commit to the "go" part of a touch-and-go landing until visually confirming that the flaps are indeed retracting. There is no excuse for taking off with the flaps fully extended.

Here are some tips to help prevent and cope with flap malfunctions:

- Operate the flaps during preflight inspections. Listen for unfamiliar sounds and be alert for anything unusual, such as jerky or uneven movement.
- Prevent overstressing flap components by observing applicable airspeed limitations. Avoiding flap operation at maximum allowable airspeeds can extend the life and reliability of flap components. (Mechanical failure due to overstressing and fatigue most often occurs where the actuation arm connects to the flap.)
- Airplane owners and operators should note that most flap failures result from insufficient maintenance and lubrication of flap components, particularly during annual inspections.

- If electrically operated flaps fail to operate, check the circuit breaker. It might be necessary to operate hydraulically actuated flaps using an auxiliary pump. Do not attempt to force manually operated flaps; this could worsen the situation.
- Do not rely on the flap position indicator during a touch-and-go landing because on some airplanes it could indicate that the flaps are retracting at a time when they are locked in position.
- Avoid extensive taxiing on unimproved surfaces with flaps extended; pebbles and rocks can be blown into flap track mechanisms and prevent retraction after takeoff. Following this rule also prevents damage to the bottom surfaces of the flaps.
- Avoid flap retraction at low airspeed very close to the ground because this is when a split-flap condition is least tolerable. Premature retraction also can result in a hazardous loss of lift and a strange sinking feeling.
- Avoid extending or retracting the flaps all at once; this increases the potential for a split-flap condition. Instead, deploy or retract flaps in increments.

Perhaps the most bizarre flap malfunction of all occurred some years ago to a Canadian pilot flying a Piper Comanche on final approach to a small airport in Manitoba. As soon as the flaps had been extended, they immediately and alternately began to retract and extend without stopping, no matter what the pilot did with the flap switch. Turning off the master switch, fortunately, arrested the flapping flaps, and a normal landing was made.

Chapter 6 **The Downwind Turn**

For most of recorded history, man was convinced that the Earth was flat and that the sun and stars revolved around him. Even Plato and Socrates left this dogma unchallenged. So when Galileo espoused that the Earth was a sphere revolving about the sun, it was no surprise that he should be found guilty of heresy.

It is incredible that in this age of technological sophistication, there still survives the Flat Earth Society, whose members defiantly maintain that the Earth is flat. They rely on Biblical interpretations and contrived experimental data to justify their position. No amount of scientific proof can convince these believers otherwise.

In aviation, there exists an equally defiant core of pilots whose beliefs are founded on fallacy. They contend—also in the face of scientific proof—that a downwind turn (turning away from a headwind) is aerodynamically different than an upwind turn (turning into a headwind) when performed in a steady wind.

Advocates of this downwind-turn theory believe that dangerous airspeed and/or altitude losses can occur when turning away from a steady headwind. When climbing at low airspeeds immediately after takeoff, for example, they claim that this phenomenon can result in an inadvertent stall. Furthermore, they cite innumerable instances when cropdusters and other experienced pilots have fallen victim to the downwind turn when flying low and slow. The stronger the headwind—so the theory goes—the greater the airspeed and/or altitude losses to be expected. An identical low-altitude turn in calm air, it is claimed, does not produce these same dangers.

The downwind-turn theory goes something like this: Assume that an airplane is climbing into a headwind shortly after takeoff and has a relatively low groundspeed. If a rapid turn is made away from the headwind and into a tailwind, so the theory goes, the airplane must accelerate rapidly to some faster groundspeed. And because the airplane may be incapable of such rapid acceleration, something must give in the process. That something, we are told, is airspeed. Bilge.

Logic compels one to ask, "How can an airplane in flight possibly sense and respond aerodynamically to the wind?" It obviously cannot. A pilot can

The Myth....

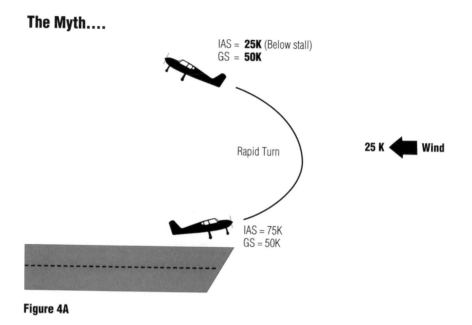

IAS = **25K** (Below stall)
GS = **50K**

Rapid Turn

25 K ◄ Wind

IAS = 75K
GS = 50K

Figure 4A

...and The Reality

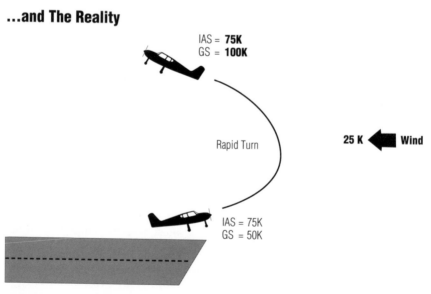

IAS = **75K**
GS = **100K**

Rapid Turn

25 K ◄ Wind

IAS = 75K
GS = 50K

Figure 4B

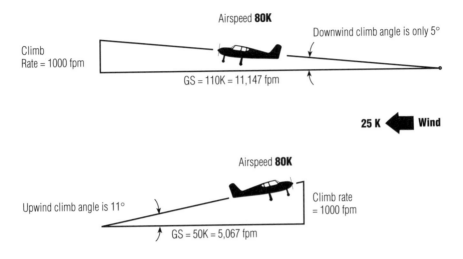

Airspeed **80K**

Downwind climb angle is only 5°

Climb
Rate = 1000 fpm

GS = 110K = 11,147 fpm

25 K ◀ **Wind**

Airspeed **80K**

Upwind climb angle is 11°

Climb rate
= 1000 fpm

GS = 50K = 5,067 fpm

In this example, climb angle decreases from 11° when climbing upwind
to only 5° when climbing downwind.

Figure 4C

detect drift and a difference between airspeed and groundspeed, but these are
navigational factors that have nothing to do with aircraft behavior and performance within a homogenous air mass.

If the downwind-turn theory had merit, a pilot could then expect to gain
airspeed and altitude when turning from downwind to upwind. Furthermore,
when executing a gliding turn into the wind, the pilot should anticipate a
substantial reduction in sink rate, or perhaps a climb, should the wind be
strong enough. Soaring enthusiasts, who spend much of their time circling at
slow airspeeds in strong winds, are unlikely to agree with any of this nonsense.

Although Newtonian physics can be used to disprove the downwind-turn
theory, I am not qualified to present such a mathematical treatise. Nor, I
suppose, would you be interested in dredging through such heavy-handed
mathematics. Instead, it is easier and more fun to resort to empirical methods
of debunking the downwind-turn theory.

If it existed, such a phenomenon also would be detectable at altitude. It
could be experienced simply by executing a continuous series of 360° climbing turns at low airspeed and full power under the influence of a strong,
steady wind. The pilot would notice a decrease in airspeed and climb rate

when turning downwind, and a comparable increase in performance when turning into the wind. Does this occur? As an airline captain who has spent my share of time holding in a jet stream, I can tell you emphatically that it does not.

If it were possible to detect changes in performance when turning downwind and upwind, then a pilot wearing an IFR hood should be able to determine from his instruments the approximate wind direction simply by sorting out — during each 360-degree turn — the points at which the performance changes occur. Some years ago, I extended a challenge to anyone who believes he can demonstrate such a phenomenon. No one has yet to accept this challenge, even when a sizable wager is offered.

Inertially, the change in groundspeed is no different when turning downwind than when making a similar turn in calm air. Assume that an airplane is climbing at 100 knots into a 25-knot headwind. Groundspeed is obviously 75 knots. The pilot then executes a 180-degree turn so that the wind is on his tail. The new groundspeed is 125 knots. The net change in groundspeed is determined by combining a groundspeed of 75 knots in one direction with a groundspeed of 125 knots in the other, which results in a net change of 200 knots.

If the same turn were made in calm air, the net change in groundspeed would be determined by combining a groundspeed of 100 knots in one direction with 100 knots in the other, which also results in a net change of 200 knots.

In other words, the net change in groundspeed is the same irrespective of whether the turn is executed in a moving air mass or when the wind is calm. In each case, the acceleration causing the net change in groundspeed is a direct result of the aerodynamics of a turn, and is the same in each case.

An airplane's airspeed is analogous to the speed of a man jogging on the deck of an ocean liner. Assume that the jogger is running at 5 knots toward the rear of the ship, and that the ship is steaming in the opposite direction at the same speed, 5 knots. The groundspeed (or "seaspeed," if you will) is nil. When the jogger reaches the stern of the ship and begins his wide turn, does he sense a change in running speed as his "seaspeed" accelerates to 10 knots? Of course not. He can run circles around the deck of the ship and have no idea which way the ship is moving.

Those who believe in the downwind-turn theory are correct about one thing: Low-altitude downwind turns are inherently more hazardous than low-altitude turns made into the wind, but not for the reason cited. After all, where there is so much smoke, there must be fire somewhere. The following explains why the downwind turn is far more dangerous than similar turns made into the wind:

- When climbing into a strong headwind immediately after takeoff, a pilot peripherally senses an unusually steep climb angle. But as he turns downwind, the increasing groundspeed and relatively constant climb rate result in a flatter climb angle. This apparent reduction in climb performance (angle, not rate) can cause a pilot to sense that he has inadvertently allowed the nose to drop somewhat. He counters this by subconsciously raising the nose in an attempt to maintain the original (upwind) climb angle. The result is airspeed decay and a possible stall. (*See* Figure 4C.)

- Low-altitude turns into the wind most commonly are made when turning from downwind or base leg to final approach. A pilot might perceive the resultant decrease in groundspeed as a decrease in airspeed and add power. There is nothing dangerous about this; a surplus of airspeed usually does no harm. But when turning downwind soon after takeoff, this sensation is reversed, and the groundspeed increase can be subconsciously interpreted as an increase in airspeed. This—along with the flatter climb angle—reinforces the pilot's perception that he has allowed the nose to pitch downward. A common tendency is for the pilot to react to this by applying back-pressure on the control wheel. The result can be a potentially dangerous low-altitude loss of airspeed that comes at a time when the throttle is already wide open and reserve power is unavailable.

- When climbing into a strong headwind, wind velocity usually increases steadily as altitude is gained between the ground and 2,000 feet AGL (the frictional layer of the atmosphere). During the initial climb, therefore, the airplane often encounters an "increasing headwind" type of wind gradient, or shear, that tends to increase airspeed. If a climbing turn is made downwind at such a time, the gradient becomes an increasing tailwind kind of shear that tends to reduce airspeed momentarily. Many of those who believe in the downwind-turn theory undoubtedly have been victimized by such a shearing gradient. This matter of wind shear, however, has nothing to do with the notion that downwind turns are aerodynamically different than upwind turns when executed in a three-dimensional steady wind.

- When the wind is gusty, the shearing effect of gusts has a direct effect on airspeed. Because the largest gusts most frequently represent increases in the mean wind, an airplane flying into the wind most often encounters an "increasing airspeed" type of shear. But when turning downwind, these gusts strike the aircraft from behind, and these have the effect of reducing airspeed and performance.

- Wind has no effect on aircraft performance relative to the air mass in which the aircraft flies, but it does have a profound effect on navigation and ground track. Figure 5A shows a crop-duster making a 180-degree turn in still air in preparation to spray an adjacent field. As expected, the track over the ground is circular, as long as airspeed and bank angle remain constant throughout the turn. In Figure 5B, the pilot executes an upwind turn, and the wind pushes the turning portion of the track away from the field. Consequently, the pilot has ample time and space to roll out of the turn and align the aircraft with the strip of land. In Figure 5C, however, the pilot turns downwind. The wind pushes the aircraft toward the adjacent field so that the aircraft will be over the boundary of the field before the turn has been completed. Sensing that he is running out of room, the pilot steepens the bank angle and possibly cross-controls the ailerons and rudder so as to complete the turn prior to reaching the boundary. This steeper bank angle (and possible skid) increases wing loading and the likelihood of a low-altitude stall. This partially explains why cropdusters contend that downwind turns are the most hazardous. The cropdusters' conclusion is correct; the reasons they cite, however, may not be.

- Finally, any low-altitude turn can be dangerous, especially when bank angles are large and G loads high.

There is no question, however, that, for the reasons given, downwind turns close to the ground are more hazardous than turns made into the wind. But to attribute the danger to some mystical force that presumably alters the physics of turning flight serves only to obscure the facts.

Man has maintained his myths throughout history. Just as the Flat Earth Society continues to survive in this age of galactic exploration, there is no doubt that there will always remain those who believe that downwind turns in a steady wind differ aerodynamically from upwind turns, even though their contentions lack scientific support.

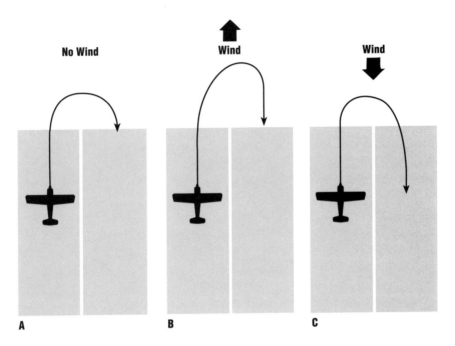

Figure 5. Wind effect on ground track

Chapter 7 **V Speeds (A through Z)**

In the early days of aviation, when airplanes were slow and simple, pilots managed airspeed by interpreting the sound of wires whistling in the wind. They were adept at sensing when the machine was about to stall or when airspeed was so great that it threatened to rip or break something. In those carefree days, a pilot had only two airspeed limits to observe: too slow and too fast. Everything in-between was fair game.

As airplanes became faster and more complex, "seat-of-the-pants" flying became less reliable, if not impossible. Pilots had to become more precise with their airspeed control. Advances in aerodynamic knowledge gave pilots a better understanding of aircraft performance. This knowledge soon was reflected in certification requirements that emphasized the need to determine an airplane's optimum airspeeds. The "seat of the pants" was replaced with "flying by the numbers."

Most of these numbers are known as V speeds (the "V" stands for velocity) and are listed in the accompanying table. Unfortunately, the brevity and simplicity of these definitions belie the complexity of many of the underlying concepts. Although a thorough understanding of these limiting airspeeds requires a knowledge of aerodynamics and aircraft performance, an attempt is made here to simplify the concepts without sacrificing the important operational aspects.

Limiting and Recommended V Speeds

V_1 .... Takeoff decision speed

V_2 .... Takeoff safety speed

V_{2MIN} .... Minimum takeoff safety speed

V_A .... Design maneuvering speed

V_B .... Design speed for maximum gust intensity

V_C .... Design cruising speed

V_D .... Design diving speed

V_{DF} .... Demonstrated diving speed

V_{FC} .... Maximum speed for stability characteristics

V_{FE} .... Maximum flap-extended speed

V_H .... Maximum speed in level flight with maximum continuous power

V_{LE} .... Maximum landing-gear-extended speed

V_{LO} .... Maximum landing-gear operating speed

V_{LOF} .... Liftoff speed

V_{MCA} .... Minimum control speed with critical engine inoperative out of ground effect

V_{MCG} .... Minimum control speed with critical engine inoperative during takeoff roll

V_{MO} .... Maximum operating-limit speed

M_{MO} .... Maximum operating Mach number

V_{MU} .... Minimum unstick speed

V_{NE} .... Never-exceed speed

V_{NO} .... Maximum structural cruising speed

V_R .... Rotation speed

V_{REF} .... Reference speed for final approach

V_S .... Stall speed or minimum steady flight speed at which the airplane is controllable

V_{S1} .... Stall speed or minimum steady flight speed obtained in a specific configuration

V_{S0} .... Stall speed in the landing configuration

V_{SSE} .... Minimum safe single-engine speed

V_X .... Best angle-of-climb speed

V_{XSE} .... Best single-engine angle-of-climb speed

V_Y .... Best rate-of-climb speed

V_{YSE} .... Best single-engine rate-of-climb speed

When a designer begins to develop a new aircraft, he knows about how fast it must be able to fly. This maximum airspeed is known as V_D, the design diving speed. In theory, the airframe is designed to withstand the aerodynamic forces at V_D and be free of flutter, control reversal, and buffeting.

Once the design evolves into hardware, the test pilot must determine if the airplane lives up to expectations. He does this by diving the airplane to V_D (in very smooth air) and, once there, attempts to verify that flutter cannot be induced. Flutter is not difficult to detect. Each part of an airframe, especially the control surfaces, has a natural vibration frequency and begins to flutter like a flag in a breeze at certain critical airspeeds. If flutter begins, it could become catastrophically divergent, which is an engineer's way of saying that it worsens until the aircraft is destroyed, even if airspeed is reduced as soon as flutter begins.

Some aircraft are incapable of reaching V_D because of insufficient power or excess drag. In such a case, the test pilot dives to the maximum speed possible, which is called V_{DF}, the demonstrated diving speed.

Those who are not test pilots have no business flying at V_D or V_{DF}. We are limited to V_{NE}, the redline or never-exceed speed, which is no more than 90 percent of V_{DF}. For instance, if V_{DF} is found to be 200 knots, V_{NE} must be 180 knots or less.

Although an airplane can be flown safely at V_{NE}, pilots should avoid this limit because the structural integrity of the airframe has substantially less tolerance for turbulence at the redline than at slower speeds. Even in smooth air, pilots cannot preclude the possibility of unexpected turbulence. The G loads imposed by turbulence can easily overstress an airplane flying at V_{NE}. The dangers of flight at V_{NE} are further compounded by poorly rigged control surfaces and balance assemblies, and improperly adjusted control rods and cables. These deficiencies can lead to flutter-induced airframe failure at high airspeeds.

If a pilot inadvertently reaches V_{NE}, he should slowly roll the wings level (if applicable), reduce power, and gingerly raise the nose.

V_{NE} applies only to piston-powered airplanes. Turboprop and jet aircraft are limited by V_{MO}, the maximum operating limit speed. (M_{MO} indicates a maximum allowable Mach number.) In practice, V_{NE} and V_{MO} are treated the same; each represents a maximum speed limit. V_{MO}, however, provides a wider margin of safety because it is only 80 percent of V_{DF}. This is necessary because turbine-powered airplanes (including turboprops) do not decelerate as well as piston-powered aircraft and cannot be slowed up rapidly in case of a turbulence encounter at high speed. This explains also why converting a piston airplane to a turboprop necessitates a lower redline.

If an aircraft exhibits undesirable stability characteristics under certain high-speed conditions, this alone could result in reducing allowable airspeed to something less than V_{NE} or V_{MO}. Such a restriction is called V_{FC}, the maximum speed for undesirable flight characteristics, and must be regarded with the same respect as a conventional redline. Otherwise, instability could develop beyond a pilot's ability to cope.

At the opposite end of the speed spectrum are the stall speeds. The first is V_S, which is the minimum steady flight speed at which the airplane is controllable. By itself, however, V_S is only a generic term and usually does not represent a specific airspeed. It is used only when discussing stalls in general. Notice that a stall is not necessarily characterized by the nose pitching down. An aircraft is said to be stalled whenever the critical angle of attack of its wings is reached or exceeded. In this condition, airspeed is insufficient to maintain attitude about any axis in smooth air.

Specific stall speeds must be defined. V_{S0}, for example, generally is determined with the airplane in the landing configuration: engine(s) idling, propeller(s) in low pitch, wing flaps in the landing position, cowl flaps closed, center of gravity (CG) at the maximum allowable forward limit, and the aircraft loaded to its maximum allowable gross weight. It is found by maintaining a wings-level attitude and decelerating at 1 knot per second. If deceleration is excessive, an increased load factor—even though imperceptible—can cause a premature or accelerated stall. V_{S0} is represented by the lower limit of the white arc on the airspeed indicator.

Many pilots wonder how landing-gear or cowl-flap position can affect stall speed. When underwing gear is extended, it forces some of the oncoming air to flow up and over the leading edge of the wing in the manner of leading-edge flaps or slats, thereby reducing stall speed slightly, if at all. When open, sufficiently large cowl flaps can deflect downward enough air to produce lift, thereby supplementing the wings in carrying the load and reducing stall speed. Decreasing gross weight or moving the CG aft also decreases stall speed. The maximum-allowable V_{S0} for single-engine airplanes and many light twins is 61 KIAS (70 mph).

V_{S1} generally is regarded as the "clean" (gear and flaps up) stall speed as represented by the lower limit of the green arc of the airspeed indicator. But this is not always the case. Technically, V_{S1} is the stall speed in a specified configuration. It could represent the stall speed with flaps in the takeoff position or with the aircraft configured in any of several different ways. It all depends on what is being considered at the time. The clean stall speed, therefore, is designated as "V_{S1} clean." By itself, V_{S1} is meaningless.

Closely related to V_{S0} is the reference speed, V_{REF}, which the FAA recommends as the final approach speed. Because V_{REF} is 1.3 times V_{S0}, it is easy to determine without a pilot's operating handbook (POH). Simply note the airspeed indicated by the low end of the white arc and increase it by 30 percent. For instance, a V_{S0} of 50 knots suggests a V_{REF} of 65 knots.

There are five V speeds involved with takeoff and climb. The first is V_{MU}, the minimum unstick speed, which is the slowest speed at which an airplane can become airborne. V_{MU} seems to have originated in the era of the de Havilland Comet, the world's first jet transport. During one particular take-off attempt in a Comet, the captain raised the nose so high and so prematurely that the resultant increased drag prevented further acceleration and liftoff. V_{MU} tests subsequently were established to ensure that future transports could take off with the tail touching the runway and maintain this attitude until out of ground effect. Such a hazardous maneuver is required only during aircraft certification trials and ordinarily should not be attempted.

Although general aviation aircraft do not undergo V_{MU} testing, there are lessons to be learned from the Comet problem. Inexperienced pilots flying heavily loaded and frequently underpowered airplanes from high-density-altitude airports often display impatience at the time and distance required to reach a safe takeoff speed. Consequently, they raise the nose prematurely. This adds considerable drag and could prevent the aircraft from ever becoming airborne or climbing out of ground effect. If conditions are insufficient for accelerating to a safe takeoff speed, it is best not to take off at all.

Recommended takeoff speed usually is found in the POH. Such a speed also is known as V_{LOF}, the liftoff speed. Usually, however, it is recommended that a pilot raise, or rotate, the nose at some lesser speed, which is known as V_R. The optimum takeoff technique consists of applying back-pressure at V_R in such a way that the aircraft continues to accelerate during rotation and lifts off at the recommended takeoff speed. If the aircraft becomes airborne at an airspeed lower than V_{LOF}, rotation is excessive; if it becomes airborne at an airspeed higher than V_{LOF}, rotation is insufficient.

The lowest climb speed for lightplanes generally should not be less than V_X, the speed that results in the best (or greatest) angle of climb. V_X, however, is not a fixed airspeed as is implied by most handbooks. The speed provided usually is valid only when the aircraft is at sea level at maximum-allowable gross weight with the wing flaps in the takeoff position. For most lightplanes, V_X increases with altitude (about one-half knot per 1,000 feet) and flap retraction; it usually decreases with a reduction in gross weight. Although a headwind increases climb angle and a tailwind decreases it, V_X does not vary with wind.

The speed for best rate of climb, V_Y, is always faster than V_X and usually is provided only for a flaps-up, gear-up configuration. Like V_X, V_Y decreases as gross weight is reduced, but unlike V_X, it decreases with altitude, something many pilots fail to consider during prolonged or high-altitude climbs.

V_Y also is very close to the speed at which the lift-to-drag ratio of an airplane is at a maximum and, therefore, is close to being the most efficient speed. Lacking other information, a pilot can consider V_Y a reasonable substitute for the best glide speed or the maximum endurance speed, which is useful for minimizing fuel burn when holding. Maximum range normally is achieved with an airspeed that is 10 to 20 percent greater than V_Y.

There are two cruise-related V speeds. The first, V_H, is primarily of concern to racing pilots and those who prepare advertising brochures. It represents the maximum speed in level flight with maximum continuous power. Ultralights are limited by FAR Part 103 to a V_H of 55 knots/63 mph.

The second is V_C, the design cruising speed, which many pilots consider to be aircraft cruising speed. But this is incorrect; a given aircraft may cruise slower or faster than V_C. The design cruising speed is of concern only to designers and is the greatest speed at which an aircraft can safely withstand the FAA's standard 50-fps gust.

There actually are several values of V_C for a given aircraft, but the lowest normally is used to designate V_{NO}, the maximum structural cruising speed. This speed is of critical importance to a pilot and is indicated by the beginning of the yellow arc, or caution range, on the airspeed indicator.

When flying at V_{NO}, a pilot knows only that the aircraft can tolerate the FAA's mathematically defined 50-fps gust. Because a pilot has no way of measuring gust intensity and because an airplane's gust tolerance decreases substantially when flying beyond V_{NO}, it behooves a pilot to avoid flight within the yellow arc whenever turbulence is present or expected. Structural engineers concede that most airplanes cannot safely withstand the most severe gusts nature has to offer. It is the pilot's responsibility to take over where the designer leaves off by avoiding such conditions in the first place or by penetrating severe turbulence at a relatively low airspeed.

The vast majority of lightplanes have been certified according to the requirements of FAR Part 23. A few, however, conform to the more stringent dictates of FAR Part 25, which were developed for Transport-category aircraft. These aircraft have a speed designated as V_B, the design speed for maximum gust intensity. Depending on the airplane and the philosophy of the manufacturer, V_B may be designated as the recommended turbulence-penetration speed to protect the structure against 66-fps gusts.

In addition to protecting the airframe as much as possible against turbulence, designers also must protect the aircraft against structural loads imposed by rapid and maximum deflection of the flight controls. This protection is available only when flying at or below V_A, the design maneuvering speed.

Most pilots realize that rapid and full up-elevator deflection when at or below V_A causes the aircraft to stall before damaging load factors can develop. But this form of aerodynamic relief cannot protect against the loads imposed by rapid and full deflection of the ailerons and rudder. Instead, the structure simply must be built strong enough to withstand such abusive control application. When flying at speeds above V_A, a pilot has no such assurances and must be cautious about manhandling the controls. This is particularly applicable when flying in turbulence because the combination of loads imposed by gusts and maneuvering is cumulative. Whenever in doubt about the structural integrity of an airplane, reduce airspeed as much as is practical. (Consider also that V_A usually decreases as the gross weight of an aircraft decreases.)

A structural engineer designs the flaps to be operated at a maximum airspeed of V_F, the design flap speed. If the finished product is as anticipated, the actual maximum flap-extended speed, V_{FE}, will be the same as V_F and will be designated by the upper limit of the white arc on the airspeed indicator.

Although it is allowable to operate the flaps at V_{FE}, there is no reason to subject the flap hinges, actuating mechanisms, and related structures to such abuse. Habitually extending the flaps at V_{FE} increases fatigue and may result in a premature failure of a flap system component. Proper care of an aircraft suggests that flap extension be delayed—when possible and practical—until airspeed is somewhat less than V_{FE}.

Pilots should consider also that the positive limit-load factor for normal-category airplanes usually is reduced from 3.8 Gs to 2.0 Gs when the flaps are extended. Similarly, the negative limit-load factor is reduced from -1.52 Gs to 0. Unless necessary, it may be advisable not to deploy flaps when substantial turbulence is anticipated.

Care also should be taken not to extend or retract the landing gear consistently when at or near V_{LO}, the maximum landing-gear operating speed. In most cases, V_{LO} is limited by the relative vulnerability of wheel-well doors to high air loads. On some aircraft, the wheel-well doors close after the gear is extended. In such a case, it may be permissible to exceed V_{LO} and accelerate to V_{LE}, the maximum landing-gear-extended speed. Protecting the doors during gear retraction also requires being at or below V_{LO}.

The rest of the most frequently used V speeds are used when operating multi-engine airplanes. V_{MC}, for example, is the minimum-controllable airspeed with the critical engine inoperative. (The critical engine is the one that, upon failing, has the most adverse effect on directional controllability and—assuming clockwise propeller rotation—is the engine located furthest outboard on the left side of the aircraft.)

An engine failure in other than center-line-thrust aircraft (such as the Cessna 336/337 Skymaster) results in a strong yawing moment created by the thrust on one side of the aircraft and the drag of a windmilling propeller on the other. Directional control is maintained by countering this asymmetrical condition with rudder in the direction of the operative engine. If airspeed is reduced, however, the rudder loses effectiveness. If airspeed is allowed to decrease below V_{MC}, even full rudder cannot prevent a yaw toward the dead engine.

It is extremely dangerous to fly a multi-engine airplane at or below V_{MC}—especially during the takeoff phase. V_{MC} is usually only 10 to 15 knots higher than a light twin's stall speeds. A pilot who climbs out at or below V_{MC} will face an uncontrollable yaw in the direction of a faded engine. If airspeed is allowed to dissipate, this yawing can be accompanied by a stall, and this stall will be asymmetric. The slower-moving wing—the one with the failed engine—will stall first, and the thrust of the operating engine can force the airplane into a spin. The severity of these reactions is much more pronounced when the critical engine fails.

V_{MC} usually is determined with the critical engine inoperative (and its propeller windmilling) and the remaining engine(s) producing takeoff power. Also, the flaps are in the takeoff position, the landing gear is up, and the cowl flaps are open. The aircraft must be banked no more than 5 degrees (toward the operative engine) and be loaded to the maximum-allowable takeoff weight at the aft CG (center of gravity) limit.

V_{MC} as applied to light and medium twins is more correctly termed V_{MCA} because it refers to an airborne situation. V_{MCG} (minimum controllable airspeed on the ground) is the minimum speed necessary to maintain directional control of Transport-category aircraft following an engine failure during the takeoff roll.

V_{YSE} and V_{XSE} (the SE stands for single engine) are the speeds for best rate and angle of climb with the critical engine inoperative, and apply only to Normal-category twins. They are used in the same manner as V_Y and vary with altitude and gross weight. V_1 and V_2 are terms applicable to multi-engine Transport-category aircraft, although they are sometimes applied erroneously to light twins. V_1 is the takeoff decision speed and is the speed below which an engine could fail and the airplane could be safely stopped on the runway. An engine failure at a speed greater than V_1 mandates that a pilot continue the takeoff roll with available power and accelerate to V_R. It would be unwise to abort after V_1 because there might not be sufficient runway within which to stop the airplane. After rotation, the aircraft should continue accelerating to V_2, the takeoff safety speed, which should be attained at approximately 35 feet AGL.

The concept of V_1 does not apply to most propeller-driven twins because they cannot continue a takeoff roll and accelerate on one engine. The pilot has no choice but to abort, even if this means overrunning the end of the runway—unless the aircraft has reached V_{SSE}, the safe single-engine speed. Although V_{SSE} is not addressed in certification requirements, the concept was developed by airframe manufacturers to establish a minimum speed (above V_{MC}) at which a proficient pilot could expect to be able to lift off, "clean up" the aircraft, and climb. (There is no guarantee how well the aircraft will climb, however.)

Although pilots usually are careful not to violate airspeed limits, they occasionally do so without realizing it. This is because airspeed-indicating systems often are in error (especially when an aircraft is more than a few years old). Moisture and other contaminants entering the aircraft's pitot-static system adversely affect the accuracy of airspeed indicators.

This should come as no surprise to those who fly twins with dual airspeed indicators. Rarely do the two instruments agree within 5 knots; discrepancies of 10 knots are not rare. (Most pilots have an unfounded bias toward believing the gauge on the left side of the instrument panel.) Those who practice formation flying also recognize that the airspeed indicators of different aircraft seldom agree.

Although the regulations require the static pressure system and altimeter of any aircraft to be flown under instrument flight rules to be checked for accuracy within the previous 24 calendar months, no such requirement exists for the pitot pressure system or the airspeed indicators. Those who would like to justify their faith in airspeed indicators might consider a biennial test of the pitot pressure system at a local instrument shop. If necessary, an airspeed calibration card will be prepared for the aircraft. After all, a pilot can fly by the numbers only if the numbers he reads are correct.

Chapter 8 **Using IFR Charts for VFR Flight**

It is said that a picture is worth a thousand words. If that picture is a sectional chart, then the cliché is an understatement. Sectionals contain so much information that a stack of books probably would be required to describe all of the information presented on one.

Ironically, however, sectionals often do not provide enough data. This is common knowledge to instrument pilots, who use a different kind of chart. Instead of sectional charts, they use IFR enroute charts. These contain almost no topographical information but are a gold mine of other data that simplifies flight planning and radio navigation for VFR pilots as well as instrument pilots. Measuring distances between stations and other navigational fixes on enroute charts is unnecessary, for example, because the lengths of all airway segments are provided; plotters are seldom required.

Enroute charts also display radio facilities that are not shown on sectional charts. These include localizers (which are similar to VOR radials and can be used to track along an extended runway centerline to an airport) and independent DME stations that are not co-located with VOR stations.

Enroute charts provide substantial information that simplifies altitude planning when flying either VFR or IFR. Every airway segment displayed on an enroute chart is assigned a minimum enroute altitude. An MEA provides at least 2,000 feet of clearance above enroute obstacles when the route is over mountainous terrain and 1,000 feet when the segment overlies non-mountainous terrain. An MEA also assures reception of navigable VOR signals along the entire route segment for which it applies. (VHF communications usually are available at the MEA, but not always.)

Consider, for example, the pilot flying along the airway in Figure 6. Mountains along his route reach up to 6,000 feet MSL. The MEA, therefore, ordinarily would be 8,000 feet MSL. But this would fail to guarantee the availability of VOR signal coverage along the airway segment because each VOR is in a shadow of steeply rising terrain. Line-of-sight limitations make it impossible for a pilot at 8,000 feet to navigate by VOR along the entire segment. In this case, the MEA must be raised to 12,000 feet, which is the minimum altitude that assures both obstacle protection and suitable VOR coverage.

If this pilot were concerned only with obstacle protection and were willing to sacrifice VOR guidance for a brief period, he could fly at the minimum obstruction clearance altitude (MOCA), which also is shown on enroute charts (when appropriate). The MOCA shown in Figure 6 is at 8,000 feet and assures the same obstacle clearance normally provided by an MEA. Although a pilot operating at a MOCA (below the MEA) can anticipate some loss of enroute VOR coverage, course guidance is assured when the aircraft is within at least 22 nautical miles of the VOR stations defining the route segment in question. A pilot cruising at a MOCA also should expect to be incommunicado for brief periods while en route.

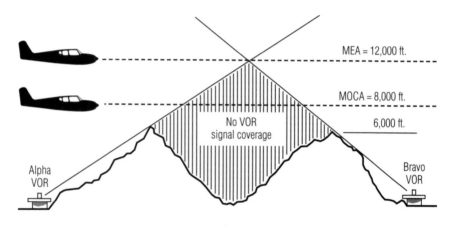

MEA = 12,000 ft.

MOCA = 8,000 ft.

6,000 ft.

No VOR
signal coverage

Alpha
VOR

Bravo
VOR

Figure 6

Instrument pilots almost always operate at or above the MEA, but sometimes it is advantageous for them to operate below the MEA (but not below the MOCA)—such as when this allows them to escape icing conditions.

When flying cross-country, VFR pilots are taught to fly outbound from one VOR until halfway to the next. At the midpoint, they change frequency and continue inbound to the next station. But instrument pilots know that this procedure is not always suitable. They even know when it is not.

Figure 7 shows an aircraft cruising between Delta and Echo, which are 150 miles apart. A pilot ordinarily would expect to navigate outbound from Delta for 75 miles until reaching the midpoint and then switch to Echo. But when flying at the MEA, this pilot will fly beyond VOR signal coverage long before reaching the midpoint.

Enroute charts warn pilots when this can be expected and advise them when to switch from one VOR to the next. The changeover point shown in Figure 7 advises that the pilot can rely on Delta for only 50 miles. He should then switch to Echo for the remainder of the route segment. A pilot flying in the opposite direction would rely on Echo for 100 miles before switching to Delta for the remaining 50 miles.

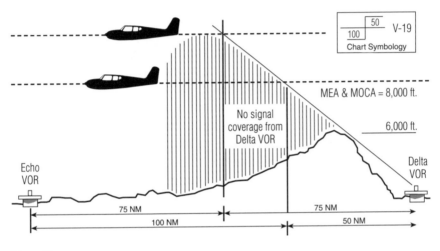

Figure 7

The heights of MEAs (and MOCAs, when applicable) vary according to the terrain below. An IFR pilot operating at an MEA must climb at the end of one airway segment because of the higher MEA of a subsequent segment. In most cases, he can wait (with the concurrence of air traffic control) until reaching the next route segment before commencing the climb to the higher altitude. Occasionally, however, a pilot must begin his climb before reaching the next airway segment. Figure 8 on the next page shows an aircraft eastbound along Victor 21 at the MEA of 3,000 feet. Zelda Intersection marks the beginning of the next airway segment, which has an MEA of 10,000 feet. If the pilot did not begin climbing until reaching Zelda, he might discover that his aircraft has insufficient performance to outclimb the steep mountain lying ahead. This explains why the enroute chart in this hypothetical example displays an eastbound minimum crossing altitude (MCA) of 8,700 feet for Zelda Intersection.

Every once in a while, an airway segment has a maximum authorized altitude (MAA). Although this limitation usually applies only to pilots operating on an instrument flight plan, it could affect those operating VFR. An MAA might indicate that the airway segment underlies restricted airspace, or flight above the MAA could result in signal interference caused by receiving two VOR stations on the same frequency.

Airway intersections are a handy way for pilots to report enroute progress. On occasion, a pilot operating at or above the appropriate MEA is too low to receive the off-course facility needed to define an intersection along his route of flight. When this occurs, the enroute chart provides the minimum reception altitude (MRA) needed to identify the intersection.

VFR pilots should recognize that the minimum altitudes shown on an enroute chart are just that—minimum altitudes applicable to IFR flight. Although they can assist a pilot in determining suitable VFR cruising altitudes, they should not be regarded as cruising altitudes unless they also conform to the hemispherical rule used to select VFR cruising altitudes.

Enroute charts are superior to sectional charts with respect to providing communications frequencies. A handy panel on each enroute chart provides every communications frequency available at every facility covered by the chart. These include, for example, ground control frequencies, which are not shown on sectional charts.

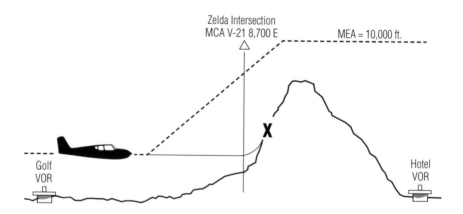

Figure 8

Perhaps the most useful communications features of enroute charts are the Air Route Traffic Control Center frequencies scattered throughout. These make it easy to determine which frequency should be used in any area to obtain radar assistance and flight-following services. Those using sectional charts are forced to call a flight service station or other source to obtain the appropriate center frequency.

Those planning to obtain an instrument rating should consider the VFR use of enroute charts before their IFR training begins. This provides a familiarity with the terminology and symbology, easing the transition into the esoteric world of IFR flight.

Although enroute charts provide an abundance of invaluable information to VFR pilots, they should be used only as supplements, not substitutes. One reason for this is that enroute charts do not adequately portray the maze of airspace restrictions placed in the way of VFR flight (such as Class B and C airspace). This is because these charts are intended for instrument pilots who ordinarily are not concerned about such restrictions. IFR pilots simply fly in accordance with clearances issued by ATC. They are confident in the knowledge that these instructions will keep them safely away from where they do not belong. In this respect, VFR pilots have a more difficult and challenging role. They alone are responsible for not violating any of the numerous airspace restrictions strewn across their path.

Enroute charts are published by the National Oceanic and Atmospheric Administration (the same federal folks who bring you sectional and other aeronautical charts) and Jeppesen Sanderson in Englewood, Colorado. They are available from either source by subscription but also are sold by pilot supply shops and fixed-base operators.

Enroute charts are issued every eight weeks and therefore are more up-to-date than sectional charts, which are issued only twice yearly. Each Jeppesen enroute chart contains an informative list of the changes that are incorporated into each new edition.

It would be remiss not to emphasize here that pilots must be careful about using only current charts. Obsolete charts—whether intended for VFR or IFR flight—compromise safety and can lead to tragedies of the worst kind.

Chapter 9 **Pilot Error**

As this book went to press, I had celebrated my 59th year on Earth and my 25,000th hour above it. Spending the equivalent of almost 3 continuous years in a cockpit entitles one to a certain right of reflection. Although hours alone do not a pilot make, they at least provide an experienced perspective of matters aeronautical. Consequently, I will use this opportunity to review some of the poor judgment and near-tragedies I have observed during 43 years of flying. These vignettes provide some interesting and entertaining object lessons.

Some years ago, a teenage pilot devised a novel way to fulfill a desire to be in the spotlight. He used his rented Aeronca Champ to fly into one of those large advertising spotlights once used to spike the night sky over Los Angeles to herald a motion-picture premiere or a supermarket opening. It was an interesting challenge, but one that almost ended his brief career.

After several attempts, he did manage to remain in the spotlight for almost a full circle, but only while turning steeply at low altitude. The aircraft was seen by thousands, a few of whom also observed it enter an inadvertent spin and ultimately recover at less than 200 feet above the ground. For the pilot, it was an illuminating experience.

Intense competition can push some people beyond the limits of reason and propriety. Such was the case when a Super Cub instructor was competing with a peer during a short-field landing contest. Instead of using an imaginary line on the runway, these pilots used the actual runway threshold from which to measure landing distance.

The third approach by the rear-seat pilot was low, and the Cub was hanging on the prop, perilously close to a stall. As the main tires passed only inches above the edge of the runway, the pilot chopped the power and pulled the control stick aft. Because there was no reserve of airspeed, the airplane did not balloon. Instead, the tailwheel came down hard and caught the lip of the concrete runway. This tore the tailwheel structure from the aft fuselage, which—in combination with aggressive braking that almost caused a noseover—resulted in the shortest landing of them all. Pride indeed goeth before the fall.

The student in the front seat of the Aeronca Champ always forgot to apply carburetor heat prior to a power reduction. So it was during this particular entry to a power-off stall. The instructor, who was in the rear seat, was about to teach his student—and himself—a valuable lesson.

As the student brought the aircraft into a nose-high attitude with the engine throttled, the instructor reached for the ignition switches (which are located to the rear of the student's left elbow and thus cannot be seen from the front seat) and stealthily turned off the magnetos. When the aircraft began to quiver during the stall entry, the student lowered the nose and pushed the throttle forward. Instead of the engine roaring to life, of course, the propeller came to a standstill. The instructor screamed at the student for having gotten them into such a precarious situation. He simultaneously turned the ignition back on, took control of the airplane, and entered a high-speed dive to get the propeller spinning once again. (No, the airplane did not have an electric starter.)

Trouble is, the prop was hung up on a compression stroke and would not budge, not even at the redline airspeed of 112 knots. With altitude and ideas in short supply, the instructor had no option other than to make an emergency landing on the beach. Fortunately, the sands were void of sun worshippers on that winter weekday. (The FAA inspector who arrived on the scene believed the instructor's story about having been victimized by carburetor ice and allowed him to take off after being assured that the carb ice had "melted." The local constable was less sympathetic and ticketed the pilot for illegal parking.)

A veteran American pilot in South Africa was about to depart Hluhluwe (pronounced shloo-`shloo-ee) in a Beech Baron twin on a flight to Skukuza on the southwestern perimeter of Kruger National Park (where some of the bugs are so large that a pilot needs a type rating and a saddle to fly one). Because the pilot had departed Johannesburg with full tanks, he knew that he had enough fuel for this second leg and did not bother to make a visual inspection of the tanks. No problem, though. The fuel gauges confirmed a more than adequate supply.

En route to Skukuza and over the desolate bushveld, the fuel-quantity indicators began to move rapidly and inexplicably toward the big E. Was there really enough fuel on board? The pilot began to wonder. Perhaps someone had drained fuel from the tanks while the airplane had been left unattended for two days. The pilot had two choices: continue over the wilderness with an unknown fuel quantity, or land at nearby Mbabane, the capital of

Swaziland, where the occupants of a South African-registered airplane might be greeted by a less-than-hospitable welcoming committee. (This was before the end of apartheid in South Africa.) But even this, he reasoned, seemed preferable to a potential forced landing amid a pride of lions.

At Mbabane, the airplane was met by a Jeep bristling with machine-gun-toting soldiers. The prospects for having to spend time in a Swazi jail seemed to be increasing. After being confronted and questioned by a general who had more medals and decorations than Idi Amin, the pilot was advised that his trespass (he had neither a visa nor an overflight permit for Swaziland) might be overlooked in exchange for an adequate supply of Yankee dollars or South African gold. After emptying his wallet and arranging to purchase fuel with his American Express card, the pilot fired up the twin and hightailed it into the air before the general had a change of heart.

How much fuel did the twin require? Not much, considering that the tanks were indeed more than half full. An inadequate preflight inspection, however, could have avoided having to pay more than $20 per gallon to top the tanks.

The young pilot and his friend had been planning this flight to Las Vegas for months, but when the big day finally arrived, the departure airport was shrouded with a blanket of zero-zero fog. Just enough visibility remained to taxi the Luscombe onto the runway and line up with the centerline. Big deal, the pilot thought. I've got 20 hours of instrument dual and an airplane equipped with a turn-and-bank indicator. I'll fly needle, ball, and airspeed until we're on top, and it'll be severe-clear the rest of the way.

The initial climb was routine (considering that neither the pilot nor the airplane were properly equipped for IFR flight), until the turn indicator began to stick. This is when the pilot learned what the big boys meant when they talked about "sweating bullets." The turn indicator could be made to function, albeit briefly, by stabbing at the rudder pedals and inducing a yaw strong enough to dislodge the needle.

That was many years ago. Today, that Luscombe pilot never departs on an IFR flight in any airplane without first S-turning on a taxiway to verify the integrity of all gyroscopic instruments.

The charter pilot was about to depart on a return flight from Mexico to Los Angeles in a Twin Beech. When his passengers arrived at the terminal building, he was preoccupied with the purchase of a souvenir. Consequently, he was not paying much attention when one of them asked where in the airplane they could stow the tequila.

"Stick it in the rear of the cabin," the pilot advised. "The baggage compartment is already full." He directed his passengers to the airplane, attended to the filing of a flight plan, and finally arrived at the large taildragger, where he found his passengers seated and ready to go.

Everything appeared normal during the takeoff roll until the pilot pushed forward on the yoke in an attempt to raise the tail. There was no reaction; the airplane remained in a three-point, nose-high attitude.

Well, the airplane is a bit heavy, the pilot thought. We just need a little more airspeed. But acceleration was agonizingly poor in such a tail-low attitude, and the Model D-18 was running out of runway. There soon was insufficient room to abort, and the tail remained stubbornly low, even though the control wheel was shoved to its forward limit. Finally—and with only scant feet of runway remaining—the airplane slowly levitated into the air in a dangerously nose-high attitude.

Without taking time to explain, the pilot screamed for the passengers in the rear of the cabin—who coincidentally were the heaviest—to get up and move as far forward along the aisle as they could. This shift in the center of gravity did make the airplane more manageable, and the passengers were allowed to return to their seats after the gear and flaps had been raised and cruise-climb established.

The pilot discovered to his chagrin that the tequila earlier mentioned by his passengers had consisted of several cases weighing hundreds of pounds. Rather than risk landing with such an extremely aft CG, the pilot insisted that his passengers dispose of the tequila—one bottle at a time—through an emergency exit and into the Pacific Ocean. Needless to say, the pilot never again left the loading of an airplane up to his passengers. (Nor did those passengers ever again charter his airplane.)

The elements common to the events just described are carelessness and poor judgment, factors contributing to the majority of aviation accidents. That each pilot managed to survive his own stupidity, however, is no credit to his skill or cunning. Were it not but for the finger of fate, we might just as well have read about these misadventures amid the sobering reports issued frequently by the National Transportation Safety Board.

Each pilot received a valuable object lesson, but the methodology was intolerable. Safe flight demands also that pilots recognize their fallibility and vulnerability to error. Pilots must be willing to learn from the mistakes of others and accept the advice of their mentors. Good pilots are not the product of repeated exposure to unnecessary risk. The best pilots are those who never tempt fate or confront a hazard of their own making. It is only during the struggle for perfection that we can at least attain some level of excellence.

In each case I've described, the pilot deserved the harshest criticism for exposing himself and others to such unnecessary dangers. But what makes these misdeeds even more fascinating is that they were not committed by several pilots. They were the reprehensible acts of one. And that pilot, I am hesitant to confess, is me.

Chapter 10 **Declaring an Emergency**

In his Pulitzer Prize-winning novel, *The Caine Mutiny*, Herman Wouk eloquently describes a situation where an officer of the USS *Caine* finds it necessary to override the captain's command authority. This occurs when the captain, Lieutenant Commander Phillip Queeg (brilliantly portrayed by Humphrey Bogart in the film adaptation), places his ship in danger of capsizing by mishandling it during a typhoon.

As you may recall, Queeg had previously shown signs of incompetence and acute paranoia. For example, he had allowed his ship to overrun its own tow line during a 360-degree turn, turned tail under fire, and became obsessed with finding an imaginary key to a food locker after discovering that a quart of strawberries was missing. Another overt sign was Queeg's response to stressful situations: He had a compulsive habit of clicking a pair of ball bearings in the palm of one hand.

During the subsequent court martial, it was determined that the executive officer had exercised his "emergency authority" under Article 184 of Naval Regulations and was not guilty of "conspiring to make a mutiny."

Pilots also have the right, and perhaps the obligation, to exercise their emergency authority when confronted with a crisis. The FAA's equivalent of Article 184 is Federal Aviation Regulation 91.3(b), which states, "In an in-flight emergency requiring immediate action, the pilot in command may deviate from any rule of [Part 91] to the extent required to meet that emergency." It must be emphasized that nothing in this discussion is intended to encourage anyone to violate regulations in the course of routine operations. What follows is intended only as advice that might be applicable during emergency conditions.

It would be appropriate at this point to define an emergency, even though this may seem unnecessary. For most of us, it usually is recognizable as a time when the mouth becomes dry, adrenaline begins to flow at a furious rate, and a large knot forms in the pit of the stomach.

The FAA, however, defines an emergency in the *Aeronautical Information Manual* (AIM) as "a distress or urgency condition." That is somewhat vague, but the FAA goes on to say (on a different page) that distress is a "condition of being threatened by serious and/or imminent danger and of requiring immediate assistance." An engine fire and a major structural failure are obvious examples of distress conditions.

Notice, however, that a situation does not need to be that dire to constitute an emergency. This is because an urgency condition also is regarded as an emergency. The AIM defines urgency as being a "condition concerning the safety of an aircraft or other vehicle, or of [a] person on board or in sight, but which does not require immediate assistance." According to the AIM, "an aircraft is in at least an urgency condition the moment the pilot becomes doubtful about position, fuel endurance, weather, or any other condition that could adversely affect flight safety."

This definition of an urgent condition is significant because it points out that an emergency can exist without the sense of imminent danger associated with the popular concept of an emergency. In other words, if a pilot senses concern or "becomes doubtful" about the safety of his flight or his passengers, he should regard the situation as an emergency and act accordingly.

As one veteran pilot puts it, "The severity of an emergency is inversely proportional to the options available." Because many emergencies are slow to develop and frequently are the result of a chain of events, it is incumbent upon the pilot to do whatever is necessary to prevent the available options from dwindling in number. If resolving an emergency results in violating regulations, do not hesitate to do so. The FAA provides the necessary authority. (Some attorneys contend that a pilot is negligent if he fails to exercise his emergency authority at a time when this would be an appropriate course of action.)

A pilot obviously must not abuse this emergency authority; he must have a valid reason for using it. But if he perceives either a distress or urgency condition, he must be prepared to take appropriate action to protect the safety of those involved. Safety is a pilot's highest priority, and he must do whatever possible to preserve it.

Pilots generally are a law-abiding group. Unfortunately, their respect for regulation occasionally is carried to an extreme. Consider, for example, the case of a private pilot flying a Grumman American Yankee on a 150-nautical-mile cross-country flight. Nearing his destination, the pilot of this no-radio aircraft noticed that his fuel supply had rapidly and inexplicably become almost nil. (It was determined later that a loose fuel line was responsible for a substantial leak.) Rather than fly through the intervening Class C airspace without the ordinarily required radio contact, this pilot complied with regulation and circumnavigated a portion of the restricted airspace to reach the nearest airport. He ran out of fuel a mile short of the runway. Fortunately, neither occupant was injured, although the aircraft was substantially damaged during the off-airport landing.

A similar situation occurred some years ago when a well-known stunt pilot for the motion-picture industry was scud-running over and between some hills while en route to his home base at Santa Ana, California. He ultimately flew headlong into rising terrain. This pilot could have resolved his emergency simply by climbing into the overcast and out of harm's way (assuming that a turn was not possible because of high-rise terrain on both sides of the aircraft). Considering his emergency authority, this would have been authorized and prudent—with or without a clearance from air traffic control.

Many accidents occur because pilots fail to act while there still is time to do so. Conditions must not be allowed to deteriorate to a point beyond which extrication from the emergency may not be possible.

One reason that pilots are reluctant to exercise their emergency authority is their fear of recrimination by the FAA. But consider that it is the FAA that authorizes appropriate deviations in the first place. Pilots are expected to use this authority whenever necessary.

If a pilot does violate any of the regulations in Part 91, he is not required to put himself on report. FAR 91.3(c) says that a pilot who violates a regulation in accordance with his emergency authority is required to submit a report of the deviation only when requested to do so. However, a pilot who uses his emergency authority is encouraged to submit a report of the incident to the Aviation Safety Reporting System (ASRS), which is administered by the National Aeronautics and Space Administration. According to FAR 91.57, the FAA may not use any of the submitted information against the pilot except for "information concerning criminal offenses or accidents which are wholly excluded from the program." In a sense, pilots who file ASRS reports are immunizing themselves against possible legal action by the FAA; many pilots consider it essential to have an ASRS form available whenever they fly. Should the FAA request any information regarding a violation of regulations, a pilot should consider allowing an attorney to reply on his behalf.

Although pilots do receive substantial training with respect to specific emergencies, such as engine and systems failures, they often are not given emergency training of a general nature. If they were to receive such training from the airlines or the military, they would receive the following advice:

- An emergency often dictates expeditious handling, but never be in such a hurry as to worsen matters (such as the multi-engine pilot who feathers the wrong engine).

- No matter what the emergency, never allow it to distract you from controlling the airplane.
- Acknowledge—at least to yourself—that an emergency exists. Do not bury your head in the sand and attempt to minimize the situation.
- Remind yourself of the need to remain calm and rational despite the severity of the problem. Resolution of an emergency requires clear thinking.
- Commit to memory the initial steps required to cope with the most serious emergencies (such as an electrical fire or a power loss). Have emergency check lists immediately available. They are of little value if not readily accessible.
- Emergencies can be resolved as long as options are available. Keep options open by taking action in a timely fashion. Unnecessary delay can result in tragedy. No situation is hopeless as long as the aircraft is still flying and the pilot is capable of controlling it.
- If a spare receiver is available, use it to monitor the emergency frequency. You might be the only communications link with someone in distress.
- In many cases, pilots create or allow the development of an emergency that could have been avoided.

A pilot frequently is in contact with ATC when an emergency develops. At such a time, he should not use the emergency frequency. It is more efficient to use the ATC frequency because communications already have been established. Assistance is more immediately available than if a distress call is made "in the blind" on 121.5 MHz.

Years ago, virtually all FAA facilities guarded the emergency frequency, but not now. Some facilities either do not guard 121.5, or they have the volume turned down so low that no one would hear a distress call. Also consider that the emergency frequency capability of air route traffic control centers normally does not extend to their radar coverage limits. In other words, centers often "see" farther than they can "hear."

If communications have been established, a pilot should not automatically squawk the emergency code (7700) on his transponder. This is done only when necessary to attract attention. A controller, however, may request that the pilot squawk 7700 so that other controlling facilities will recognize that an emergency is in progress.

History shows that a pilot often is reluctant to declare an emergency after one has developed. One reason for this may be his fear that such a declaration might be interpreted as a failure on his part, something he might not be willing to concede to a controller, his passengers, or himself. (He also may not want to alarm his passengers.) Because of his desire to present a macho image, he may not want anyone, including himself, to believe that he cannot handle an emergency without assistance. Finally, some pilots are reluctant to declare an emergency because of perceived consequences, even though there usually are none. Not declaring an emergency, however, can have far graver consequences than those originally feared by the pilot. Declaring an emergency should not be taken lightly, of course, but it must be done before the condition worsens. Obtain all the help you can as soon as you can. Air traffic controllers are not mind readers. They will go to extremes to provide all possible assistance, but only after being apprised of the difficulty.

According to the controller's handbook, Air Traffic Control, if a controller considers a situation to be an emergency or a potential emergency, he is to handle it as if it were an emergency. If a pilot conceals his difficulty, though, a controller will have no reason to suspect that an emergency is in progress. Consequently, he might not offer needed services or advice.

When declaring an emergency, pilots should use "Mayday" repeated three times as a communications preface. This advises a controller in no uncertain terms that you have an emergency and want all possible assistance. Although sounding a "Mayday" might seem overly dramatic, it helps to cut through the formalities with a minimum of fuss and bother. It also commands silence on the frequency so that a pilot in distress will have a clear channel of communications.

"Mayday" is used when a distress condition exists. In an urgency situation, the initial call should be prefaced with the word "Pan" repeated three times. This warns others on the same frequency not to interfere with communications. For some reason, pilots are often reluctant to use "Mayday" and "Pan," but they should not be. These phrases command more immediate attention and quicker service than the pilot who calmly says (with a Chuck Yeager-like drawl), "Say, Center, I have a problem up here."

After declaring an emergency, a pilot might become bombarded with well-intended questions and suggestions. If this interferes with your handling of the emergency, advise the controller that you are busy and will get back to him when time and conditions permit. Do not allow a controller "into the cockpit" until you are ready for him.

Some pilots tend to regard controllers as authority figures, but always bear in mind that the pilot—not the controller—is responsible for the operation of the aircraft. Accept assistance, but only when this appears beneficial. If an ATC clearance is unsuitable, for example, refuse it. Do whatever is necessary to resolve the emergency, whether the controller likes it or not.

Can a controller approve a violation of the regulations? He cannot, but a pilot does not need such approval. His emergency authority is blanket approval to deviate from any regulation when necessary to resolve an emergency.

Some controllers have access to a tool that only a few pilots know about. It is the emergency obstruction video map (EOVM). This can be invaluable to a pilot unable to maintain a minimum terrain/obstacle clearance altitude (because of structural icing, for example). EOVM enables a controller to provide emergency vectoring at lower altitudes than would ordinarily be available. Such a service, however, is provided only when the pilot declares an emergency or the controller has determined that an emergency exists because of a pilot's inability to maintain an appropriate altitude.

Pilots often wonder whether a particular act is legal or illegal (with respect to Part 91). Generally speaking, anything is allowed as long as there is not a regulation prohibiting it. To this, however, must be added a caveat, a catchall regulation (FAR 91.13), which states that "no person may operate an aircraft in a careless or reckless manner so as to endanger the life or property of another."

Assume, for example, that a pilot flying solo in his own airplane wants to land on a long, smooth dirt road in the desert. Would this be legal? Yes, because there is no regulation in Part 91 prohibiting such a landing (local ordinances notwithstanding). But the pilot must be certain that "the life and property of another is not endangered." (It would appear that the regulations are not particularly concerned about the safety of the pilot.)

Are pilots required to abide by procedures detailed in the AIM? No, because the AIM is not law. A pilot should realize, however, that the AIM spells out how a prudent pilot is expected to conduct his flight. Lawsuits for injury and damage have been lost because pilots have failed to conduct themselves in a reasonable and prudent manner. In other words, if the FAA does not get you, the courts will.

Preventing an emergency clearly is preferable to having one, but should a pilot have an emergency, it is vitally important that he recognize the condition and be prepared to exercise his emergency authority.

Chapter 11 **Investigating Lightplane Accidents**

One of the simplest yet most profound observations ever made states that those who do not learn the lessons of history are destined to repeat it.

This philosophy motivates the National Transportation Safety Board to meticulously analyze aircraft accidents for probable cause. Lessons learned from the mistakes of others can be used to prevent similar tragedies in the future.

The news media, however, often and irresponsibly jump to erroneous conclusions with respect to accident causes. These judgments sometimes are printed or broadcast even before investigators have arrived at the crash site. Pilots often are the most flagrant Monday-morning quarterbacks. The deceased pilot, obviously unable to defend himself, usually is the designated scapegoat.

It is remarkable that blame or cause can be so rapidly assessed when it can take trained specialists and investigators months of painstaking study to fit all of the puzzle pieces together. (Occasionally the puzzle is never solved because of missing pieces.)

Accident investigation is a complex science that places the history of a given flight under microscopic examination. This detailed study often requires the expertise of a wide variety of specialists who probe the facts without prejudice. These "detectives" include metallurgists, aerodynamicists, pathologists, toxicologists, human factors specialists, meteorologists, biomechanical experts, powerplant and propeller engineers, and many others. A key member of the team often is an accident reconstructionist, who—like "all the king's horses and all the king's men"—tries to put the pieces back together again. By the time an investigation is complete, very little evidence has escaped detection.

This attention to detail, however, is typical only of major tragedies with fatalities, such as those involving an air carrier, or other accidents of a sensational nature. Because of time, budget, and manpower constraints, most general aviation accidents are not investigated as thoroughly. Consequently, many such accident reports contain hasty and erroneous conclusions. Because most accidents inevitably lead to litigation (for the purpose of assessing liability), independent investigations often are conducted to pick up where the NTSB leaves off.

Accident investigation usually involves delving into four major areas of concern: the pilot or crew, the aircraft, the weather, and air traffic control, if involved.

It is crucial that a qualified investigator arrive at the crash site as soon as possible after the accident to note and photograph evidence before it disappears or is altered. Structural icing, for example, often melts before investigators arrive, and a valuable clue vanishes forever. Also, tracks made by the aircraft in mud or snow soon may be masked by subsequent precipitation. In some cases, valuable evidence is removed by souvenir hunters or thieves before investigators arrive.

Other clues—such as broken trees or shrubs, gouges in the terrain, or scars on boulders or buildings—assist the reconstructionist in estimating aircraft speed, track, and descent angle immediately prior to impact.

The wreckage pattern reveals valuable information about the nature of the crash. Norman L. Horton, a reconstructionist who has investigated hundreds of accidents over the past 30 years, states that there are six basic patterns:

- A hole in the ground is caused by a high-speed dive into the ground at a nose-down attitude of between 45 and 90 degrees. Heavier aircraft components, such as engines, usually are found at the bottom of the crater (or beneath the bottom if impact speed is sufficient). Ruling out suicide, this type of accident usually indicates loss of control. In such a case, an autopsy of the pilot is warranted because of the stronger than usual possibility of incapacitation.

- Spin accidents result in a shallower crater because of the relatively low speed associated with spins. Indications of spin rotation often can be found in the form of ground scarring outside the impact crater. One scar is created by the inside wing, which usually is the first part of the airplane to strike the ground. Because the aircraft is spinning at the moment of impact, the outside wing also creates a ground scar but at a point more or less than 180 degrees (with respect to the impact crater) from the markings created by the inside wing. The wreckage and ground scars indicate the direction of spin rotation. Also, damage to the leading edge of the inside wing can be assessed to approximate aircraft attitude at the moment of impact. Although the typical spin is characterized by a nose-down, banked attitude, some aircraft tend to spin flat. In these cases, the ground scars created by the wings are more diametrically opposed.

- Spiraling impacts are typified by the inside wing striking the ground first (as in the case of a spin) followed by the engine and then the outside wing. This wreckage pattern, however, is unlike that resulting from a spin. Instead, debris is spread over a relatively large, fan-shaped area. The engine usually separates from its mounts and remains near its first point of impact. The wings often are torn from the aircraft and come to rest some distance from the fuselage.

- High-speed, small-angle-of-impact accidents are characterized by long, fan-shaped debris patterns. The aircraft often breaks into many pieces, with the heavier parts traveling farthest forward in the pattern. The first marks on the ground usually are made by the tires or propeller(s). If the accident occurs in a wooded area, the wings may damage treetops long before contacting the ground. Because aircraft components and pieces often are spread over a large distance, many are never found, which complicates the process of reconstruction. This type of accident is caused by controlled flight into the ground, such as when flying at too low an altitude in IFR conditions. In the same category is the low-speed, small-angle-of-impact accident, which might be the result of a forced landing. Airframe damage is substantially less, and survival probability is high.

- In-flight disintegration leaves an unmistakable signature. Major parts of the aircraft usually are scattered over a wide pattern without apparent rhyme or reason. The fuselage usually free-falls and is compressed or flattened upon impact. Some aerodynamic components, such as flight controls, may be undamaged and remotely located from the main wreckage. Reconstruction is most valuable following this type of accident because properly piecing the parts together might reveal the sequence of disintegration. If speed, direction of flight, and altitude above the ground immediately prior to disintegration can be determined, an analyst can construct a "fly-back" diagram that may point toward a particular component failure. Structural failures occur for various reasons, and each may leave unique telltale signs that reveal the nature of the failure. Common causes include flutter, fatigue, massive overstress, corrosion, lightning strike, in-flight fire or explosion, upset and overspeed, and midair collision.

- Wire strikes continue to plague general aviation, especially those involved in low-level flights (such as helicopter and agricultural operations). Although it might appear that the cause of this type of accident is self-evident, an investigator cannot afford to simply assign the cause to pilot error and close his book on the subject (especially if the pilot is killed). Other, less conspicuous reasons may explain why the pilot was unable to avoid the hazard.

After examining the overall wreckage pattern, investigators then turn their attention toward the components. For example, a forward bend in the propeller blades indicates that the engine was developing significant power at the time of impact. Blades bent rearward signify that little or no power was being developed. An S-shaped propeller (one blade bent forward and one blade bent aft) also suggests a power-off condition.

Much can be determined by inspecting the flight and engine instruments. The clock, for example, often stops at the instant of impact and records the time of the accident.

The direct indications of some gauges are of little value because the pointers usually move to random positions during collision. Valuable data, however, can be obtained indirectly. During catastrophic deceleration, an instrument pointer may bend forward momentarily (in reaction to impact forces) and mark the face to reveal what the instrument was indicating at the instant of impact. Data also can be obtained by inspecting the internal mechanism of an instrument for impact markings.

Empty fuel tanks do not necessarily indicate fuel exhaustion. The fuel may have spilled after impact, a situation indicated by ruptured fuel tanks and soil saturated with fuel stains. Fuel starvation or exhaustion is best determined during the subsequent engine teardown, when investigators may find that the fuel lines and other fuel system components (such as the carburetor bowl) are bone dry. Or investigators might find contaminants or the wrong grade of fuel in the system.

The trained eye also can distinguish between an in-flight and a post-crash fire. An in-flight fire is indicated when fire damage and soot is downstream of protrusions on the aircraft exterior. Also, relative wind causes beads of molten aluminum to be blown downwind (aft) along the fuselage. A post-crash fire is indicated by a widespread pattern of soot and fire damage that lacks the effects of downwind streaming.

Substantial information about the history of a flight can be obtained by studying voice recordings routinely made by air traffic control of all two-way communications. These tapes, which contain superimposed time signals, normally are kept for only 15 days unless an accident warrants keeping them for evidence.

Voice recordings are not the exclusive property of the FAA. The Freedom of Information Act provides that copies of recordings are to be made available to anyone requesting them. This should be of more than casual interest to a pilot who gets into difficulty with an ATC facility and needs a copy of the tape to support any contentions he might need to make (at a hearing, for example). Otherwise, the evidence may be destroyed, and it becomes a matter of your word against that of the FAA (and you know who will win that argument).

Recordings made by an ATC facility for any specified time period may be obtained (for any reason) by submitting a written request for a copy of the tape within 15 days of the event in question to the FAA's chief counsel at the appropriate regional headquarters. A nominal charge is made for this service. Recordings also are available of telephone briefings that a pilot obtains from a flight service station.

Another valuable investigative tool is the ATC radar tape. You may not realize it, but every time your transponder is interrogated by an ATC radar facility, the transponder reply also is recorded and saved for 15 days. In other words, the geographic position and altitude (in the case of transponder code Mode C) of your aircraft is recorded for posterity (and possible certificate action) every four to five seconds when being tracked by an automated radar terminal system (ARTS III), and every 6 to 12 seconds when being tracked by air route traffic control center radar.

These recorded radar "hits" can be used to prepare a tabular printout that shows aircraft position in longitude and latitude against altitude and time. This data is then used to plot an aircraft's track on an aeronautical chart. By applying winds aloft data, groundspeed and airspeed between any two hits is easily determined.

The NTSB and NASA's Ames Research Center have developed a computer software program that expands the data available from radar tapes. Aircraft position, altitude, time, performance data, and winds aloft can be analyzed to provide a description of aircraft attitude, performance, and power setting(s) at any given point along the flight path. This narrows substantially the field of difficulties that a pilot might have had and how he handled the aircraft. These data can even be used to prepare an animated videotape that seems almost as authentic as an actual movie of the events leading up to the accident.

Primary radar targets (aircraft without transponders) usually are not recorded except when a controller uses a special electronic device that tracks such a target across his screen. If all of this sounds as though Big Brother is coming, you are wrong; he is already here.

In many accidents, weather plays a major role. Fortunately, it is easy to retrieve weather data. Would you like a copy of the sequence reports for Kennedy International Airport for July 4, 1966? Or a satellite photograph of the western United States that was taken last Christmas? Or copies of the applicable forecasts for Colorado on August 8, 1975? Simple. Just call the National Climatic Data Center in Asheville, North Carolina. For a nominal fee, the NCDC will provide certified copies of any weather documents you might need. These data can be used by a meteorologist to paint a very accurate picture of the conditions that existed at the time of an accident.

A pilot also may be subjected to scrutiny. Pathologists probe body cavities for hidden clues, toxicologists test for foreign substances in the blood, activities prior to the flight are investigated, FAA records are reviewed, and so forth. (Every pilot is entitled to a copy of his FAA file, which contains certificate and rating applications, written examination results, violations, address changes, and so on. This file is like an official diary of your aviation career and can be obtained—for a small fee—by writing to the FAA's Airman Records Branch in Oklahoma City, Oklahoma).

Logbooks also play a role in the investigation process. A pilot might be accused (either in court or in an accident report) of violating regulations when it appears that he was not qualified to make a night flight, for example, because he had not logged three night takeoffs and landings within 90 days prior to the accident. There is a lesson here for those who fail to log recent flight experience as required by the Federal Aviation Regulations.

Witnesses obviously contribute to an investigation. Although witnesses who saw the same event may describe it differently, a common element in their stories might eventually lead to establishing an accident cause.

Without passing judgment on the crushing effect that litigation has had on the sharply rising costs of product liability insurance, undeniable benefits have accrued. The process of pre-trial investigation and discovery has resulted in numerous safety improvements and object lessons that have contributed significantly to general aviation's improving accident record.

Section 2

IFR Operations

In the world of instrument flight, becoming proficient on instruments can be compared to becoming an experienced VFR pilot. Just as a new private pilot certificate is a license to learn, so, too, is an instrument rating. The next seven chapters are designed to provide some of the additional insight needed to develop IFR proficiency during a variety of situations.

Chapter 12 **Category I, II, and III ILS Approaches**

My first instrument instructor told me that once I learned to shoot an ILS approach at home, I would be able to do the same wherever else in the world I might wander. "This," he said, "is because all ILS approaches are the same. Master one and you've mastered them all."

That might have been true in 1956 when there was only one type of ILS approach. Today, there are several. The conventional ILS is a Category I, or CAT I, approach. It has a decision height (DH) of no less than 200 feet and a minimum visibility of no less than a half-mile (or a runway visual range [RVR] of 1,800 feet if the runway has centerline lights).

In 1962, in response to a growing need by the airlines for reduced approach minimums, the FAA issued a notice of proposed rulemaking that sought comments on what eventually would become known as a Category II approach (with a DH of no less than 100 feet and a minimum RVR of 1,200 feet).

AOPA's Michael V. Huck responded to the NPRM by stating that "light aircraft are far more maneuverable and can operate more safely under…lower minimums than can transport aircraft. Therefore, we suggest that the…minimums for light aircraft performing a standard instrument approach be just half those established for transport aircraft."

Huck persevered and ultimately became the first general aviation pilot to be certificated for CAT II approaches. This set the stage for the drama that unfolded at John F. Kennedy International Airport on April 2, 1968. The weather reported there included a 100-foot ceiling with the RVR down to 1,200 feet. This forced many jetliners to divert while others (I was a copilot aboard one of them) held helplessly, hoping for conditions to improve. Huck had arrived in the area on a personal flight from Washington, D.C., and neither diverted nor held. Instead, he guided his Piper Aztec toward the runway and made the first-ever CAT II approach at JFK. (You cannot imagine how embarrassing it was for the captain to tell our Boeing 707 passengers that the only aircraft to land at JFK that morning was a "Piper Cub.")

This eventually led the FAA to enact the regulation that allows general aviation pilots to become certified for CAT II approaches when operating Category A aircraft (those with an approach speed of less than 91 knots).

The airlines currently have the edge over general aviation when it comes to CAT III approaches. This is because the airplane must be equipped with a sophisticated head-up display or an auto-flight system capable of making an automatic landing.

There are three types of CAT III approaches. CAT IIIa allows an approach and landing with an RVR of less than 1,200 feet but no less than 700. CAT IIIb permits approaching with an RVR of less than 700 feet but no less than 150. No aircraft has yet to be certified for CAT IIIc, which eventually will allow an approach and landing during zero-zero conditions.

In a sense, the first CAT IIIc, or "blind" approach and landing, was performed on September 24, 1929, by then-Lieutenant James H. Doolittle. He used a Consolidated NY-2, the first airplane ever equipped with an attitude horizon and a directional gyro (designed for this flight by Elmer Sperry, Jr.). The biplane also was equipped with a Kollsman precision (sensitive) altimeter and a system of vibrating reeds that enabled Doolittle to follow a radio beam aligned with the runway. The landing gear was reinforced to absorb excessive shock.

On that historic morning at Mitchel Field in New York, Doolittle climbed into the front cockpit of his biplane and pulled a canvas hood over the entrance so that he could not see outside the aircraft. A safety pilot, Lieutenant Ben Kelsey, sat in the rear.

Doolittle took off toward the west, climbed to 1,000 feet, made a one-eighty to the left, and then flew several miles until he was sufficiently east of the airport. He made another one-eighty, intercepted the beam, descended to 200 feet, and leveled off. After passing a fan marker near the end of the runway, he began another descent and "flew the plane down to the ground using the...procedure that [he] had developed."

The first automatic landing was made in 1937 by Army captains Carl J. Crane and George V. Holloman at Wright Field in Ohio. They used a Fokker-designed, high-wing monoplane, the General C-14B, equipped with a Sperry gyropilot.

The first airplane certified with an autoland system was the Lockheed 1011 TriStar in 1972. The autoflight system was designed by Lockheed, Collins, and Lear-Siegler, and was based on the one developed for the space shuttle. It still is regarded by many as the autopilot of choice when making a CAT III approach.

Most of my CAT III experience has been in Paris, where dense ground fog is both common and persistent. It never seems to burn off until after the CAT III-qualified aircraft have landed and the others have scattered to their alternates.

My crew and I usually learn about the need to shoot a CAT III approach at Paris after crossing the Atlantic at night. The sun rises and bursts into the cockpit, our wake-up call, an intrusive signal that it is time to prepare for the challenge. Fortunately, the CAT III approach is a no-brainer. I could teach any pilot to do it—as long as nothing goes wrong. Follow along.

After descending into the Paris area and being vectored toward the localizer, we select autoland mode and engage the second autopilot. If one of the two should fail, a missed approach would be required, even though the remaining autopilot could complete the approach and landing.

The first officer calls out, "Localizer alive," and the big Lockheed gently rolls onto the final-approach course. A minute later, he calls, "Glideslope alive." We deflect the flaps from 10 to 22 degrees and then lower 10 wheels from their wells.

The glideslope needle centers, and we extend the flaps fully to 33 degrees. The nose of the TriStar dips slightly, and the dual autopilots establish an initial sink rate of 680 fpm, which approximately parallels the glideslope. Seconds later, they make the corrections needed to intercept and track the glideslope. The wings slice into the undercast, and the autothrottles almost imperceptibly move to maintain the indicated reference speed of 138 knots.

For the remainder of the approach, the signals from both ILS receivers will be fed into a "vote-and-veto box." If a suspect signal is received, the computers reject it and allow the approach to continue on the basis of what are considered the most reliable signals.

The outer marker flashes blue dashes as we pass overhead. I call out, "Outer marker," and the flight engineer—who is in the best position to monitor flight instruments and their fail flags on both sides of the panel—calls out, "Flags checked."

The dual radio altimeters (also known as radar or absolute altimeters) indicate that we are passing through 1,500 feet AGL. This signals the autopilots to roll in some nose-up trim to prepare the TriStar for the possibility of a missed approach. The autopilots also take control of the rudder. This means that they now can automatically prevent the yaw created by the failure of an underwing engine during the remainder of the approach (without any pedal-pushing help from the pilot, thank you).

The tower clears us to land, and in the same breath reports that the ceiling is zero and that the touchdown, mid-runway, and rollout RVRs are holding steady at 300 feet. It seems ironic that although we can land with such poor visibility, we would not have the 600 RVR required for a takeoff.

At 500 feet, the first officer calls out, "One hundred and thirty-eight knots, sink seven."

My left hand holds the yoke loosely; my index finger rests lightly against the go-around switch, just in case. For example, if a pilot taxiing toward the active runway were to inadvertently trespass into the ILS critical area, the proximity of his aircraft to the ILS transmitters might interfere with the localizer or glideslope signals. This could displace one of our ILS needles, and the dual autopilots would dutifully follow the errant signal with the tenacity of a bulldog. This is why it is so important that taxiing pilots pay attention to the special double-yellow lines that indicate the boundary of an ILS critical area during low-visibility operations.

My right hand is on the throttles, and I can feel them making slight and occasional thrust changes. I also can sense my pulse rate picking up a bit.

Until now, the autopilots have been crabbing the airplane to remain on the localizer. But at 150 feet AGL, they dip a wing to compensate for the crosswind and add top rudder to align the Lockheed with the runway. Although the autoland system has demonstrated an automatic landing with a 44-knot direct crosswind, CAT III landings are not allowed with more than a 10-knot component.

The middle marker spews a short stream of dots and dashes, the radio altimeter shows that we are descending through 100 feet, and the ILS needles remain centered, yet there is no sense of being so close to the ground, no approach lights reflecting through the dimensionless world of gray, no nothing. I shift ever so slightly in my seat and try not to let my crew notice. It's crunch time.

For most airplanes executing a CAT III approach, the pilots must use a 50-foot DH. This means that a missed approach is required if the touchdown zone lights cannot be seen when the landing gear is 50 feet above the runway threshold.

A few types of aircraft (including the L-1011) benefit from an exemption. Pilots of these aircraft do not have to see anything outside the aircraft prior to touchdown, which eliminates the need for a DH. They instead use an alert height of 50 feet. This is simply the height above which a missed approach must be made if a required ground or airborne component fails. The approach and landing may be continued, however, if a component failure occurs when below the 50-foot alert height.

A small amber light on the radio altimeter signals that the main landing gear wheels are descending through the 50-foot alert height, and the autoland system shifts to the flare mode. I feel the throttles moving aft. The attitude indicator confirms that the flare has begun. At 10 feet, the auto throttle system retards the thrust levers fully and nonchalantly trips itself off. The computers program the flare so that the aircraft will touch down with a 2-fps sink rate. We still cannot see anything through the milky mist. The radio altimeter shows 10 feet, 5 feet. We can almost feel the main landing gear reaching, stretching for the ground.

The mains touch with a mild thump, the ground spoilers deploy, and still we see nothing. The autopilots lower the nose at a programmed rate, and then just as the nosewheel is about to touch, we make out a short stream of centerline lights disappearing beneath the nose. I pray that no vehicle has strayed onto the runway. We would have no warning of the impending collision.

The autopilots have shifted to the rollout mode and remain locked onto the localizer by steering the nosewheel.

I engage the thrust reversers, which seem more effective at making noise than slowing the airplane. The first officer calls out, "Eighty knots," which is the signal to come out of reverse and apply normal braking. I also disconnect the autopilots, resume manual control of the aircraft, and steer toward the ghostly image of a high-speed taxiway.

It is humbling to execute CAT III approaches and landings in an L-1011. They compel us to concede that the autopilots make good landings more consistently than human pilots.

In a sense, CAT III approaches are safer than CAT I and II approaches made without the benefit of autoland (or a CAT III-approved, head-up display). CAT III operations do not expose pilots to the danger associated with transitioning at 100 feet to visual conditions and then landing manually with as little as a 1,200-foot RVR.

Perhaps the most hazardous aspect of a CAT III operation is finding one's way to the gate without bumping into something on the way.

Not even the great Jimmy Doolittle had to accept that challenge.

Chapter 13 **Circling Approaches**

All motion involves risk. Stepping out of a bathtub, walking across the street, or flying an airplane cannot be totally without hazard. Most of aviation's risks, however, are well understood and usually can be avoided or minimized by planning and precaution. There are exceptions. One is the circling approach.

During a recent three-year period, there were 45 accidents resulting from circling approaches. Similar accidents continue to occur with alarming regularity. Most pilots understand that the circling approach is inherently dangerous, a form of legalized scud running in limited visibility. But many circling accidents occur because of factors about which most pilots know very little.

While researching this topic, I interviewed 38 professional pilots, half of whom were airline captains, and found that most of them do not appreciate what is necessary to safely complete a circling approach, particularly at night and in mountainous terrain. These pilots are not alone. Many—and perhaps most—FAA inspectors and examiners also harbor dangerous misconceptions about the circling approach. Even the National Transportation Safety Board demonstrates ignorance about the subject by arriving at erroneous conclusions and probable causes with respect to accidents involving circling approaches.

The reason for this confusion is regrettably simple: The FAA does not publish or make available the information and guidance necessary for pilots to understand the critical elements of a circling approach. What is available in the FAA's Instrument Flying Handbook and Aeronautical Information Manual, two bibles for instrument pilots, is woefully inadequate and archaic. Some straight talk about circling approaches is long overdue.

The circling approach consists of four phases: the instrument- approach procedure (IAP), the circling maneuver at or above the minimum descent altitude (MDA), the descent from MDA to touchdown, and—when necessary—the missed-approach procedure. The instrument-approach phase is technically not a circling approach. It is a conventional approach (usually nonprecision) designed to allow a pilot to arrive at the MDA and visually identify the airport prior to reaching the missed approach point (MAP). If the airport cannot be seen prior to arriving at the MAP, a missed approach is mandatory.

The first critical error often is made when the pilot sights the airport and abandons the published approach course to begin the circling maneuver. If the instrument approach is abandoned when too far from the airport, the pilot unwittingly places his aircraft in a position where absolutely no obstacle protection is provided, and a controlled crash into terrain could result. This raises the question: How close to an airport must the airplane be so as to remain safely above all obstacles while circling at the MDA? This is one of those critical pieces of the puzzle that the FAA fails to include in any of its publications for pilots. The information is available, however, in a book titled *United States Standard for Terminal Instrument Procedures.* Unfortunately, this publication, colloquially referred to as TERPS, is intended for those who design instrument approaches and is not available in the general marketplace. (Pilots should make an effort to obtain a copy of TERPS from the Government Printing Office because of the insight it provides regarding all IFR procedures.)

According to TERPS, a pilot is assured of at least 300 feet of obstacle protection while visually circling an airport at the MDA, but only when within what is called the circling approach area. This area, however, is much smaller than you might imagine.

Figure 9 shows how a circling approach area is determined. An arc is swung from the center of the approach end of each runway. The radius of this arc is the distance shown in Figure 10. For example, the radius of the circling area for aircraft in Category C (those with approach speeds of 121 to 140 KCAS) is only 1.7 nautical miles. The final shape and size of the circling area is determined by connecting the arcs with lines tangent to the arcs (as in Figure 9). This may sound complicated, but the result is startlingly simple: A Category C aircraft is assured obstacle protection only when within approximately 1.7 NM of the airport. By flying even slightly outside this area, a pilot risks colliding with high terrain that he might not be able to see at night, for example. It should be obvious, therefore, that to remain safely and laterally distant from any obstacles that might lurk immediately outside the circling area, a pilot flying a Category C aircraft should never fly much more than a mile from the airport while circling at the MDA. That is why the circling approach used to be called a "close-in circling approach" (and probably still should be).

As shown in Figure 10, maximum safe distances from the airport vary from 1.3 to 4.5 NM, depending on aircraft approach speed. This explains why faster aircraft usually have higher minimums. As the size of the circling area expands, the MDA must be raised so as to remain at least 300 feet above

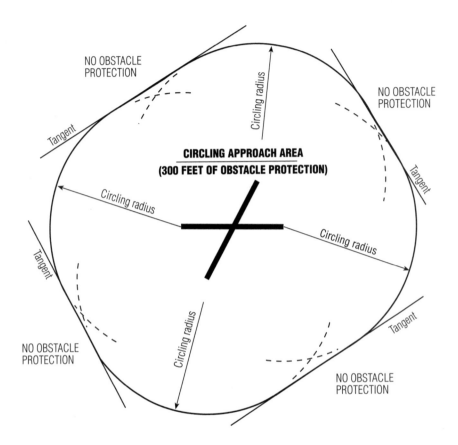

NO OBSTACLE
PROTECTION

NO OBSTACLE
PROTECTION

Tangent

Circling radius

CIRCLING APPROACH AREA
(300 FEET OF OBSTACLE PROTECTION)

Tangent

Circling radius

Circling radius

Tangent

Circling radius

NO OBSTACLE
PROTECTION

Circling radius

Tangent

NO OBSTACLE
PROTECTION

Figure 9. Determining a circling approach area

Aircraft Approach Category (based on 1.3 V_{SO} calibrated airspeed at maximum certificated landing weight)	**Radius of Circling Area**	Standard (lowest) Circling Minimums	
		HAA	**Visibility**
Category A Less than 91 knots	1.3 NM	350 feet	1.0 SM
Category B 91–120 knots	1.5 NM	450 feet	1.0 SM
Category C 121–140 knots	1.7 NM	450 feet	1.5 SM
Category D 141–165 knots	2.3 NM	550 feet	2.0 SM
Category E More than 165 knots	4.5 NM	550 feet	2.0 SM

Figure 10. Maximum safe distances during a circling approach

higher terrain that might be immediately outside a smaller circling area. It is permissible and safe for a pilot to maneuver outside the circling area for his particular aircraft category. To do so, however, he must remain within the larger circling radius specified for a faster aircraft, as shown in Figure 10. He also must abide by the higher MDA that might be specified for that faster category of aircraft.

Now, back to our original question: How close to the airport must the airplane be to remain safely above all obstacles while circling at the MDA? The answer is: Never abandon the final approach course until safely within the applicable circling radius shown in Figure 10 if obstacle protection is desired while circling at the MDA. Any maneuvering performed outside the circling area is at the pilot's risk and should not be attempted unless all obstacles are clearly visible (such as during the day with good visibility). This also explains why tower controllers may not instruct a pilot executing a circling approach to extend his downwind leg or widen his traffic pattern. Following such an instruction might cause a pilot to leave the circling area and lose his obstacle protection.

Figure 10 shows that the radius of the circling area increases as approach speed increases. This is because faster aircraft obviously need more room within which to maneuver. A pilot, however, may perform the circling maneuver at any airspeed of his choosing (aircraft limitations permitting). But if a pilot opts to increase his airspeed so as to change his circling category, he must abide by the higher MDA of that new category.

Maneuvering within the circling area and at the MDA may continue indefinitely as long as the pilot remains in visual conditions and can keep the airport in sight at all times. If an identifiable part of the airport does not remain distinctly visible during such a circling maneuver while at or above the MDA, a missed approach is mandatory (unless the inability to see the airport is caused only by banking the aircraft). Because operating within the circling area at the MDA guarantees only 300 feet of obstacle protection, pilots should recognize the foolishness of descending even slightly below the MDA to avoid reentering clouds, for example. Three hundred feet is a slim margin of safety when flying over high terrain at night or in reduced visibility.

Most pilots (and most flight operation departments) erroneously believe that circling at high MDAs is safer than circling at lower altitudes. It does not matter how high the MDA is above the airport because there is only 300 feet of obstacle protection in any event. The higher the MDA, the higher the terrain. There is, however, a unique hazard associated with a combination of high MDAs and cold ambient temperatures: altimeter errors become larger and more dangerous as altitude above the airport increases.

Consider, for example, the 3,700-foot-AGL MDA associated with the NDB-D approach at Missoula, Montana. When the temperature on the ground is 0°C, a pilot flying that high above the airport actually is 170 feet lower than he thinks he is. With a reported temperature of -10°C, the altimeter is in error by 320 feet, which could be 20 feet below the top of an obstruction that is supposed to be 300 feet below the circling MDA. Colder temperatures, of course, produce significantly larger altimeter errors. This is another one of those critical factors about which the FAA is silent.

Another question: Must the in-flight visibility while circling at or above the MDA be at least the minimum visibility specified for the approach? Curiously, it need not be. Any visibility is legal and will suffice as long as the pilot can remain in visual conditions and keep the airport in sight. The minimum visibility specified for the approach is required, however, to operate below the MDA.

The obvious purpose of circling the airport at MDA is to position the aircraft at a point from which a normal descent can be made from the circling area to the runway of intended landing. This maneuvering should be made as close to the airport as practical, not only to avoid straying outside protected airspace, but also to prevent losing sight of the airport. If the visibility while circling is 1 mile, for example, and the pilot gets more than a mile from the airport, it is likely that visual contact with the airport will be lost, and a missed approach will be necessary.

One way to judge distance from the airport is to use the runway as a gauge. A 7,500-foot-long runway, for example, is about 1.5 statute miles long. A pilot using such a runway and not wanting to be more than a mile from the runway knows not to get farther away than a distance equivalent to two-thirds of the length of the runway. A pilot is not likely to get too far from the airport, however, as long as he reminds himself that he might be circling deep within a granite bowl the sides of which cannot be seen but are immediately outside the circling area. This indicates how perilous it can be to stray very far from the airport, particularly when operating in mountainous terrain at night or in poor visibility.

Circling ordinarily should be made to the left (unless prohibited by a notation on the approach chart) because this provides the pilot with the best view of the airport.

According to the regulations, a pilot may leave and continue to operate below the MDA only if:

1. the flight visibility is not less than that prescribed for the approach,
2. at least one of the visual references (as specified in the Federal Aviation Regulations) for the runway of intended landing is distinctly visible and identifiable to the pilot, and
3. the aircraft is in a position from which a descent to a landing on the intended runway can be made at a normal rate of descent using normal maneuvering.

Contrary to popular belief, once a pilot leaves the haven of an MDA during a circling approach, he sacrifices all obstacle protection. This is unlike other IFR approach procedures that protect a pilot from colliding with the ground as long as he complies with the dictates of the approach procedure. In other words, a pilot operating below an MDA while circling must provide his own obstacle protection. Many accidents could have been avoided had the pilots been aware of this simple fact.

Any pilot contemplating a circling approach at night or in poor visibility should make it a point to learn in advance as much as possible about the terrain and other obstructions in the vicinity of the airport. Unfortunately, sectional and terminal area charts do not provide sufficient detail to serve this purpose. Small hills (into which many circling aircraft have crashed) often are not shown. Topographical aeronautical charts portray only the general nature of the terrain in the vicinity of airports. Nor can instrument approach charts be relied upon because these show only selected spot elevations that are not intended to be used for obstruction avoidance. (Some experts contend that all obstructions should be deleted from instrument approach charts to prevent pilots from believing that they can rely on such information to avoid obstructions while circling below the MDA.) The FAA's *Airport/Facility Directory,* which often includes comments about obstructions in the vicinity of airports, might be helpful. Regardless of whatever information a pilot may or may not have about the obstructions surrounding an airport, none of this relieves him of the responsibility to visually establish and maintain a safe descent profile. In other words, if you cannot see well enough to avoid obstructions, you have no business continuing the approach.

This raises an interesting point with respect to night circling approaches in mountainous terrain. A pilot can break out of the overcast, circle the airport at a relatively high MDA, and then begin a visual descent to landing with unlimited visibility beneath the clouds. Although he can easily see the distant lights, this does not mean that he can see a dark hill or mountain directly in front of the airplane. Many pilots have fallen into this trap, which helps to explain why VFR flight after sunset is not permitted in some foreign countries. If a pilot cannot see sufficiently well to avoid any obstacles that might be in his way during a circling approach (day or night), he has no business being there. Instead, he should consider biting the bullet and executing a missed approach.

This inconvenience certainly is preferable to the potentially catastrophic alternative. During my research of this subject, the FAA's Office of Flight Standards replied in a letter to me that "it is particularly important to note that the conspicuity of obstacles in areas of high terrain may not be possible at night." The same warning applies to those flying circling approaches during the day under conditions that make it difficult or impossible to see obstructions (such as when they are obscured by snow or heavy rain).

There obviously are numerous hazards associated with circling approaches at low altitude and in adverse weather. The FAA could take a giant step forward by revising the *Instrument Flying Handbook* and the *Aeronautical Information Manual* (AIM) to include material that clarifies what is expected of pilots during circling approaches. Continuing to ignore the problem will result in the perpetuation of the circling-approach accident.

Chapter 14 **Altimetry**

There is more to an altimeter than meets the eye. When several pilots were asked to read an altimeter shown in a photograph taken at an airport near the Dead Sea in Israel, most noted an indicated altitude of 8,780 feet MSL. This is because they failed to notice that the 10,000 foot pointer (the small, third hand of a three-hand altimeter) was slightly left of zero. After careful inspection and explanation, they ultimately agreed that the indicated altitude was actually 1,220 feet below sea level, an error of exactly 10,000 feet.

Altimeters not only are misread occasionally, they often are misleading because of system errors that are either misunderstood or dangerously underestimated.

Pilots learn early that altimeters indicate correctly only when using the proper altimeter setting. An incorrect setting results in an altitude error of 1,000 feet per inch of mercury (of atmospheric pressure). An altimeter misset by a tenth of an inch results in a 100-foot error.

We know also that when using too high an altimeter setting, the aircraft is lower than we believe it to be; true altitude is less than indicated altitude. Typically, this occurs when flying from a high to low pressure area without resetting the altimeter enroute. From this stems the mnemonic "from high to low, look out below."

The function of a sensitive altimeter is to measure how high the instrument is above a point where the barometric pressure is equal to the altimeter setting. An altimeter set to 30.00 inches, for example, indicates height above sea level only when the atmospheric pressure at sea level also is 30.00 inches. If the aircraft proceeds into the low-pressure system, the altimeter—still set to 30.00 inches—continues to measure height where the pressure also is 30.00 inches. However, this dips further and further below sea level. In other words, the altimeter displays height above reference points that are situated below sea level.

This altimeter error—the difference between true and indicated altitude—is eliminated by resetting the altimeter. When the altimeter is reset to the sea-level pressure, 29.60 inches, for example, it then indicates how high it is above that point where atmospheric pressure is 29.60 inches. This height coincides with the altitude of the instrument above mean sea level; true and indicated altitudes are the same. (Mean sea level is defined as "the average height of the surface of the sea for all stages of tide." Actual sea level at any given place and time also is affected by swell and wave height. This explains why a properly set altimeter cannot be used to determine height above the water at extremely low altitudes.)

The concept of pressure altitude is not as clearly understood. It is the altitude indicated when the altimeter is set to 29.92 inches and generally is regarded only as a figure needed to compute density altitude and true airspeed. In reality, pressure altitude is the height of an aircraft above that point where the actual pressure is 29.92 inches. Such a point is above sea level when flying in a high, and below sea level when in a low. In other words, pressure altitude is how high an aircraft would be if the actual atmospheric pressure at sea level were 29.92 inches.

Pressure altitude is significant to those who fly at high altitude (above 17,500 feet MSL). When at low altitude (17,500 feet and below), pilots are required to use appropriate and current altimeter settings. In this manner, true and indicated altitudes are approximately the same, and pilots can remain aware of their vertical proximity to nearby high-rise terrain. Also, vertical traffic separation depends on all pilots using a common altimeter setting when operating in a given area. When at high altitude, however, pilots are not concerned about obstructions because the highest terrain in the 48 contiguous states is California's Mt. Whitney, the summit of which is only 14,495 feet MSL. Consequently, when above 17,500 feet, altimeters are set to 29.92 inches.

The resultant pressure altitudes, however, are referred to as flight levels because true altitude is unknown. A pressure altitude of 18,000 feet, for example, is referred to as Flight Level 180, which is written as FL180. A pressure altitude of 35,000 feet is FL350, and so forth. An advantage of flight-level flying is that pilots—particularly those operating at high speed—do not have to fret about resetting their altimeters every several minutes. When at FL180 and above, 29.92 inches is used no matter how far-flung the destination.

The true altitude of an aircraft maintaining an assigned flight level does vary as it progresses from one pressure system to the next, but because the pilot is maintaining a constant indicated altitude, he is unaware of these changes. Nor does he care. Also, vertical traffic separation is enhanced at high altitude because all altimeters are adjusted to a common setting.

An interesting situation develops when flying through an area of low pressure at FL180. Because the altimeter is set to 29.92 inches, the actual altitude of the aircraft might be 17,500 feet, for example. At such a time, an IFR aircraft cruising at FL180 would be at the same true altitude as opposite-direction VFR traffic at 17,500 feet. This explains why air traffic control will not assign or allow to be used one or more of the lowest flight levels when altimeter settings in a given area are less than 29.92 inches.

Pilots are taught (for the purpose of taking FAA written examinations) that barometric pressure decreases 1 inch per 1,000 feet of altitude, but this occurs only at very low altitudes. Otherwise, you would run out of atmosphere at 30,000 feet. Pressure does change (during standard conditions) 1.07 inches between sea level and 1,000 feet, but the change between 10,000 and 11,000 feet is only 0.79 inches. Between 20,000 and 21,000 feet, it is 0.57 inches, and between 30,000 and 31,000 feet, it is only 0.40 inches. In other words, the pressure lapse rate decreases with altitude.

Because pressure change per 1,000 feet at high altitude is less than at low altitude, altimeter accuracy (sensitivity) also decreases with altitude. For this reason, aircraft at very high altitudes are provided with increased vertical separation. At the lower flight levels, east- and westbound aircraft are separated vertically by 1,000 feet, but beginning at FL290, 2,000 feet of vertical separation is provided. Eastbound traffic cruises at FL290, FL330, FL370, and so forth; westbound traffic cruises at FL310, FL350, FL390, and so forth.

A reduced pressure lapse rate at high altitude allows pilots to descend rapidly without as much ear-popping discomfort as would be experienced at lower altitudes. A pilot descending through FL200 at 4,000 fpm, for example, experiences a pressure change of only 2.47 inches during the first minute. An equally rapid descent from 4,000 feet to sea level, however, results in a pressure change of 4.08 inches. This explains why an emergency, unpressurized descent from 35,000 feet or so is not as uncomfortable as you might imagine (until reaching the lower altitudes). If a rapid descent is necessary, passenger and pilot suffering can be minimized by descending steeply at first and less rapidly at lower altitudes.

An interesting piece of trivia involves flying in areas of extremely high pressure. No matter how high the pressure, ATC is not allowed to provide an altimeter setting in excess of 31.00 inches. This is because many altimeters cannot accept a higher setting. When given a setting of 31.00 inches, therefore, consider that the actual altimeter setting might be higher. This rarely is a problem except when shooting an IFR approach to minimums. A pilot might have to execute a missed approach because his indicated altitude at such a time will be above his true altitude. This prevents him from descending to genuine minimums (in terms of height above airport or height above threshold). The highest altimeter setting ever recorded in the contiguous United States was 31.40 inches at Helena, Montana, in 1962. The highest pressure ever recorded anywhere was 32.01 inches at Agata, Siberia, in 1968. The lowest surface pressure ever recorded near sea level in the free atmosphere was 26.35 inches, which occurred when a hurricane passed over Long Key, Florida, in 1935. The normal range of altimeter settings is considered to be 28.00 to 31.00 inches.

Although pilots are generally conscientious about using current altimeter settings, they often are not as aware of errors caused by substandard temperatures. Such errors can be much larger than you might imagine, and although altimeters can be corrected for pressure variations, they cannot be corrected for temperature variations.

Ask most pilots about the effect on an altimeter of flying into a cold air mass, and many will say that this is like flying into a high (because cold air is denser than warm air). In other words, they believe that substandard temperatures cause indicated altitude to be less than true altitude. Actually, just the opposite is true. Flying in cold air has the same effect as flying into a low; the aircraft is lower than the pilot believes it to be. The mnemonic mentioned earlier should be revised to read "from high to low, or from warm to cold, look out below."

But if cold air is denser than warm air—which it is—why does it have the same effect on the altimeter as flying into lowering pressure? This seems to make no sense whatsoever. To unravel the paradox, assume that the barometric pressure at two sea-level airports is the same, 30.00 inches. The only meteorological difference between them is surface temperature. Because airport A is experiencing a heat wave, the air above that airport has less than normal density. As a matter of fact, the air is so thin that a pilot must gain much more than 1,000 feet to experience a 1.0-inch pressure drop. In this case, he must climb to 1,300 feet in the "thin" air to get to where the pressure is 29.00 inches. (The pressure lapse rate is less in warm air than in cold.) The temperature at airport B is extremely cold. The air is so dense that a pilot needs to climb only 500 feet before experiencing a 1.0-inch pressure loss. In other words, the pressure at 500 feet above airport B is 29.00 inches.

Now assume that a pilot is at an indicated altitude of 1,000 feet above airport A while using an altimeter setting of 30.00 inches. His true altitude obviously is 1,300 feet, but as the flight progresses toward B, the pilot must descend to 500 feet MSL to maintain a constant indicated altitude of 1,000 feet. Without realizing it, he has lost 800 feet while flying from warm air to cold. This obviously is an exaggerated example, but it helps us to visualize the principle.

It is worth emphasizing that when flying from a high to a low, or from warm air to cold, the loss of true altitude cannot be detected. This is because ambient pressure does not change during the descent. The altimeter and vertical speed indicator are fooled into believing that the aircraft is maintaining a constant altitude. Can such a shallow descent affect performance? You bet it can. An airplane flying even slightly downhill does have somewhat more airspeed than when flying uphill in the opposite direction (depending on the distance over which the atmospheric changes occur).

Nevertheless, pilots generally do not appreciate how low they really might be when operating in frigid climes. Consider an airplane at a true altitude of 10,000 feet at a time when the mean temperature of the air between the airport and the aircraft is -10°F. The indicated altitude will be 1,090 feet higher than true altitude. Temperature-induced errors can exceed 3,000 feet during extreme conditions.

Pilots do not have to be in the dark about true altitude when operating in unusually cold temperatures. They should sometimes use an appropriate computer to determine true altitude. The result might inspire an expeditious climb, especially at night or when in instrument meteorological conditions (with or without an appropriate ATC clearance).

Although temperature-related errors increase with altitude above the station providing the altimeter setting, they cannot be ignored at low altitude. When on an IFR approach, for example, the FAA allows aircraft to pass only 300 feet above obstacles on final approach or while circling at minimum descent altitudes. At such times, no amount of altimeter error can be tolerated.

Canadian pilots, who know something about cold weather operations, use a government-provided chart to determine how much altitude should be conservatively added to the minimum altitudes shown on approach charts when temperatures are significantly below standard. (A pilot may adjust procedural altitudes shown on approach charts once cleared for an approach. With rare exception, these are minimum altitudes, and a pilot may fly above them. He may not, however, adjust assigned altitudes, but he may refuse them.)

As a point of interest, the coldest surface temperature ever recorded was -127°F (exclusive of any wind-chill factor) at Vostok in Antarctica in 1960; the hottest was 136°F (in the shade) at Azizia, Libya, in 1922. (While I'm on a meteorological roll, the wettest place in the world is Mt. Waialeale, Kauai, Hawaii, where the average annual rainfall is 460 inches per year; the driest is Arica, Chile, which averages 0.03 inches of rain per year.)

During January 1989, an intense continental-polar air mass blanketed Alaska and brought with it surface temperatures as low as -85°F and altimeter settings as high as 31.85 inches. This resulted in a density altitude at Anchorage International Airport of 14,000 feet below sea level. Assuming that a pilot can start an engine in such a climate, can you imagine what airplane performance must have been like?

Other altimeter errors include being provided an incorrect setting (it happens), flying through strong winds over mountainous terrain, and using an unreliable altimeter.

According to the FAA, a pilot noting an altitude discrepancy of 75 feet while on the ground with a properly set altimeter should refer the problem to an appropriate repair station. Although the FAA does not designate a maximum-allowable altimeter error for either IFR or VFR flight, common sense should dictate what is safe and what is not. (Maximum-allowable errors stipulated for passing a biennial static system test are applicable only at the time of the test.)

Also, if an altimeter is slightly in error, the FAA prefers that the pilot use the altimeter setting—not airport elevation—to set the altimeter before departure. This is because the error noted may not be consistent throughout a flight.

The question "how high is up?" may be of philosophical interest to some people, but it is a subject that pilots can ill afford to ponder.

Chapter 15 **Minimum Vectoring Altitude**

A few years ago, a Cessna 172 departed Van Nuys, California, on an IFR flight plan to 12-mile-distant Santa Monica. An instrument flight instructor was in command. Shortly after takeoff, he was given a radar vector that ultimately was to have led the aircraft to the final approach course. Moments later, however, the controller who issued the vector was relieved by another controller who might not have been made aware of the Cessna. The flight came to an abrupt end when the aircraft struck the towering San Gabriel Mountains, which separate the Los Angeles Basin from the Mojave Desert. According to the subsequent investigation, the aircraft crashed while maintaining the assigned heading and altitude. Both occupants perished.

There is always some Monday-morning quarterbacking following an aircraft accident, but a tragedy of this nature seems to divide opinion. Some pilots place total blame on the controller(s) for vectoring an aircraft into terrain. There can be no doubt that the controller in such a case often is guilty of a procedural error; when vectoring an aircraft, it is his or her responsibility to keep the aircraft at or above the minimum vectoring altitude (MVA) and out of harm's way. Other pilots criticize the pilot because he is responsible for maintaining a safe altitude at all times. In other words, the pilot presumably should always know his position relative to obstructions and terrain. This apparently is true even while being vectored in instrument conditions.

According to the *Aeronautical Information Manual* (AIM), a clearance "is not authorization for a pilot to deviate from any rule, regulation or minimum altitude nor to conduct unsafe operation of his aircraft." The National Transportation Safety Board apparently agrees that this responsibility applies to a pilot accepting radar vectors. During its investigation of several airline and general aviation CFIT (controlled flight into terrain) accidents, the NTSB has indicated that pilots are expected to always be aware of their position relative to nearby terrain and obstructions.

The logical conclusion is that both pilot and controller are responsible for terrain avoidance. The AIM goes on to say that "the responsibilities of the pilot and controller intentionally overlap in many areas, providing a degree of redundancy. Should one or the other fail in any manner, this overlapping responsibility is expected to compensate, in many cases, for failures that may affect safety." Unfortunately, the redundancy mentioned in the AIM does not seem to exist during radar vectoring. Consequently, the pilot is caught in a dilemma because he is responsible for maintaining a safe altitude at a time when he may not have a viable means of determining his proximity to high-rise terrain. This is a particularly acute problem during low-altitude vectoring within any of the designated mountainous areas defined in the AIM.

Radar vectoring obviously is a commonplace procedure, especially in high-density terminal airspace. Its purpose is to provide traffic separation, to keep aircraft away from noise-sensitive areas, and to obtain an operational advantage for either the pilot or the controller. With respect to the controller, radar vectoring is used primarily as a method of sequencing aircraft so as to prevent aerial logjamming or conflict. The pilot takes advantage of vectoring either to simplify navigation or to capitalize on the short-cut routings that vectoring often provides. The pilot complies with vectoring clearances simply by maintaining assigned headings and altitudes. According to the AIM, however, the pilot also is responsible for questioning any assigned heading or altitude believed to be incorrect. But how can a pilot have a basis for believing a clearance to be incorrect at a time when he does not have the tools needed to arrive at such a conclusion?

Figure 11 shows the MVA sectors for the Burbank, California, Terminal Radar Approach Control (Tracon). It is a video map that overlies the controller's radar screen and shows the complex array of MVAs established for all airspace within a 60-nautical-mile radius of the radar antenna. These are the lowest altitudes to which a pilot may be cleared while being vectored. In most cases, the MVA is below the MEA (minimum enroute altitude) for any given airway passing through the area. In other words, a pilot flying along an airway and subsequently receiving a radar vector could expect a clearance to descend below the MEA for that airway segment. Unfortunately, he has no method of independently confirming that a descent below the MEA is safe. (Because of radar limitations, an MVA occasionally is higher than an MEA.)

The MVA for a given sector is at least 1,000 feet above the highest obstacle within 3 miles of any sector boundary. This means that a pilot being vectored can expect to be as close as 3 miles to an obstacle that looms above his assigned altitude. There are times when this leaves pitifully little room for error. (An MVA also must be at least 300 feet above the floor of controlled airspace.)

When a pilot navigates along a published route segment, he can determine at a glance the applicable MEA and MOCA (minimum obstruction clearance altitude). This is an example of the safety redundancy mentioned in the AIM because both pilot and controller are aware of the minimum safe altitude for each route segment. Should the controller inadvertently issue an unsafe descent clearance, the pilot can refer to his chart and have a logical basis for questioning the clearance. Similarly, the controller knows that he cannot honor a request that would allow the aircraft to descend below the applicable MEA or MOCA. This check-and-balance system is one major reason that flying IFR is ordinarily so safe.

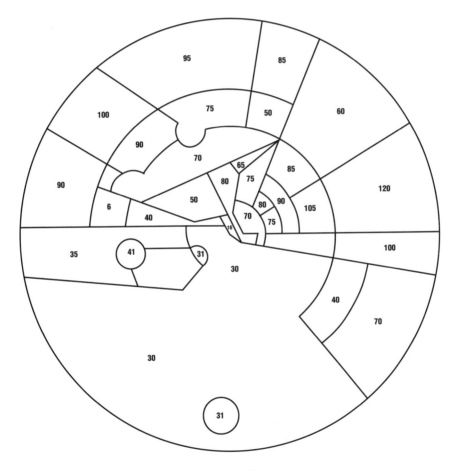

Figure 11. Burbank, California TRACON–MVA sectors

But when a pilot is given an off-route vector or is descended to an MVA along an airway, the safety afforded by redundancy is eliminated. The controller knows the applicable MVAs as the aircraft passes from one sector (as shown on the MVA video map) to another, but the pilot does not. Although he theoretically shares the responsibility for terrain avoidance, the pilot does not have sufficient information in a usable format to remain aware of his proximity to nearby obstructions, which could be only 3 miles distant (or less if the controller errs). Consider also that pilots can become somewhat disoriented (especially with respect to the proximity of terrain) during periods of prolonged vectoring that involve numerous large heading changes.

During investigative hearings about CFIT accidents that involved air carriers, a number of professional pilots candidly admitted that they do not have the tools necessary to maintain adequate terrain awareness while being radar vectored. These pilots complained that vectoring often places them in navigational limbo. In a way, their command authority is usurped—to quote one veteran Boeing 747 captain—"by a controller whose greatest risk is falling off his chair."

Most pilots being vectored over and around irregular terrain during actual IFR conditions probably have sensed gnawing doubt and discomfort because of not knowing exactly where the obstructions were, but we generally have faith in the controller and abide by his every instruction. The point is, however, that such feelings of concern are intolerable. Pilots shouldn't have to endure the kind of uneasiness that vectoring often creates. There is something wrong with the system when its users cannot feel secure and confident at all times.

Some people regard this problem as being overstated because there were only 44 CFIT accidents during a recent 18-year period. Although 2.4 accidents per year does not seem particularly dramatic (unless you are one of those involved), consider that a scientific study conservatively claims that during a recently concluded 25-year period, more than 5,000 aircraft inadvertently missed high terrain by less than 500 feet. So perhaps there is some justification for feeling a bit uneasy when navigational "command" shifts to a controller. Although the pilot is legally responsible for the safe operation of his aircraft, radar vectoring essentially compels him to rely almost totally on the controller for terrain avoidance.

It is natural to ask how an aircraft can be vectored into terrain. Such accidents usually are caused by communications irregularities that lead to confusion (of either the pilot or the controller, or both), a controller who assigns an incorrect MVA, a pilot who accepts and acts upon a descent clearance intended for someone else, failed radar systems, or a loss of communications. In some cases, a controller simply forgets about an aircraft that is being vectored toward high terrain (such as what apparently happened to the aircraft discussed at the beginning of this article).

When a pilot approaches his destination and is given a radar vector, he typically begins to relax and becomes somewhat complacent because he has been relieved of the navigational burden. For obvious reasons, however, this phase of flight—particularly when in the vicinity of mountainous terrain—demands a more heightened awareness of aircraft position, but even the most conscientious crew cannot cross-check the controller without plotting fixes on a topographical chart (a most impractical and distracting chore when flying in cloud at low altitude). Instead, the pilots typically do as they are trained to do: Tune in the approach facilities, identify them, and prepare for the approach.

If worrisome doubts begin to form about nearby obstacles while being vectored, do not hesitate to speak up. Question the controller about the MVA for the sector you are in and the one you might soon be entering. Request your position relative to nearby obstructions. Ask for a lost-communications procedure that can be used to avoid high terrain ahead of the aircraft, just in case. Discretion remains the better part of valor. Also, an obviously alert crew helps to keep the controller alert (even though this is usually not a problem).

If a pilot senses that he is dangerously close to terrain, he can exercise his emergency authority and begin an expeditious climb. This might be a pilot's only option during a two-way communications failure (which also can be caused by a stuck microphone button or a saturated frequency). But how many of us are willing to do this when it might involve climbing into overhead traffic? (It is interesting to note that 80 percent of CFIT accidents involve aircraft striking terrain within only 300 feet of mountain ridges and peaks.)

Some pilots erroneously believe that the minimum sector altitudes (MSAs) portrayed on approach plates (shown within the circle at the top of Figure 12) can be used to determine a minimum safe altitude while being vectored in the vicinity of an airport. Although MSAs provide a 1,000-foot clearance above the highest obstacle within 25 NM of the specified navigation facility, they often are much higher than the MVAs, MEAs, and MOCAs found within 25 NM of an airport. Consequently, they have virtually no value during the course of normal operations. Even the august NTSB has misinterpreted the relevance of MSAs by formally criticizing pilots involved in CFIT accidents for having descended below the MSA. (The pie-shaped MSA sectors, by the way, are not the same as the irregular sectors established for designating MVAs.) MSAs were developed in the dark ages of IFR flight as altitudes that could be used to approach an airport during an unspecified emergency situation. Some experts speculate that MSAs eventually will be deleted from approach plates because they are essentially inapplicable in today's IFR environment.

Recognizing the terrain-awareness problem associated with radar vectoring, Jeppesen Sanderson portrays the general layout of terrain on its terminal area charts and appropriate approach plates, including color contouring. Although these features do help a pilot to appraise the nature of surrounding topography during off-route navigation, they do not make it any easier to maintain positional awareness during radar vectoring. Also, area charts are available for relatively few destinations. (Instrument area charts published by the U.S. Government, it should be noted, make no effort to portray topography.)

Can a pilot reliably use obstacles shown on an approach plate to determine minimum safe altitudes? Not really. Figure 12 shows an ILS approach to Runway 8R at Phoenix. Assume that an aircraft is south of the airport in the vicinity of the 3,407-foot (MSL) obstruction. Approach control clears the pilot to descend to 3,000 feet. Would this be safe? It is difficult to know without knowing the precise position of the aircraft. Additionally, the spot elevation shown on the approach plate is just that, a spot elevation. What is not shown are other nearby obstructions (such as lengthy ridges) that might be only slightly below the spot elevation yet above the newly assigned altitude. Approach charts clearly cannot be used as tools for terrain avoidance at low MVAs.

The minimum safe altitude warning (MSAW) was developed in the late 1970s as a computer program for the FAA's automated radar terminal system III. It provides a computer-generated warning to controllers whenever an aircraft descends below a predetermined safe altitude. MSAW does prevent many accidents but does not solve the problem completely. The warning must be quickly relayed by the controller to the pilot, and this is not always possible because of communications difficulties and saturated frequencies. Consider also that when an aircraft is too low for a given MVA sector, intervening terrain can make VHF communications impossible. Nuisance warnings notwithstanding, MSAWs would be more effective if they could be transmitted directly to the pilot. This could be done via up-link transmissions when aircraft are appropriately equipped.

Some people have suggested that pilots could be kept in the safety loop by providing them with the type of MVA charts used by controllers. (MVA charts are difficult to obtain; my attempts to obtain MVA charts from three different terminal radar facilities were fruitless.) Such charts, however, are not the answer. This is because the complex shapes and locations of MVA sectors do not correlate to VOR/DME indications. MVA sectors are plotted with respect to a radar antenna site, which usually is not collocated with a VORTAC transmitter. Any attempt by a pilot flying on instruments to fix his

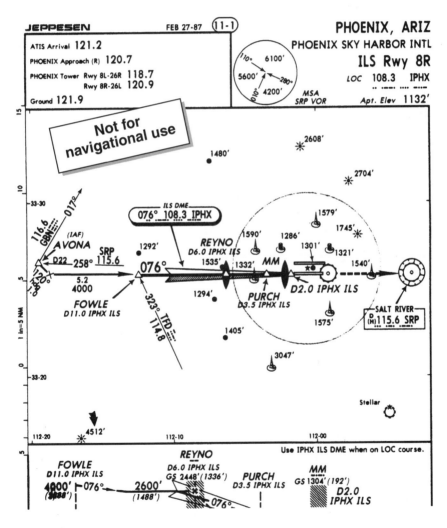

Figure 12

position with respect to MVA sectors would result only in distraction and confusion. (The U.S. Air Force once tried to incorporate MVAs on its instrument approach charts, but the attempt was abandoned because the results were too difficult to interpret.)

One immediate step could be taken to provide the kind of safety redundancy clearly lacking during off-route vectoring. GPS and Loran receiver manufacturers could store MVAs in their databases and develop a selectable mode to display the applicable MVAs to the pilot. As the aircraft moves from one MVA sector to the next, the MVA indication on the display would change automatically. Pilots would be brought back into the safety loop because they could verify at a glance the minimum safe altitude at all times, not just when flying along a published route.

In the meantime, pilots must make do with what is available now. Just as "eternal vigilance is the price of liberty," it also is the price that must be paid to ensure safety in flight.

The author wishes to thank John M. McCormick, Jr., for data provided from his award-winning abstract, "In-Flight Access to Minimum Vectoring Altitudes—A Pilot's Perspective," published by the Society of Automotive Engineers.

Chapter 16 **Avionics Failure**

The Federal Aviation Regulations are very specific about the procedures to follow should an instrument pilot encounter two-way communications failure while flying in cloud. This is because air traffic control needs to know where such a pilot would go and at what altitudes. Otherwise, ATC would have difficulty anticipating the pilot's course of action and have to clear large chunks of airspace to avoid the possibility of a traffic conflict (or worse).

Two-way communications failure is, thankfully, rare. This is because most IFR-equipped aircraft have two or more radios, and for both of these to fail requires the failure of a common component. Fortunately, there are very few of these. One, for example, is the audio amplifier, but a pilot can combat such a failure simply by donning a headset.

The most likely cause of two-way communications failure is the failure of the entire electrical system, but this would also render the navigational systems and transponder inoperative. About this dilemma—the most likely cause of communications failure—the FAA is silent.

But one March day, David W. Berglund could have used some advice. This was when a wet low-pressure area was crawling across southern California, bringing with it widespread low ceilings and visibilities. Berglund had taken off from Oxnard (northwest of Los Angeles) in his Piper Saratoga on an instrument flight plan, bound for Riverside (east of L.A.). Although the forecast called for heavy rain and widespread turbulence, the flight promised to be otherwise routine.

Approaching the halfway point of the 90-NM flight at an assigned altitude of 5,000 feet, Berglund began to hear a loud squeal from the overhead speaker, even though he was using headphones at the time. He also noticed that the displays of various pieces of avionics began to flash erratically.

Sensing some sort of electrical anomaly, he pressed the voltage function button on his Stormscope. He was immediately informed that battery voltage was only 10.4 volts and falling.

Berglund followed the book: Everything but essential electrical appliances was turned off, and he advised SoCal Approach Control that he was experiencing an electrical system malfunction and needed an immediate clearance to nearby Van Nuys Airport for an ILS approach to Runway 16.

The controller immediately cleared Berglund to 7,000 feet and issued a radar vector to Umber Intersection, which is on the final approach course to Van Nuys. Not a major problem, Berglund thought. After all, the battery would last long enough to complete the approach.

But seven minutes later, the battery expired. It had not been charged for part or perhaps all of the flight. Anything and everything electrical became dead weight.

Thankfully, Berglund had a hand-held transceiver complete with VOR guidance. But even this presented an unanticipated problem, because it was difficult to maintain control of the airplane under such adverse conditions while setting up the hand-held for communications and navigation. Consequently, he was receiving an intense and unwelcome refresher course in recovering from unusual attitudes.

Berglund advised the controller of his deteriorating situation and asked where the nearest VFR conditions could be found. Heading toward better weather, he believed, would be safer than attempting a VOR approach with a hand-held.

The controller advised that William J. Fox Airfield in the western tip of the northern desert was reporting a 4,000-foot overcast. He also cleared Berglund to proceed direct to the Palmdale VOR, which is on the desert floor north of the mountains ringing the Los Angeles Basin.

After turning toward Palmdale, Berglund had to incessantly switch back and forth between the nav and com functions of the hand-held. Finally, he was given welcome relief in the form of a radar vector. Although his transponder was obviously inoperative, Joshua Approach Control tracked the aircraft using its primary radar return.

Just as Berglund began to breathe a bit more easily, the batteries in the hand-held also failed. With few options remaining, he continued northbound and dead-reckoned his way toward Fox Field. Soon, however, he spotted the desert floor through small holes in the clouds. He took one large gulp and pushed the nose down, praying that he would not encounter anything solid on the way down.

After landing, Berglund discovered the source of his electrical nightmare. It was a worn belt (similar to a fan belt) that was slipping and incapable of turning the alternator.

He also learned not to rely on nicad batteries retaining a charge for very long. He now recharges them with regularity and carries several alkaline batteries because of their relatively long shelf life.

Berglund continues to wonder what fate might have had in store had there not been VFR conditions within range of his fuel supply. He prefers not to think about it. But part of every preflight briefing now includes determining where he could go should history be repeated.

He also learned the hard way why the FAA offers no advice to instrument pilots regarding navigation failure. There is precious little to give.

Chapter 17 **Flying DME Arcs**

Of all the black boxes in an airplane, the DME ranks as one of the simplest to use. All a pilot has to do is glance occasionally at the slowly changing numbers to determine his slant-range distance from a given VORTAC. But when he is confronted with having to maintain a circling track at a specific distance from the station, DME usage assumes an entirely different complexion. Tracking DME arcs can be a new and frustrating experience, especially when winds aloft are strong.

Some years ago, DME arcs were relatively uncommon, and IFR pilots didn't have to worry much about them. But times changed, and the FAA increased the use of DME arcs as prescribed paths to be followed during the initial phases of IFR approaches.

The Feds even went so far as to create an IFR approach procedure incorporating a final approach that is defined by the 24 DME arc of a nearby VORTAC. That's right; the "straight-in," VOR/DME approach to Runway 10 at NASA Wallops Station at Chincoteague Island, Virginia, requires flying a circular track all the way from the intermediate approach fix to the runway threshold.

Because such an approach procedure is so rare, it obviously does not dictate an urgent need to become proficient in flying DME arcs. But the proliferation of DME arcs as "initial" IFR approaches does.

A DME arc is simply a circular course at a specific slant range (DME distance) from a given VORTAC. An arc typical of the type most likely to be encountered is shown in Figure 13, which is a simplified view of a back course approach to Runway 21 at Amarillo, Texas. A pilot who arrives at the initial approach fix (IAF) south of the AMA VORTAC (aircraft number 1) and is then "cleared for the approach" is expected to track along the 8 DME arc (a radius of 8 miles from the DME) until near the localizer. Because he might have only one navigation receiver, (and that would have to be tuned to the AMA VORTAC while tracking the arc), a pilot needs to be warned when nearing the localizer to prevent him from unknowingly flying through the final approach course.

This warning is provided in the form of a "lead radial," which, in this case, is the AMA 056-degree radial. After tracking the 8 DME arc and upon

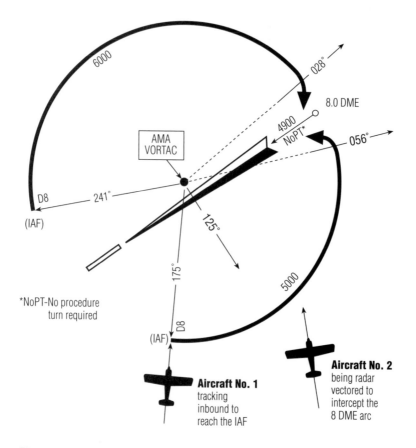

Figure 13. Approaching a DME arc

reaching the lead radial, the pilot should simultaneously tune in the ILS and turn to intercept the localizer.

It is also possible that a pilot might be radar-vectored to intercept the DME arc at a point other than at an IAF. Aircraft number 2 in the figure has been cleared to maintain a given heading and intercept the 8 DME arc, at which point he should begin orbiting the VORTAC as shown on the approach plate.

It is interesting to note that each circular initial approach, like conventional initial approaches, is provided a minimum enroute altitude (MEA). The arc northwest of the AMA localizer, for example, has an MEA of 6,000 feet, but the southeastern arc has an MEA of 5,000 feet. It is imperative when tracking such an arc that a pilot does not descend to the applicable MEA unless either "cleared for the approach" or cleared to the specified altitude. Otherwise, he must maintain the last assigned altitude.

Assume that a pilot has been cleared for the approach and is tracking the northwesterly arc at 6,000 feet. Upon crossing the 028-degree lead radial, he begins an inbound turn to intercept the localizer. Is he then free to descend to 4,900 feet, which is shown on the plate as the MEA when inbound from the "8.0 DME" fix along the localizer course? Emphatically not. Descent must be delayed until the localizer has been intercepted. Crossing a lead radial is not an authorization to descend; intercepting the localizer is.

Another requirement for arc flying is shown in Figure 14, a simplified view of the VOR-A approach to Cheyenne, Wyoming. Lead radials are not needed to warn a pilot that he is nearing the final approach course because the same NAVAID (CYS VORTAC) is used throughout the entire procedure.

Pilots should be aware that when DME arcs are used as initial IFR approaches, maximum obstacle protection is provided only when within 4 miles of the arc. In other words, when tracking a 17 DME arc, for example, a pilot must remain between the 13 and 21 DME arcs that provide him with an 8-mile-wide band of maneuvering protection.

Additionally, as the DME radius becomes shorter and the circle becomes smaller, flying the arc becomes more difficult. To prevent imposing too much of a workload on pilots, civilian DME arcs are limited to a minimum radius of 7 miles.

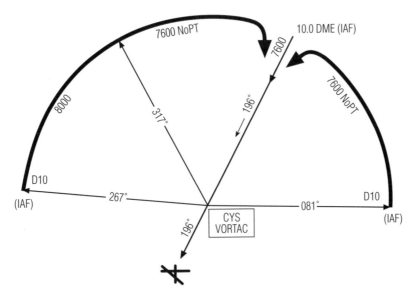

Figure 14. VOR-A approach with arc transitions

At first glance, tracking a DME arc appears to be a relatively simple affair. It's just a matter of flying a wide, sweeping circular track in such a way as to keep the indicated distance constant.

Maintaining a precise track along a DME arc on a windless day theoretically requires an extremely shallow banked turn with an almost infinitesimal turn rate. For example, if a pilot were tracking an arc with a 30 DME radius while flying at a true airspeed of 100 knots, 1.9 hours would be required to fly the entire 188-NM circumference. To do so while constantly turning would require a turn rate of only one-twentieth of a degree per second. Only a computer is capable of such excruciating precision.

In practice, therefore, tracking an arc necessitates flying a series of short, straight segments, each of which spans a 10-degree sector of the arc. The result is a 36-side polygon that approximates a circle.

To intercept the 20 DME arc shown in Figure 15, for example, the pilot tracks inbound on the 140-degree radial (as shown). When approximately one-half mile from the arc (20.5 DME), the pilot turns to a heading perpendicular to the inbound course (either 050 or 230 degrees in this case, depending upon the desired direction of flight).

Because the pilot in the figure plans to fly a counter-clockwise arc, he turns 90 degrees right to a heading of 050 degrees. This results in an initial track very nearly the same as the desired course. (A half-mile lead usually prevents overshooting the arc and is satisfactory for aircraft with airspeeds of 150 knots or less; proportionately larger leads are required for faster aircraft.)

During the latter part of the intercepting turn, he closely monitors the DME. If the DME indication is something less than 20 miles (aircraft A), the arc has been overshot, and the turn should be continued beyond 90 degrees to reintercept it. If the DME indicates more than 20 NM (aircraft B), the arc has been undershot, and the turn should be terminated prematurely.

Upon intercepting the arc, the pilot returns to the original 050-degree heading and makes whatever small heading corrections are necessary to maintain a constant DME indication of 20 NM.

Once established on the arc, it is theoretically possible (on a windless day) to remain on track by flying perpendicular to the radial being crossed at any given instant. This, however, requires changing the omni-bearing selector (OBS) in 1-degree increments throughout flight along the arc and is an arduous procedure. Instead, it is satisfactory to use radials spaced 10 degrees apart.

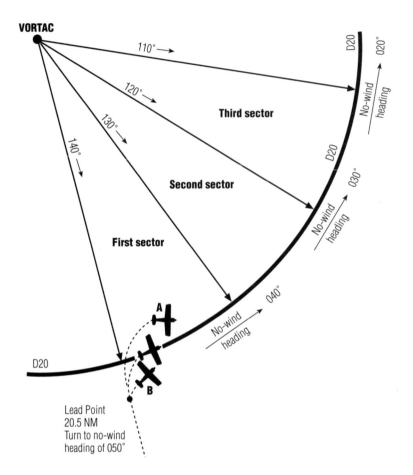

Figure 15. Intercepting a DME arc

While passing through the first sector in Figure 15, therefore, the pilot should rotate the OBS to 130 degrees, which is 10 degrees from the radial used to intercept the arc.

As this radial of 130 degrees is approached, an approximately perpendicular heading (040 degrees) should be used to track the arc. This heading, 040 degrees, is simply a guide—a no-wind reference heading. If the DME indication tends to decrease, the pilot is drifting inside the arc and should correct slightly to the right. If the DME indication tends to increase beyond 20 miles, then a correction to the left is required.

After crossing the 130-degree radial, the OBS should be set to 120 degrees. The new reference heading while traversing the second sector is 030 degrees and is perpendicular to the newly selected 120-degree radial.

If it is determined that a crosswind necessitates crabbing while crossing one sector, don't neglect to apply a similar drift-correction angle to the reference heading of the next sector. As progress around the arc continues, however, the effect of the wind changes gradually. A correction used on previous segments of the arc may be insufficient or excessive on subsequent segments.

Quite obviously, this is a thinking man's game and requires constant analyses of heading versus bearing from the station versus wind correction versus distance from the station. All these factors must be considered continuously to maintain a reasonably circular track. When the winds are strong, the mental gymnastics compound proportionately.

Orbiting in a strong wind can be simplified somewhat by flying slightly inside the arc. In this manner, the arc is constantly "turning" toward the aircraft, and interception usually can be accomplished by holding a constant heading. If the aircraft is outside the arc, the curved course constantly "turns" away from the aircraft, and larger heading corrections are required to intercept.

Because the FAA makes use of DME arcs in terminal areas, it is logical to assume that it would have developed a more simplified method of arc tracking. Yes, it is logical but incorrect. The FAA offers pitifully little information about orbiting procedures.

After querying FAA officials about this, I was told that arc flying is considered more a matter of technique than procedure, and was referred to the FAA's only published work regarding the subject, an advisory circular that is more than 20 years old. The circular contains a noteworthy comment: "Unless the pilot is highly proficient in the use of [VOR/DME] equipment and in performing [DME arcs], it is recommended that [orbits] be flown only when RMI (radio magnetic indicator) equipment is available."

Because most general aviation aircraft are not so elaborately equipped, this places most pilots between a rock and a hard place when confronted with the need to fly a DME arc, especially when the winds are strong.

The RMI, of course, does simplify orbiting. With a needle that points to a VOR station the way an ADF needle points to a radiobeacon, all a pilot must do is keep the needle pointed approximately toward the inside wing tip while making small heading corrections to maintain a relatively constant

DME indication. The RMI is invaluable in this regard because it helps a pilot to visualize the relative location of the VORTAC station.

Orbiting without RMI is almost like "turning about a point" without looking at the pylon. A pilot has to visualize the relationship of the aircraft to the VORTAC station by using the changing variables of heading, bearing, and distance.

Flying a DME arc was once simpler than it is now. An early model Narco DME receiver incorporated an orbit indicator, a left-right needle that assisted a pilot in precisely tracking a given DME arc. But that function did not meet expectations and was quietly dropped. In the meantime, pilots must cope with DME arcs using only raw data.

Tracking a DME arc is one of those maneuvers that is easier to perform than to describe, but before it can be executed proficiently, considerable practice is required. Fortunately, this can be done in VFR conditions and requires neither a hood nor an IFR clearance. But before embarking on a practice mission, one additional piece of equipment is required: a competent observer to watch for traffic. Orbiting can be a mentally distracting affair, and the student of DME arcs rarely has time to both concentrate on the problem and watch for traffic.

Initially, a pilot should practice with a large-radius arc, one at least 20 DME from the station. Arcs of large radii have relatively "flat" curves and are easier to track. A relatively low groundspeed should be maintained during the orbit; high speed requires more skill because of the greater rate of course deviation and correction. After he becomes comfortable with the large arc, a pilot can increase groundspeed and tackle DME arcs with progressively shorter radii.

When these skills have been developed, a pilot is ready to practice under a hood on a windy day. Those who boast that orbiting is simple probably have never flown a short-radius DME arc under the demanding and difficult conditions that can arise during an actual IFR approach.

Although flying in circles may not be the shortest way from A to B, it occasionally is the only way.

Chapter 18 **Radar Approaches**

Most pilots believe that radar approaches are the easiest IFR approaches to perform. They appear to be little more than "monkey hear, monkey do" procedures. During an ASR (airport surveillance radar) or PAR (precision approach radar) approach, the pilot presumably does little more than what he is told; the thinking is done by the controller.

Although there is some truth to this, no IFR procedure should be regarded so casually. Every maneuver on instruments, including a radar approach, requires a considerable amount of know-how and proficiency.

Unfortunately, today's pilot is afforded little opportunity to become familiar with radar approaches. And because a practice approach can delay traffic and tie up a controller for as long as 15 or 20 minutes, the average approach control facility is reluctant to provide the service except when necessary.

Although almost every terminal radar approach control (TRACON) facility has the equipment necessary to provide an ASR approach, the procedure is available only at those relatively few airports where the ASR approach has been flight-tested and trained personnel are available. At a location where the procedure normally is not available, a trained TRACON controller might be available to provide an ASR approach in an emergency.

As far as PARs are concerned, you can forget them; they are relics of a past era and have been removed from the pilot's bag of tricks.

So what are a pilot's options after losing all navigational capability when flying on instruments and beyond range of the nearest ASR facility?

If a genuine emergency (such as the loss of nav receivers or gyros) dictates the need to execute a radar approach, head for the nearest military airport. Almost every one can provide a ground-controlled approach (GCA), the military equivalent of a PAR. These facilities are spread about the country and are available to civilian pilots during an emergency.

To appreciate just how many GCA approaches are available and where they are located, refer to the communications panel on any Jeppesen low-altitude enroute chart of the United States. All military airports are listed there, and virtually all such listings contain the notation GCA, indicating the availability of this approach.

One might wonder why the Air Force, Navy, and Marines still use a procedure long ago abandoned by the FAA, especially considering that most military airports also have complete ILS facilities.

The answer is that military pilots and controllers need to remain current with radar approaches because they never know where in the world such procedures might be required. If a temporary, remote base must be rapidly established in the middle of Saudi Arabia, for example, a mobile GCA unit can be readily transported there to provide a precision IFR approach. ILS facilities cannot be installed so easily.

Although practice GCA approaches are discouraged or banned at some military installations, they are allowed at others. March Air Force Base, which is east of Los Angeles, for example, gave me permission by radio to execute a practice approach, but I was advised not to land there. The only way to determine the policy at a specific military installation is to call the facility on one of the frequencies shown on the Jeppesen chart.

It is likely, however, that a pilot's first radar approach is going to be for real without benefit of a dress rehearsal. Notice from the following that there is more to the procedure than obeying commands from the ground.

Controller: *Bonanza Six-Zero-Three-One-Three, this will be a surveillance approach to Runway Eight. Squawk three-four-four-three and ident. Descend to and maintain eight thousand. Turn right, heading two-six-zero for radar vectors.*

Unlike the maneuvering required during conventional radar vectoring, turns executed while preparing for an ASR approach should be performed at the standard rate (3 degrees per second). When on final approach, however, turns should be executed at half-rate while maintaining a relatively constant airspeed. This gives the controller an opportunity to observe and become accustomed to the aircraft's turn radius and better enable him to provide accurate guidance.

Controller: *Bonanza Three-One-Three, the missed approach point is one mile from the runway.*

It is important for a pilot to correlate the distance of the missed approach point from the runway to the reported visibility. If the visibility in this example is 2 miles, the pilot can expect to see most of the runway when beneath the overcast at the MAP. But if the runway visual range (RVR) is only 3,000 feet, he probably would not see the runway upon arrival at the MAP. (Proceeding visually beyond the MAP is permissible if the pilot can see only the runway environment, which includes the approach lights.)

An ASR approach usually requires at least a 250-foot ceiling and 1-mile visibility, but lower minimums are approved in a few cases.

Controller: *Bonanza Three-One-Three, if no transmissions are received for one minute while in the pattern or fifteen seconds when on final, execute a missed approach.*

A missed approach almost always necessitates navigating to a radio fix. This is unfortunate for the pilot executing an ASR approach because of inoperative navigation receivers. Because he cannot comply with such a route, he will be issued instead a clearance requiring only an expeditious climb to a given altitude on a given heading.

If two-way communications cannot be reestablished during the missed approach, the pilot may be beyond help.

Controller: *Bonanza Three-One-Three, turn left heading zero-eight-zero. Your position is eleven miles west of Albuquerque International Airport. Contact the final controller on one-three-four point one.*

When executing ASR approaches, some pilots are nervous about giving up "control" of their aircraft to someone sitting safely and cozily on the ground. There is something disturbing about descending to minimums without being able to independently verify one's position during the approach. After all, aircraft have been vectored into mountains, and it is the pilot who is first to arrive at the scene of the crash.

But there is no cause for concern. Controllers providing ASR service use a large video presentation with a scale of almost one-half mile per inch. They can easily guide an aircraft to within 500 feet of the runway's extended centerline. Also, if an ASR approach is approved for a specific airport, controllers there are required to maintain ASR currency. This is why pilots occasionally are asked to accept an ASR approach at times when such a procedure is wholly unnecessary. Cooperating affords practice not only for the pilot, but also for the controller.

If an emergency ASR is being executed at an airport that does not have an approved radar procedure, the controllers there probably are not current. This may or may not affect approach accuracy; it depends on the controller's previous ASR experience.

Final controller: *Bonanza Six-Zero-Three-One-Three, this is the Albuquerque final controller. How do you read me? ... Roger, Three-One-Three. Do not acknowledge further transmissions. Prepare to descend in two miles. The minimum descent altitude is five-thousand-seven-hundred feet. Turn right heading zero-eight-two.*

The point at which descent to the MDA commences usually is the final approach fix. Prior to reaching this point, therefore, prepare the aircraft for landing and complete the before-landing checklist. When descent begins, the pilot should be free to concentrate solely on instructions from the controller.

Also, if the ASR procedure is to be concluded by a circling approach to another runway, confirm that the final controller understands this and has issued a possibly higher MDA, predicated on both the need to circle and the aircraft approach category (A, B, C, or D, depending on normal approach speed, 1.3 V_{S0}, at maximum certificated landing weight).

Final Controller: *Bonanza Three-One-Three, you are six miles from the runway. Descend to your minimum descent altitude. Turn left, zero-seven-eight.*

ASR approaches generally require an average sink rate of 300 feet per mile, which equates to an approximately 3-degree descent path. Several years ago, controllers provided recommended altitudes as the aircraft descended and progressed inbound from the final approach fix. A controller might have said "four miles from the runway, recommended altitude one-thousand-five-hundred feet... three miles from the runway, recommended altitude one-thousand-two-hundred feet." These altitudes, however, no longer are volunteered. They are issued only upon request. Should recommended altitudes be requested during an ASR approach? Yes, but only when the terminal weather is known to be relatively good. When conditions are marginal, adhering to recommended altitudes can blow the approach. Notice in Figure 16 that—because of cloud cover irregularity (a common situation)—it is possible to conform to a normal descent profile, reach the MAP, and never establish visual contact with the ground, even though the reported ceiling would suggest otherwise. In such a case, the result is an unnecessary miss.

The descent to MDA during an ASR approach should be treated like any other nonprecision approach. After passing the final approach fix, descend expeditiously to the MDA (unless intervening altitude restrictions are communicated by the controller). As shown in the figure, the pilot has more time to spend at MDA searching for the airport. During marginal conditions, this increases significantly the probability of a successful nonprecision approach.

Final controller: *Slightly right of course. Turn left zero-seven-four ... Correcting nicely... Four miles from runway... On course. Turn right zero-seven-six.*

The importance of precisely holding assigned headings cannot be over-emphasized. The controller assumes that a pilot is doing exactly as instructed. Any variation from the assigned heading appears to the controller as wind drift, which makes it necessary for him to issue a correction. The result is that

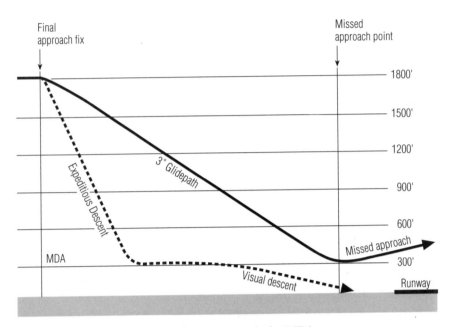

Figure 16. Using an expeditious descent to reach the MDA

the pilot probably will wind up overshooting the final approach course when turning to the next assigned heading. If such sloppy heading management recurs, the controller may be unable to provide adequate guidance and have to call off the approach.

For example, assume the assigned heading is 050 degrees, but the pilot is lax and has been holding 045 degrees. The controller notes a left "drift" and calls for a new heading of 055 degrees, a correction of 5 degrees right. Instead, when the pilot turns from an incorrect heading to the newly assigned heading of 055 degrees, he will have turned 10 degrees, doubling the necessary correction and making it difficult for the controller to get a feel for actual wind conditions.

But if a pilot notes that he has been holding an incorrect heading for any period of time, he should not arbitrarily turn to the correct heading. Such an unannounced turn also appears on radar as drift. Finally, when the controller assigns a new heading, the pilot should not turn to it but only the number of degrees separating the new and previously assigned headings.

For similar reasons, never reset a precessed heading indicator during a radar approach; that should be done prior to beginning the approach.

Final controller: *Bonanza Three-One-Three, drifting slightly left. Turn right zero-seven-niner [3 degrees right of the previously assigned heading] ... Over the missed approach point. If approach lights not in sight, execute missed approach.*

The ASR approach has ended. Either the pilot can proceed visually, or he must execute a missed approach—right now, immediately, without hesitation.

The procedures for executing a military GCA are, of course, similar but involve much more precision, both laterally and vertically. The GCA, in essence, is an ILS approach with verbal directions instead of the visual cues provided by cross-pointer needles. Operationally, the most significant difference between an ASR and a GCA is altitude management after passing the final approach fix. Instead of descending rapidly to an MDA, the pilot is guided gently down and must remain on a precise glidepath that is portrayed on the controller's radar screen.

Final controller: *Bonanza Three-One-Three, you are approaching glidepath... The decision height is three-hundred and seventy feet... Begin descent... Tower advises you are cleared to land.*

After intercepting the glidepath ("begin descent"), a sink rate should be established that approximates a 3-degree descent angle. The required rate of descent is dependent on groundspeed and will be issued by the final controller if requested.

But there is a rule of thumb that enables a pilot to easily determine a target sink rate. Simply add a zero to groundspeed and divide the result by two. For example, a 90-knot groundspeed requires an approximately 450-fpm sink rate to maintain a 3-degree glidepath. (The exact figure is 484 fpm, but 450 is close enough.) Or the sink rate can be determined from any ILS approach plate containing a 3-degree glideslope.

Another difference between the ASR and the GCA is that the latter requires almost constant contact with the controller while on final. A missed approach is required whenever there is more than a 5-second pause in communications (compared to 15 seconds during an ASR approach).

Final controller: *Heading zero-eight-zero, on course, slightly above glidepath, increase sink rate slightly... On course, approaching glidepath... Going slightly right of course, turn left zero-seven-eight... On glidepath, resume normal sink rate... One mile from touchdown... Going slightly below glidepath... Lined up with the left shoulder of the runway, turn right zero-seven-niner... On glidepath... At decision height.*

Unlike an ASR approach, the pilot is not told upon reaching the missed approach point to either execute a missed approach or continue visually. In this respect, the GCA is identical to an ILS approach. The pilot must make that choice on his own at or prior to the decision height.

Also similar to an ILS approach, but unlike an ASR approach, the pilot will continue to receive course and glidepath guidance after descending below DH and while continuing visually.

Final controller: *Over the approach lights, on course; slightly above the glidepath; over landing threshold, on course, on glidepath.*

The precision characteristic of GCA equipment leads to the natural question: "In an emergency during zero-zero conditions, could a pilot be talked all the way to touchdown?" That depends on the experience and expertise of the final controller, or stick man, so called because he dictates movement of the control stick (or wheel). Using the proper voice inflections and tones, yes, a competent final controller can "massage" an experienced pilot into executing the minute corrections necessary during such a critical maneuver.

If an extreme emergency dictates a GCA talkdown to a blind landing, execute the approach and landing with flaps retracted (if possible and practical) to increase the likelihood of a nose-up touchdown.

While this kind of radar approach can and has been done many times, its use is limited only to dire emergencies, and it is unlikely that you will ever have to resort to one.

It would be a good idea for more pilots to practice ASR and GCA approaches as part of maintaining their proficiency. Electrical problems on board an airplane in instrument conditions can make the radar approach the only alternative for a safe approach, and difficulties can crop up at the most inopportune times.

Section 3

Turbine Operations

Most general aviation pilots are limited to flying piston-powered airplanes (usually for economic reasons). To advance the thrust levers of a turbine-powered airplane, however, is to rocket into an entirely different world of flight. This section consists of a short course in the art and science of turbine operations. It is designed to provide the piston pilot with an understanding of the significant differences between flying "jugs" and jets. It is the only section in this book in which the chapters should be read sequentially.

Chapter 19 What it is Like to Fly a Jet

My close friend Hal Fishman and I were driving around the local airport soaking up the ambiance and browsing at aircraft. It is a pastime that we jokingly call "taking inventory."

We soon came upon a Bonanza with its engine removed. The cowling, though, was in place, which gave the aircraft an almost normal appearance except for the missing propeller.

"Hey, look," Hal said kiddingly, "a jet Bonanza."

"Don't you wish."

"Wonder what it would be like to fly one."

"It would be a lot easier to handle than your Bonanza," I said matter of factly.

He glanced at me with a hint of disbelief.

"Think about it, Hal. There would only be one engine control, a thrust lever, which is similar to a throttle. You would no longer have to be concerned about propeller pitch, cowl flaps, mixture, or alternate air source.

"The preflight check and runup would be a snap," I added. "That's because there wouldn't be any. You wouldn't even have to warm up the engine; just light the fire and go."

Hal was beginning to get the picture. When it comes to operating a turbine engine—irrespective of size—there is little to do.

This reminds me of when I went through Boeing 747 training in 1982. When the powerplant portion of ground school began, the other students and I eagerly anticipated what the instructor would have to say about those mammoth engines.

"You've all flown turbine aircraft before," he began. "Well, the JT9D engines on a 747 are the same as all the others. They're just bigger. Now let's move on to something else."

There is, of course, more to flying a jet than just pushing and pulling on the thrust lever. Some handling characteristics are significantly different.

For example, there is no difference between power-on and power-off stall speeds. This is because there are no propellers to reduce stall speed by "blowing" additional air across the wing and reducing its angle of attack.

When flying conventional airplanes, adding power causes the nose to rise and reducing power causes it to drop. But the absence of prop-wash across the tail of a turbine aircraft means that changing power has little or no effect on pitch. The only immediate result of adding power is an increase in speed, and vice versa.

Nor is there any p-factor, the force that causes a propeller-driven airplane (especially singles) to yaw left when flown at high-power settings and large angles of attack. You can climb steeply in a jet with feet flat on the floor. This is why aerobatic maneuvering is so much easier in turbine-powered aircraft.

Most observers (including pilots) misjudge the climb angle of departing jet aircraft. They estimate that jetliners, for example, climb initially with body angles of 30 or 40 degrees. This is an illusion. The maximum deck angles of the Boeing 727, 747, and 767, for example, are limited to 17, 17, and 20 degrees, respectively.

The high-altitude capability of turbine aircraft leads to the popular misconception that jet engines develop rated power at altitude. This is incorrect. A turbine engine is like a normally aspirated piston engine. Both lose power with altitude. At 36,000 feet, for example, a turbine engine typically can produce only one-fourth of its rated power.

This explains why climb rates decrease dramatically with altitude. A pilot who does not fly heavily loaded, widebody jetliners, for example, might be surprised to learn that such an aircraft often struggles at less than 100 fpm as it approaches its assigned altitude.

I occasionally have the opportunity to take a general aviation pilot for his first flight in the cockpit of a jet airplane. Having a somewhat sadistic streak, I particularly enjoy telling him during cruise flight to be certain that his safety belt and shoulder harness are securely fastened.

"Why?" he usually asks with obvious apprehension.

"Well, I'm going to turn off the ignition and want you to be safely and securely seated."

"Wha!?!"

I reach for the ignition switches and turn them off in quick succession. He is momentarily horrified. But when absolutely nothing happens and he sees that I am trying desperately to hold back my laughter, his fear quickly fades.

He learns the hard way that once a jet engine has been started, the fire in the burner section(s) continues to rage as long as it is provided an uninterrupted supply of kerosene. A source of ignition is no longer needed. In that respect, the jet engine is like a bonfire, which will not go out as long as you keep adding logs.

The propellers of piston-powered aircraft create enormous drag when the engine is idling, so retarding the throttle on a conventional lightplane results in rapid deceleration. The windmilling propeller acts like a huge air brake.

But retarding the thrust levers of a turbine aircraft does not result in such aerodynamic braking. Without windmilling propellers, deceleration is hardly noticeable. You almost have to study the airspeed indicator to detect changes. This is why turbine aircraft have spoilers. "Popping the boards" often is the only way to slow up and go down at the same time.

Another advantage of turbine engines is that they are impervious to the shock cooling that can be so harmful to piston engines. The valves, for example, cannot be damaged by retarding the thrust lever too rapidly because a turbine engine does not have valves. Nor does it have other components that are subject to harm by frequent and rapid changes in engine operating temperatures. A pilot can open and close the throttle(s) rapidly and without concern.

This explains why a descent, whether in a 747 or a Lear, typically begins by retarding the throttles from a cruise setting to idle. Most of the descent is a power-off glide.

Programming a descent from high altitude is a snap. Just multiply cruise altitude (in thousands of feet) by approximately 3 (depending on the aircraft and winds aloft) to determine the approximate distance needed to lose that altitude. For example, a 35,000-foot descent typically requires 3 times 35, or 105 nautical miles.

Turbine aircraft have outstanding glide performance, the result of aerodynamic cleanliness and no propeller drag. Most such aircraft—even the jumbos—can glide along a 3-degree glideslope with all engines idling. This equates to a 20:1 ratio, which is more than double that of a typical propeller-driven airplane.

Multi-engine turbine airplanes also are easier to control than their piston-powered counterparts, especially when an engine fails. This is because there is no propeller to feather. And minimum-controllable airspeeds usually are so low that they are of no concern.

Also, a multi-engine turbine aircraft does not have the type of critical engine associated with conventional multi-engine, propeller-driven aircraft. This is because the failure of any turbine engine (except one located on the aircraft centerline) produces the same amount of yaw as would the failure of its counterpart on the other side of the aircraft.

In the late 1950s, when airline pilots were learning to fly first-generation jetliners (consisting mostly of 707s and DC-8s), there was great concern about the jet engine's inability to spin up quickly from idle and provide power on demand. During a rejected landing, for example, the pilot would advance the throttles from idle and perhaps wait several critical seconds for the engines to "spool up" and deliver power. On a few occasions, the power came too late, which resulted in some spectacular accidents.

Almost all modern turbine engines are turbofan engines. These are much more responsive than older designs, which were called "pure jets." This is because the outer sections of the compressor blades of turbofan engines are similar to ducted fans, or high-speed propellers, that "bite" the air (like propellers) and produce thrust almost as soon as the throttles are advanced.

Another reason that turbofan engines (also called fanjets) are so responsive is that they generally have high idle speeds. Idling turbofans can produce so much thrust that the pilot must ride the brakes while taxiing to prevent a lightly loaded aircraft from accelerating to rotation speed.

Such high idle also contributes to glide performance. Without so much idle thrust, turbine aircraft would not glide so well. They would, however, still have significantly better glide ratios than most propeller-driven aircraft.

An abundance of idle thrust, however, is detrimental during a normal landing. This is because excessive power inhibits speed bleed during the flare and partially explains why a full-stall landing should be avoided. The time required to lose all that airspeed can consume most of the runway and not leave enough for the landing roll.

A typical landing in a turbine aircraft involves flaring the aircraft just enough to eliminate almost all of the sink rate. The aircraft is then flown onto the runway.

The pilot deploys the thrust reversers immediately after touchdown to eliminate the counterproductive effects of idle thrust. With respect to producing a significant amount of reverse thrust that can be used to help slow the aircraft, most pilots agree that reversers are noisier than they are effective.

Landing a jet in a crosswind requires the same techniques and considerations that are used when landing propeller-driven aircraft, unless you happen to be flying a Boeing 747.

Imagine that a pilot is crabbing a 747 into a 30-knot, right crosswind while on final approach. He is doing a great job and has the runway centerline nailed. He passes directly over the numbers and kicks out of the crab and into a slip—and crashes.

The pilot failed to consider the length of the 747. It is so long that when he (and the nose of the aircraft) passed over the centerline of the runway threshold while in a crab, the main landing gear, which is a mile or so behind the cockpit, was over the weeds to the left of the runway. To compensate for this problem, 747 drivers landing in a crosswind sight along the upwind edge of the runway so that the main landing gear will be over the runway.

The only difficulty that a newcomer might have when transitioning to a jet is learning to keep up with the aircraft. Higher speeds require thinking further ahead.

Adapting to speed, however, is not difficult. It is not unlike when the pilot of a Piper J-3 Cub, who is accustomed to cruising at 70 knots, checks out in a turbocharged Beechcraft B36TC Bonanza, which flies three times as fast. Adaptation comes quickly. It just takes experience.

The most difficult aspect of checking out in a turbine aircraft is learning and becoming intimate with its systems. This is what truly makes flying one jet airplane different than flying another. It also explains why the FAA requires a pilot to have a type rating for each type of turbine aircraft he intends to fly as pilot in command.

Perhaps someday I can demonstrate to you how genuinely pleasant and relatively easy it is to fly a turbine aircraft. Oh, don't let me forget. There is something I'd like to show you about the ignition.

Chapter 20 **Jet Takeoff Techniques and Performance**

One of the most misunderstood performance terms is V_1, the takeoff decision speed. It is applicable primarily to the operation of Transport-category, multi-engine airplanes (including business jets).

V_1 also is colloquially known as the go/no-go speed.

If an engine failure occurs during the takeoff roll and prior to V_1, the pilot is expected to abort. A failure at or above V_1, however, requires that he continue the takeoff in conformance with a standard profile. This involves using the remaining engine(s) to accelerate to rotation speed, V_R, and then raising the nose to the appropriate climb attitude so as to reach the minimum-allowable takeoff safety speed, V_2, at 35 feet above the runway. (V_2 is 1.2 times the stall speed of the aircraft in takeoff configuration.)

This explains why the concept of V_1 does not apply to aircraft certificated in the Normal and Utility categories. These aircraft—especially the singles—do not have sufficient performance and controllability to accelerate, take off, and climb following an engine failure. There are, however, a few exceptions. The Beechcraft King Air 350, for example, complies with the takeoff performance requirements of Transport-category aircraft.

V_1 applies not only to an engine failure. An abort is recommended when any serious threat to safety occurs prior to V_1. If such a hazard occurs beyond V_1, it should be regarded as an in-flight problem.

It is difficult to understand the significance of V_1 without considering another concept, the balanced field length.

Assume that an engine fails at V_1 (Figure 17A). Notice that the distance required to abort is the same as the distance required to continue the takeoff profile. A balanced field length is said to exist because the accelerate-stop distance is the same as (or is "balanced" with) the accelerate-go distance. The balanced field length represents the minimum runway length that presumably enables a pilot to cope with an engine failure no matter where it might occur during takeoff. (If the failure occurs before or after V_1, the runway distance required is less than if the failure occurs at V_1.)

The value of V_1 obviously is critical. Figure 17B, for example, shows what can happen when V_1 is too high. Continuing the takeoff following an engine failure at such a high V_1 would be relatively easy because very little accelera-

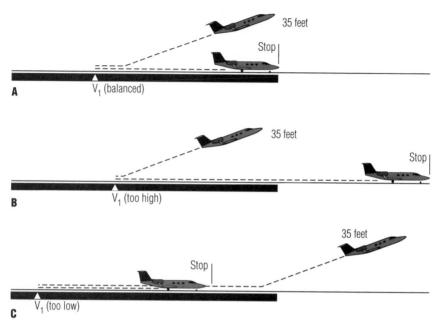

Figure 17

tion would be needed to reach V_R. But an abort following an engine failure at such a high V_1 would be impossible without running out of runway.

Conversely, Figure 17C shows what happens when an engine failure is experienced at a low V_1. There is plenty of room within which to abort, but the takeoff profile could not be completed within the confines of the runway. This is because the aircraft must accelerate through a greater speed range while handicapped with a significant power loss.

Some may wonder why it is important to reach 35 feet (and V_2) by the end of the runway following an engine failure at V_1. This is because a pilot conforming to the minimum-required climb profile with one engine caged is guaranteed only 35 feet of protection above obstacles along the extended runway centerline until reaching 1,500 feet above the runway elevation.

In other words, a pilot performing flawlessly during an engine-out climb in an aircraft with a large wingspan could expect to strike an obstacle with a wing tip by banking too steeply while struggling to 1,500 feet. Do yourself a favor. Try not to think about this minuscule margin when executing such an engine-out departure during IFR conditions.

The balanced-field concept was devised to provide a safe option irrespective of where an engine failure might occur during the takeoff roll. If an engine fails prior to V_1, the pilot aborts; if it fails at or beyond V_1, he continues. It is a simple theory. The problem, however, is that a pilot who initiates an abort at or immediately prior to V_1 probably will bend metal. This is because only superhuman pilots operating mechanically perfect airplanes are capable of performing as required when runway length is critical. There are several reasons for this:

- The accelerate-stop distance of an aircraft is determined by a factory test pilot who expects an engine failure and is spring-loaded to react as necessary (after a 2-second delay) to stop the aircraft in the minimum distance possible.

- The average pilot ordinarily does not anticipate an engine failure during takeoff and needs 5 or 6 seconds to recognize and react to one.

- The average pilot aborts by first closing the throttles and then applying brakes, an habitual stopping sequence developed during years of executing normal landings. An abort, however, demands snapping the throttles closed and simultaneously applying a maximum braking effort. It might seem awkward to stomp on the binders while the throttles are still open, but this is how it must be done. Less than this consumes excessive stopping distance.

- Stopping distance also increases unless the aircraft is equipped with new brakes and new, properly inflated tires.

- Believe it or not, runway contamination is not considered when calculating V_1. In other words, the FAA allows pilots to assume that an airplane can stop as well on a wet runway as it can on one that is clean and dry. When departing on icy runways, most professional pilots regard V_1 and brake release as occurring simultaneously.

- The need to abort is not always as immediately recognizable as a sudden engine failure. Other causes, such as a partial power loss, dragging brakes, or a blown tire usually are less conspicuous.

- V_1 loses significance if the acceleration used to approach that speed is subnormal (as in the case of taking off in slush or with dragging brakes that go unnoticed).

- Maximum braking action might not be available if the abort is necessitated by one or more blown tires, which have less traction.

In most cases, however, runway length is not critical. There usually is more runway available than is required. At such times, it is unnecessary to predicate V_1 on the basis of the balanced field length.

Figure 18A, for example, illustrates a balanced field length. V_1 is selected so that the accelerate-stop distance is equal to the accelerate-go distance.

Figure 18B, however, shows the effect of reducing V_1. An abort begun at such a low speed obviously requires much less distance. The accelerate-go distance, however, increases because the aircraft must accelerate through a greater speed range with an inoperative engine.

Conversely, Figure 18C shows the effect of increasing V_1. An abort from such a high speed obviously consumes substantially more distance. The accelerate-go distance, however, is reduced because more of the acceleration to V_2 is accomplished with all engines operating.

In other words, V_1 can be increased or decreased when the available runway is longer than that required for a balanced field. But there are limits. V_1 must not be less than V_{MCG}, the minimum-controllable speed (when on the ground with the failure of a critical engine.) Otherwise, a pilot might try to continue a takeoff following engine failure without the speed necessary to

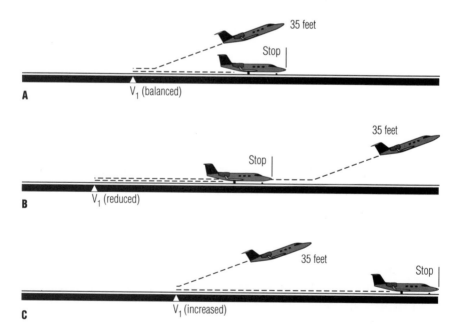

Figure 18

maintain directional control. (V_{MCG} differs from V_{MCA}, or just plain V_{MC}, the minimum-controllable airspeed when airborne, because nosewheel steering and tire traction obviously affect directional control on the ground.)

Also, V_1 must not exceed V_R because aborting a jet airplane is not a viable option once rotation begins.

It is logical to ask why anybody would want to adjust V_1. Why not just use the V_1 associated with the balanced field length and be done with it?

The answer is simple. The high-speed abort is a dangerous maneuver and has resulted in numerous disasters. In most instances, it is far safer to continue a takeoff in case of an engine failure than to abort at high speed. Consequently, reducing V_1 (when runway length permits) reduces the speed at which an abort might be required and therefore reduces the potential for catastrophe.

Lowering V_1 has become a common practice in air carrier operations. Although adjusting V_1 to take advantage of available runway length is becoming more popular with bizjet operators, most still use the V_1 associated with a balanced field length because this is the only performance data available.

It is possible to have too much of a good thing. Continuing a takeoff following an engine failure at a low V_1 can require substantial rudder input (because of the close proximity of V_1 to V_{MCG}). Consequently, a strong crosswind from the same side of the aircraft as the failed engine could require more rudder than is available.

Another increasingly popular procedure involves using reduced engine thrust for takeoff when surplus runway is available. Although this obviously reduces engine wear and tear caused by high operating temperatures and rpm, it also decreases effective runway length. An abort, therefore, is riskier than if maximum thrust were used for takeoff.

The process of rotating an aircraft with a failed engine often is taken for granted. The procedure requires finesse to reach V_2 at 35 feet and establish the aircraft in an optimum climb profile. One must not be so cavalier as to simply haul back on the yoke and jerk the airplane into the air. Business jets usually require a 3-degree-per-second rotation, while 2 degrees per second is typical for air carrier aircraft.

Pilots also should be conscientious about rotating precisely to the target attitude. Overrotation creates excessive drag, and underrotation prevents the wings from developing sufficient lift. Climb performance suffers in either event. Late rotation in a typical jet consumes about 100 additional feet of runway for each extra knot.

Preparation for the possibility of an engine failure during takeoff begins before departure. Tires, for example, should be properly inflated, and every effort should be made to minimize braking during taxi, especially when the aircraft is heavy. Overheated brakes are less effective during a maximum-effort stop.

If conditions are critical, taxi into position so as to use every foot of available runway. (Such a practice is advisable at all times.) Also consider applying full power prior to brake release because this minimizes takeoff distance.

When taxiing onto the runway, review the abort procedures and mentally prepare for the possibility of an engine failure. Although the odds obviously are heavily against an engine failure at or near V_1, don't be willing to bet your life on it. A balanced field length works much better in theory than it does in practice.

Chapter 21 **Airspeed in a Jet**

When the typical general aviation pilot sits in the cockpit of a turbine-powered airplane for the first time, he will notice many unfamiliar controls, instruments, and systems. Even the familiar ones may appear strange.

For example, the airspeed indicator in piston-powered lightplanes is decorated with colorful arcs and radial markings, but the same gauge in a turbofan (or turbojet) airplane has none of these. Gone are the familiar white, green, and yellow arcs. And in place of a redline there may be a maximum-airspeed pointer. This often is called a barber pole because of its diagonal striping. The barber pole—as will be seen later—is more than a fancy substitute for a redline.

When flying an airplane with a reciprocating engine, the pilot does not routinely fly beyond V_{NO}, the maximum structural cruising speed. V_{NO} is represented on an airspeed indicator by the upper limit of the green arc. He may, however, exceed V_{NO} and operate in the caution range (represented by the yellow arc) when flight conditions are smooth. At such a time, he also is allowed to nudge the redline and fly at V_{NE}, the never-exceed speed.

It is relatively safe to operate at the redline in smooth air because there is little danger of inadvertently exceeding this critical airspeed. This is because the increase in parasitic drag of piston-powered airplanes in high-speed flight is so great that it imposes somewhat of an aerodynamic barrier to flight beyond V_{NE}. In most cases, a conscious effort is needed to violate the redline.

When flying turbine aircraft, however, it would be much easier for a pilot to inadvertently exceed V_{NE}. This is because these aircraft create relatively less drag when in cruise configuration. Everything else being equal, turbofan airplanes, for example, create only half as much drag as piston-powered aircraft. This is why they can glide twice as far from any given altitude. Some are so "clean" and have so much power that they can exceed the "redline" while in a climb. Even turboprop airplanes are cleaner than their piston counterparts because of reduced frontal area and the elimination of cooling drag.

Consequently, turbine-powered airplanes are limited to a relatively lower speed. The purpose of this is to provide a greater margin of safety in case the pilot inadvertently exceeds the maximum-allowable airspeed. In effect, V_{NE} (the top of the yellow arc) is reduced to V_{NO} (the bottom of the yellow arc) and is redesignated as V_{MO}, the maximum operating limit speed for turbine-powered airplanes. This applies to both turboprop and turbofan airplanes and explains why the airspeed indicators of such aircraft do not have a yellow caution range.

When a piston-powered airplane is converted to a turboprop, a pilot might be dismayed to discover that the conversion necessitates reducing the maximum-allowable airspeed. V_{NE} and the yellow arc are eliminated, and V_{MO} replaces V_{NO} (to conform with the certification requirements of turbine airplanes). In other words, the new redline on a converted airplane is where the bottom of the yellow arc used to be.

This airspeed reduction, however, is not as disheartening as it might seem. One reason is that few pilots operate routinely in the caution range (above V_{NO}), so they do not miss it when flying turboprop aircraft. Another is that these aircraft usually cruise at higher altitudes where a given indicated airspeed results in an appreciably higher true airspeed.

Even the big jets are limited by what appear to be unusually low indicated airspeeds. A Boeing 747-100 at 35,000 feet, for example, is limited to 312 KIAS. But on a standard day, this results in a true airspeed of 516 knots, which is not too shabby.

Because a turbine airplane—especially turbofan aircraft—can more easily accelerate to and beyond V_{MO}, many of these aircraft are equipped with an aural warning to alert the pilot when airspeed reaches the barber pole or redline. In some cases, aircraft are equipped with stick-pullers that apply nose-up back-pressure to the control wheel to prevent a worsening speed excursion and to initiate recovery. (Some aircraft also are equipped with stickshakers to warn of an impending stall. Others have stick-pushers that pitch the nose down sharply to prevent stalling.)

The most recent generation of aircraft take overspeed protection a few steps further. In the Boeing 767, for example, certain autopilot modes prevent the aircraft from exceeding V_{MO}. As airspeed approaches the barber pole during a steep descent, for example, the autopilot automatically raises the nose to prevent a speed violation.

When flying an Airbus 320, 330, or 340 in the normal mode, flight-control computers prevent the pilot from exceeding V_{MO} by more than a few knots even when he shoves and holds the control stick fully forward. Similarly, they prevent the aircraft from stalling despite the pilot's best efforts to the contrary.

Taking control from the captain in this manner has been the subject of heated debate. Proponents of this concept believe that limiting the pilot's control authority is likely to prevent accidents caused by violating the airplane's operating envelope. Others insist that there are times—especially during an emergency—when a pilot might need to operate his aircraft in an extreme or heroic manner. They contend that depriving a captain of these options can result in accidents that might otherwise be avoided. Accident records support both points of view; take your pick.

Turbine aircraft have two speed limits, The first is V_{MO}, which prevents flutter and limits ram-air pressure acting against the structure. The other limit is M_{MO}, the maximum operating Mach number. An M_{MO} of Mach 0.82, for example, means that the airplane may not be flown in excess of that Mach number. (Mach 1.0, of course, is the speed of sound.)

High-speed aircraft designed for subsonic flight are limited to some Mach number below the speed of sound to avoid the formation of shock waves that begin to develop as an aircraft nears Mach 1.0. These shock waves (and the adverse effects associated with them) can occur when the speed of an aircraft is substantially below Mach 1.0 (depending on the airplane). For example, a Learjet 35A has an M_{MO} of Mach 0.83 while the Cessna Conquest (a turboprop aircraft) is limited to Mach 0.55.

To observe both limits, V_{MO} and M_{MO}, the pilot of a turbofan airplane needs both an airspeed indicator and a Machmeter, each with appropriate redlines. In some general aviation jets, these are combined into a single instrument that contains a pair of concentric indicators, one for indicated airspeed and the other for indicated Mach number. Each is provided with an appropriate redline.

A more sophisticated indicator is used on most jetliners. It looks much like a conventional airspeed indicator but has a barber pole that automatically moves so as to display the applicable speed limit at all times.

Figure 19 makes it easier to understand the concept of a barber pole. It has a graph that provides the maximum operating limit speeds, V_{MO} and M_{MO}, for a Boeing 767. Notice that V_{MO} is a constant 360 knots between sea level and 26,000 feet. During a climb to FL260, the barber pole—like a conventional redline—constantly points at 360 knots.

But at 26,000 feet, V_{MO} and M_{MO} cross paths. In other words, V_{MO} and M_{MO} at 26,000 feet are the same (360 KIAS).

Now assume that the pilot continues to climb at Mach 0.86, the new limiting speed. As the aircraft gains altitude, indicated airspeed decreases as shown in Figure 19. This is because the indicated airspeed (in knots) for any given Mach number decreases with a gain in altitude.

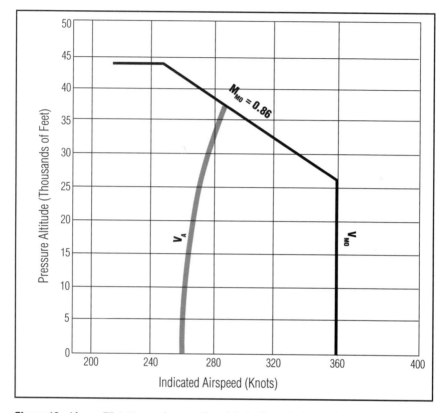

Figure 19. Above FL260, maximum-allowable indicated airspeed decreases.

In other words, Mach 0.86 is equivalent to an indicated airspeed that decreases from 360 KIAS at 26,000 feet to only 264 knots at 40,000 feet. The barber pole on a Boeing 767, therefore, decreases in conformance with the graph as the aircraft climbs above 26,000 feet. By keeping indicated airspeed below the barber pole, the pilot is assured of not violating either V_{MO} or M_{MO}.

During a descent, the reverse occurs. The barber pole of a Boeing 767 increases from 264 knots at 40,000 feet until reaching 360 knots at 26,000 feet. Below 26,000 feet, the barber pole remains fixed at 360 knots.

Climbs and descents in jet aircraft are made using indicated airspeed in the lower altitudes and Mach number in the higher altitudes. Assume, for example, that the recommended climb speeds for a particular aircraft are 280 KIAS and Mach 0.75.

After climbing through 10,000 feet (where it becomes legal to exceed 250 KIAS), the pilot accelerates to 280 KIAS, which will be used for the climb to some higher altitude. During climb at this constant indicated airspeed, true airspeed and Mach number increase steadily. Also, rate of climb gradually decreases. This is because (1) turbine engines are naturally aspirated (not turbocharged) and lose power as altitude increases, and (2) pitch attitude must be minutely and progressively reduced to maintain the 280-KIAS climb speed.

At almost 30,000 feet, the increasing Mach number reaches the recommended climb speed of Mach 0.75. At this point, the pilot continues the climb at Mach 0.75 instead of 280 KIAS. He does this by raising the nose slightly to prevent the Mach number from increasing further. This causes climb rate to temporarily increase (until the effects of higher altitudes take their toll) and indicated airspeed to decrease.

The climb is continued at Mach 0.75 until cruise altitude is reached. After leveling off, Mach number, indicated airspeed, and true airspeed are allowed to accelerate to cruise values. Cruise power is then set.

The graph in the figure also shows that V_A (maneuvering speed) increases with altitude. Well, it does...sort of. Let us back up a little.

During flight, air entering the pitot tube has no place to go. It is a dead-end system. As a result, air compresses within the pitot system. At low speed and altitude, this compression is insignificant. But at jet speeds and altitudes, compression is sufficient to increase the dynamic pressure within the airspeed indicator and cause an excessively high indicated airspeed. The greater the airspeed and altitude, the greater is the error.

Assume, for example, that an airplane is cruising at 40,000 feet with a calibrated airspeed of 275 knots (275 KCAS). Under these conditions, compression causes a 20-knot error. Subtracting these 20 knots from 275 KCAS results in an equivalent airspeed of 255 knots, or 255 KEAS. In other words, equivalent airspeed is calibrated airspeed corrected for compression. It is what would be indicated by an error-free airspeed indicator if compression were not a factor.

The graph shows that the calibrated airspeed for V_A increases with altitude. If the effects of compression are subtracted, the graph would show that V_A does not change with altitude.

During flight at jet speeds, compression also occurs immediately ahead of the aircraft. This is the result of the structure bulldozing its way through the air. Such compression causes the temperature of the air immediately ahead of the aircraft to increase.

The greater the airspeed, the greater the temperature rise. During flight at Mach 0.85, for example, air temperature measured by the probe is 30°C warmer than ambient. This heat of compression—plus the effect of friction—explains why the skin temperature of the SR-71 "Blackbird" approaches 650°C when sprinting at Mach 3.0.

General aviation pilots are taught to use V_A, the maneuvering speed, when flying through turbulence. Flight at or below this speed allows the controls to be fully and rapidly deflected without risking structural failure. Turbofan pilots, however, seldom use V_A because they are provided with something better.

According to Figure 19, V_A for a Boeing 767 at 5,000 feet, for example, is 260 KIAS. But according to the pilot's operating handbook, the recommended turbulence penetration speed for this aircraft is either 290 KIAS or Mach 0.8, whichever results in the least indicated airspeed. In other words, the turbulence penetration speed (V_B) for a 767 at 5,000 feet is 30 knots greater than its maneuvering speed (V_A). This means that there are times when turbine aircraft should be flown in excess of V_A during turbulence encounters.

Unfortunately, this intriguing data has caused some heavy-iron pilots to conclude—and teach—that small aircraft should be flown faster than V_A during serious turbulence encounters. Don't believe it. Following such foolish advice can be fatal to both the aircraft and those inside. Small piston-powered aircraft are not provided with official turbulence-penetration speeds and must not be compared to large Transport-category turbojets in this manner.

This demonstrates that birds of different feathers should not be flocked together. Each requires a separate set of skills and knowledge.

Chapter 22 **Mach Airspeed and the Speed of Sound**

Every airplane has an envelope within which it can operate safely. When drawn on a graph, the left side of the envelope defines its lower limit, or stall speed, while the right specifies the never-exceed speed (V_{NE}). The upper and lower edges of the envelope designate the limiting load factors (positive and negative).

Serious difficulties are created when operating outside the envelope. This is particularly true when exceeding V_{NE}, the redline on the airspeed indicator. The most obvious potential problem is structural damage. Air loads acting on an aircraft depend principally on ram air pressure and vary with the square of the indicated airspeed.

At 100 knots, for example, the air load exerts a force of 35 pounds per square foot. But at 500 knots, the load increases to almost 900 psf. (The tail structure usually is the first to fail; windows often are the second.)

Exceeding the redline also can cause catastrophic flutter, a situation where a control surface flaps like a flag on a windy day. Once it begins, flutter can worsen until something breaks irrespective of any corrective action attempted by the pilot. In a sense, flutter is a case of the tail wagging the dog. And finally, load factors (G loads) are particularly critical when operating near or beyond V_{NE}.

There is another speed limit, a natural one that is imposed on all aircraft except those designed for supersonic flight. This limit is Mach 1.0, or the speed of sound, which used to be referred to in melodramatic movies as the sound barrier. (It would have been more accurately described as a hurdle.)

An airplane in motion creates a wave of pressure that is similar to the ripples formed when a pebble is dropped in water. These pressure waves radiate from the aircraft at the speed of sound and serve to "warn" air ahead of the aircraft of the approaching disturbance. As a result, the air moves aside and allows the aircraft to pass with relative ease.

But when an aircraft moves at more than the speed of sound, it outruns its own pressure waves. Consequently, air ahead of the aircraft becomes compressed and is abruptly forced out of the way. This sudden displacement of air is called a shock wave, which disturbs airflow, spoils lift, and interferes with the operation of the flight controls. (Shock waves also are responsible for sonic booms. One of the most common is the cracking sound made by a whip as the tip exceeds the speed of sound.)

But it is possible to experience some of the adverse effects of supersonic flight when operating substantially below the speed of sound.

Every pilot knows that air flowing over a wing accelerates and moves faster than the true airspeed of the airplane itself. For example, if an airplane is cruising at 200 knots, the air following the camber of the wing might have a local velocity of 220 knots. If this were not so, the wing would be incapable of producing lift.

It should be obvious, therefore, that air flowing over the wing (or some other curved part of the airframe) can reach the speed of sound (become supersonic) long before the airplane itself reaches such a speed. The speed of an airplane at which airflow over the wing first reaches Mach 1.0 is called that airplane's critical Mach number, sometimes referred to as Mach "crit."

For example, if the air moving over any part of the wing of a given aircraft is flowing at Mach 1.0 while the aircraft itself is cruising at Mach 0.8 (80 percent of the speed of sound), that aircraft is then said to have a critical Mach number of 0.8.

A jet airplane typically is most efficient and cruises at or near its critical Mach number. This is because shock waves and the dramatic drag rise associated with supersonic flight begin to occur at higher speeds.

At 5 to 10 percent above Mach crit, the drag begins to rise very sharply. This is called the point of drag divergence and typically is the speed chosen for high-speed cruise.

At some point beyond high-speed cruise is the maximum-operating Mach speed (M_{MO}), a form of airspeed redline for high-altitude aircraft. As when exceeding V_{NE}, there are potential consequences for exceeding M_{MO}. These include:

1. unusual handling qualities,
2. violent and irregular movement of the aircraft about all three axes,
3. aileron buzzing (a high-frequency oscillation),
4. aileron snatching (a condition where the ailerons move abruptly and uncontrollably in one direction and then the other),
5. large and violent trim changes,
6. deterioration of trim and control effectiveness, and
7. buffeting so intense as to cause structural failure.

One of the more interesting reasons for all of this is a surprising change in the behavior of air as it reaches the speed of sound. Unlike subsonic air, which accelerates and reduces pressure as it flows through a venturi, super-sonic air—because of compression—does just the opposite; it slows down and increases pressure when constricted.

And when you think about it, the narrow throat of a venturi should cause a slowdown. This is exactly what happens when several lanes of automobile traffic merge into one.

An accurate method for measuring the speed of an object with respect to the speed of sound was first developed by Ernst Mach (1838–1916), an Austrian physicist and psychologist, after whom the Mach number is named.

The speed of sound in the atmosphere depends entirely on air temperature. At 15°C, Mach 1.0 is 661 knots (761 mph) and decreases as the temperature gets colder. At -55°C, for example, Mach 1.0 is 576 knots.

All of this explains why jet aircraft performance is described in terms of Mach number and not knots. Mach crit (the approximate cruising speed of a jet airplane), for example, occurs at a given Mach number. But the true airspeed (in knots) at such a time varies with outside air temperature. For example, if an airplane is cruising at Mach 0.8, its true airspeed would vary from 529 KTAS at 15°C to 460 KTAS at -55°C.

When a jet aircraft cruising at a constant Mach number at a given altitude enters warmer air, required fuel flow increases, true airspeed increases, and range decreases. Conversely, when outside air temperature gets lower, required fuel flow decreases, true airspeed decreases, and range increases.

When an aircraft reaches the stratosphere (which has an average base of 36,500 feet MSL), temperature remains constant with any increase in altitude and averages -55°C. As a result, there is a direct relationship between true airspeed and Mach number when operating within the stratosphere.

At such a time, there is a handy rule of thumb that can be used to determine true airspeed (in nautical miles per minute): multiply the Mach number by 10. For example, Mach 0.8 equals approximately 8 NM/minute; Mach 2.0 equals approximately 20 NM/minute, and so forth.

Indicated airspeed, however, at a given altitude and Mach number, is always and conveniently the same. For example, a Lockheed 1011 in long-range cruise at 35,000 feet (FL350) at Mach 0.83 will have an indicated airspeed of 283 knots irrespective of outside air temperature.

For those interested in trivia, there is a fascinating relationship between indicated airspeed and Mach speed. A conventional airspeed indicator determines IAS by subtracting static pressure from pitot pressure and displaying the result. But a machmeter, which is a form of airspeed indicator, displays Mach number, which is the result of dividing pitot pressure by static pressure.

Most pilots know that the indicated stall speed (V_S) of an airplane does not vary with altitude. If a Cessna 182RG, for example, stalls at 55 KIAS at sea level, then it also stalls at 55 KIAS at 10,000 feet (everything else being equal).

But the same is not true of jet aircraft operating at high altitude. Assume, for example, that a certain jetliner has a clean (gear and flaps up) stall speed of 210 KIAS at sea level. At 35,000 feet, that same indicated airspeed equates to a true airspeed of approximately 365 knots. At such a speed, air flowing over the wings and into the pitot tube is compressed somewhat. This compression causes airflow distortion over the wings and in the pitot system. As a result of these phenomena, indicated stall speed increases significantly with altitude.

At the same time, the indicated airspeed representing M_{MO} (maximum-allowable Mach speed) decreases with altitude. For example, Mach 0.85 at 30,000 feet is equivalent to 325 KIAS. But at 40,000 feet, that same Mach speed is only 259 KIAS.

So as the aircraft climbs higher and higher, the indicated speed at which it stalls increases while the maximum-allowable operating speed decreases. Eventually it can reach an altitude where there is very little difference between the two indicated speeds.

Now assume that an aircraft operating within this narrow margin begins to buffet as the result of maneuvering or turbulence. Is this a conventional low-speed, pre-stall buffet? Or is it a Mach buffet caused by a shock wave? The two are often indistinguishable, which creates a dangerous dilemma. What should be done to recover?

If the pilot assumes that the aircraft is stalling and increases airspeed, he could unwittingly force the aircraft further beyond its Mach limit. Conversely, if he believes the disturbance to be a Mach buffet and reduces airspeed, he risks deepening a stall. Either action can result in a serious loss of control (or worse). This is why the upper tip of the operating envelope is called "coffin corner" and must be avoided.

There is another interesting phenomenon associated with transonic flight in an aircraft with swept wings, which are characteristic of most jet aircraft. The thickest and most cambered part of a wing usually is near the root, which also is the forward portion of a swept wing. If air flowing over this part of the wing reaches Mach 1.0, a shock wave forms that destroys some lift in this area of the wing. Such a loss of lift is called a shock stall.

As a result of losing lift at the forward (root) portion of a swept wing, the center of lift moves aft. In other words, the wing tips (which are aft) develop more lift than the roots. This upsets the balance of forces and causes the nose to pitch down, which explains why this behavior is called "Mach tuck." (The shock wave at the wing root also reduces downwash over the tail. This causes the stabilizer to lose effectiveness, which contributes to tuck.)

During supersonic flight, the center of lift of a Concorde shifts 6 feet aft. Pulling back on the control wheel to compensate for the resultant tuck would create unacceptable drag. Instead, aerodynamic balance is maintained by pumping fuel into aft tanks (including one in the tailcone).

A pilot does not have to join the jet set to enter the esoteric world of Mach numbers because the speed of every aircraft can be expressed with respect to the speed of sound. A Cessna 152 cruising at 100 knots with an outside air temperature of 20°C is at Mach 0.15. On a standard day at sea level, a Goodyear Blimp cruises at Mach 0.05 but does not have a machmeter to prove it.

Chapter 23 **Straight Versus Swept-Wing Airplanes**

A swept wing gives an aircraft a sleek, dart-like appearance. It creates the visual impression of speed even when the aircraft is at rest. The apparent benefit of swept wings is reduced drag, but the reasons for this are neither as simple nor as intuitive as they appear.

Pilots should recall from their early study of aerodynamics that air flowing over a wing accelerates. The result is that the air hugging the wing's curved upper surface actually moves faster than the true airspeed of the airplane itself. For example, if an airplane is moving through the air at Mach 0.50 (half the speed of sound), the air following the camber of the wing might have a local velocity of Mach 0.60. If this were not so, the wing would not produce lift, and Daniel Bernoulli would be sent home packing.

As a conventional straight wing approaches transonic flight (which usually begins at Mach 0.8), air flowing above the wing might achieve a local velocity of Mach 1.0. At such a time, a shock wave begins to form and results in the dramatic drag rise associated with supersonic flight.

Wouldn't it be convenient if a wing could somehow be "fooled" at such a time into "believing" and behaving as if the airplane were being flown at a lower speed? Well, this is exactly what a swept wing does.

Notice in Figure 20 that although the aircraft is cruising at Mach 0.85, the component of airflow perpendicular to the angle of wing sweep is only Mach 0.70. Interestingly, it is characteristic of a swept wing that it responds only to the component of airspeed that is perpendicular to its angle of sweep. This means that the lift and drag characteristics of a wing with 35 degrees of sweep cruising at Mach 0.85 are the same as those of a similar straight wing cruising at Mach 0.70.

This has the effect of delaying the formation of a shock wave (and its dramatic drag rise) that would otherwise occur as the aircraft enters the transonic speed range. In other words, a swept wing can fly faster than a straight wing before a shock wave begins to form above its wing. In addition to delaying the onset of a shock wave, sweeping a wing also reduces the severity of such a wave when it does form at higher speed. (Similar reductions in drag occur by sweeping vertical and horizontal stabilizers.)

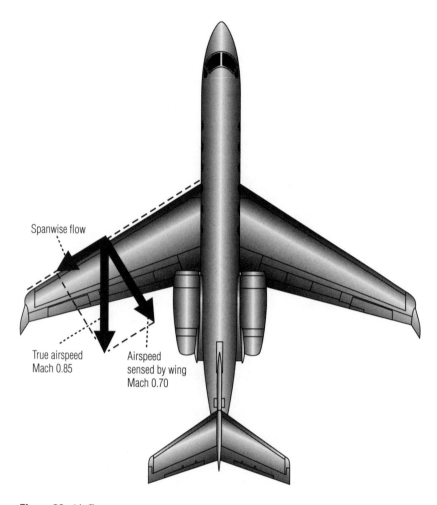

Figure 20. Airflow components over a swept wing

In the case of a Concorde, the leading edge of the wing is swept 70 degrees aft. When cruising at Mach 2.0, the wing (Figure 21), is theoretically "fooled" into believing that the relative wind has a velocity of only Mach 0.68. The supersonic transport's wing is designed to effectively behave as if the aircraft were flying subsonically. The spanwise component of the relative wind has no influence on the lift and drag of a swept wing.

The Germans usually are given credit for developing the swept wing during World War II. Credit also belongs to an American, Robert T. Jones, who independently developed the same theory for high-speed flight in 1945.

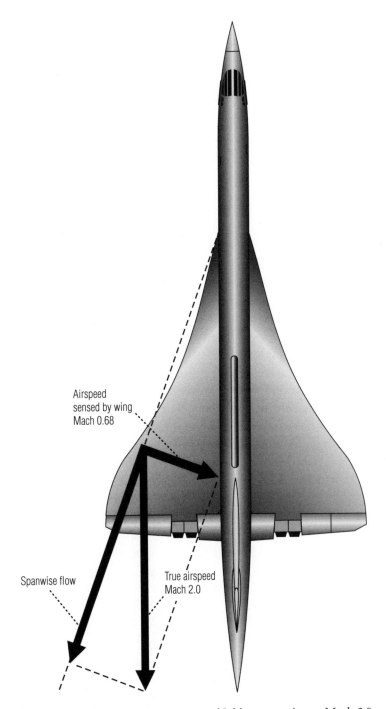

Figure 21. Airflow components over a highly swept wing at Mach 2.0

At that time, however, his revolutionary concept received a generally cool reception from myopic skeptics. One reason for this was that Jones did not have a college degree. This did not, however, prevent him from eventually rising to the position of senior staff scientist at NASA's Ames Research Center. (Jones also participated in the design of the Ercoupe, a popular lightplane of the WWII era.)

In theory, wings that are swept forward (such as those on the German Hansa jet) offer the same aerodynamic advantage as those that are swept aft. Forward sweep, however, is not as aesthetically pleasing, and poses structural complications.

Wings may be swept for other reasons. In some cases, it is necessary to sweep a wing so that its center of lift is properly positioned with respect to the airplane's center of gravity. This is because the relative position of these two points determines the nature of the airplane's longitudinal stability.

In some instances, the wing root might have to be specially placed to properly position the center of lift. In the case of the Saab Safari, a Swedish military trainer, the designer placed the wing root aft of the cockpit to improve pilot visibility. This required sweeping the wing forward to keep the aerodynamic forces properly balanced.

A disadvantage of swept wings is that they tend to stall at the tips instead of at the roots (as is the case with conventional wings). This is because the air nearest the surface of the wing (the boundary layer) tends to flow spanwise toward the tips (refer to the spanwise vector in Figure 20) and to separate near the leading edges.

Figure 22 demonstrates why this is so undesirable. The horizontal line connects the center of lift of each wing. Now upset the apple cart by stalling the wing tips and causing a loss of lift aft of this line. The result is that the center of lift moves forward. This forces the nose to rise further, which only makes matters worse.

The tendency for a tip stall is greatest when wing sweep and taper are combined. There usually is little stall warning. This is because air separating from the tips does not strike the tail and cause that familiar airframe buffeting that often is the best of all stall warning systems. There also can be a serious reduction of lateral control, particularly if the ailerons become involved in the stall.

Consequently, the designer of a swept-wing airplane must dig deeply into his bag of aerodynamic magic to create favorable stall characteristics. One of his tricks is to wash out the wing tips. This involves twisting each wing tip so

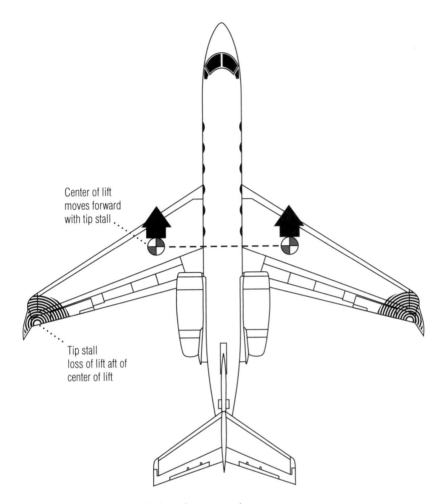

Figure 22. Stall characteristics of a swept wing

as to reduce its angle of incidence (and hence its angle of attack) so that the inboard section of the wing is the first to stall.

Also, spanwise flow can be impeded and tip stalls prevented by adding a stall fence on the upper surface of each wing. Such a fence is 6 to 8 inches tall and extends aft from the leading edge of each wing.

A wing with forward sweep usually is not plagued with the tip stall problem. This is because the spanwise flow of air moves inboard and aft, not outboard and aft as in the case of wings that are swept back.

Another unpleasant characteristic of swept-wing aircraft is Dutch roll. This is a lateral-directional oscillation that usually occurs in response to an initial disturbance in yaw. On rare occasions, it can be induced by a disturbance in roll. The oscillation consists of alternate rolling and yawing movements that are out of phase with one another and in opposite directions. It is sometimes described as a corkscrewing motion that is similar to the weave of a skater's body; hence the term Dutch roll. (In simple terms, the oscillation begins as roll due to yaw; the opposite of this, adverse yaw effect, is yaw due to roll.)

Dutch roll usually is a high-altitude phenomenon. It can be barely noticeable or become uncomfortable and continue indefinitely. In some cases, if left unchecked, Dutch roll can become dynamically unstable, divergent, and uncontrollable to the extent that an aircraft could become inverted in six or seven oscillations.

A yaw damper usually is regarded as the third axis of an autopilot and a way to keep passengers from getting airsick by eliminating yaw. But in a swept-wing aircraft, the yaw damper serves a more necessary function by preventing Dutch roll. It is the failure of a damper at high altitude that can lead to the oscillations discussed earlier. The Boeing 727 is so prone to Dutch roll that it has two yaw dampers. A total AC power failure and subsequent loss of yaw damping above Flight Level 370 could result in a hull loss. If the yaw damping system fails at high altitude, a pilot should consider descending to take advantage of the increase in natural yaw damping that occurs at lower altitudes.

Airline pilots used to receive training in Dutch roll recovery during actual training flights. This was when the Boeing 707 reigned supreme and before simulators were substituted for real airplanes during transition training.

The instructor would turn off the yaw damper at altitude and induce a Dutch roll by starting a mild skid with rudder. The recovery procedure (then and now) consists of closing the throttles (to start down) and then applying sharp and substantial aileron against the rising wing. When the aircraft stops rolling, neutralize the control wheel and mentally prepare to repeat the lateral input in the opposite direction when the other wing begins to rise, which it does very quickly. Repeat this procedure until the oscillation finally (and hopefully) subsides. Do not use rudder. Incorrect application can worsen the situation, whereas lateral control alone allows the inherent stability of the airplane to dampen the oscillation. Avoid further flight at high altitude until the yaw damper has been repaired.

It has become popular for many lightplane instructors to have their students practice and demonstrate what they erroneously describe as a Dutch roll, which cannot be performed in small, straight-wing airplanes. What they really mean is for the student to practice a series of entries and recoveries from an aileron roll. This consists of using aileron only to roll the airplane about its longitudinal axis and into a 45-degree bank and then reversing direction until the aircraft is banked 45 degrees in the opposite direction, and so forth. All the while, the student is instructed to use whatever rudder is needed to keep the nose pointed at some distant point on the horizon. Although this is a worthwhile coordination exercise, it is not a Dutch roll.

The reduction of airspeed component across a swept wing causes a loss of lift for a given airspeed at a given angle of attack. This is one reason why a swept wing does such a poor job of producing lift at low speed and explains the need for leading-edge devices and multi-slotted, trailing-edge flaps.

Another problem with swept wings is that it often is difficult for the pilot to see his wing tips because of the way the wings sweep back and away from the cockpit. In some aircraft, the pilot cannot see the wings at all, which makes it all the more difficult to taxi in confined quarters.

Swept wings also restrict the freedom of roll and pitch during takeoff and landing. Because the wing tips are so far aft of the main landing gear, rotating the nose for takeoff and while flaring for landing lowers the wing tips and places them relatively close to the ground. The tips are subject to ground damage if the airplane is banked excessively (such as when correcting for a gusty crosswind) with the aircraft in a nose-high attitude.

One of the advantages of swept wings is that they are less sensitive to turbulence than equivalent straight wings and offer a smoother ride.

The swept wing is both practical—it makes it possible for aircraft to nuzzle and exceed the speed of sound—and beautiful. It gives further credence to the old saw that great form follows superior function.

Chapter 24 **Flying Above the Weather ... Almost**

If you spend enough time in an airline dispatch office, you eventually will overhear a captain say to his first officer, "Why check the weather? We're going anyway."

Such a comment obviously is not meant to be taken literally. But it does reflect confidence in the captain's ability to overcome whatever weather obstacles might be thrown in his path. This, he realizes, is due more to the weather capability of jet aircraft than to his skill and cunning. In more than 30 years of flying turbojet and turbofan airplanes, for example, I have canceled only two departures because of weather. One was due to a persistent, dense ground fog that shrouded Los Angeles International Airport with near-zero visibility. The other was caused by a hurricane that halted operations at my destination in Puerto Rico.

During those same years, I have had to divert to an alternate only a handful of times. These were due to thunderstorms over or in the vicinity of the airport, insufficient ground visibility to begin an instrument approach, and insufficient fuel to endure projected traffic delays.

The weather capability of an airplane seems to increase in proportion to the size of its operating envelope. In other words, high-performance aircraft are less vulnerable to the whims of weather than those that fly low and slow.

The higher an airplane flies, for example, the more weather it can overfly. This is why jet airplanes in cruise flight rarely are affected by orographic (mechanical) or thermal turbulence that pummels those limited to lower levels.

Jets are affected, however, by mountain waves, which can rise to flight level 500 and beyond. This, after all, is how Robert Harris coerced his Grob sailplane in 1986 to a record-setting altitude of 49,009 feet MSL.

Although jets usually soar above the turbulence and the rotor clouds associated with mountain waves, aggressive use of the thrust levers can be required to maintain altitude. I have seen conditions so severe that the throttles would be fully retarded one moment and wide open the next. Thankfully, turbofan engines are not as susceptible to shock cooling as are turbocharged piston engines.

When near the operational ceiling of a jet aircraft, it might not be possible to maintain altitude in a strong mountain wave because of the limited power available. (Yes, turbine engines also lose power with altitude.) At such a time, the pilot has no option but to advise the Air Route Traffic Control Center of his predicament.

This is most likely to occur when crossing the Rockies or the Sierra under the influence of a strong northwesterly wind in the winter. Some say—with tongue partially in cheek—that the good news is that aircraft below are affected the same way. Traffic separation is maintained because everyone is losing and gaining altitude in unison.

Jets also are affected by CAT, clear air turbulence. This most often is caused by a strong wind gradient or shearing. Significant turbulence can be expected in the flight levels, for example, when the vertical shear (or wind change) exceeds 6 knots per 1,000 feet or the horizontal shear (or change) exceeds 40 knots per 150 miles.

Fortunately, jets have relatively high wing loadings so that a given gust is not as uncomfortable as when flying other aircraft in similar conditions. Another advantage is that the turbulence penetration speed of a jet airplane usually is very nearly the same as its cruising speed. In a Boeing 747-100, for example, it is Mach 0.82 to 0.85 or 280 to 290 KIAS, whichever is less. (Consider that 280 KIAS at FL370 is approximately 490 KTAS.)

Avoidance and escape are the obviously preferred methods of dealing with turbulence, and this is greatly enhanced by the superb climb and descent rates typical of most jet aircraft. This—plus a large selection of cruising altitudes—usually makes it relatively easy to climb above or descend below turbulence.

One must be careful not to carry this to an extreme, however. Climbing too high while still in turbulence can subject jet aircraft to high-speed stalling, and descending too low can increase specific fuel consumption and reduce range to the point where the destination cannot be reached with needed fuel reserves.

Pilots know that wind speed generally increases with altitude, but only to a point. High fliers bucking strong headwinds when flying westbound across the United States in the winter often can climb above those headwinds while simultaneously reducing fuel flow. This is because the tropopause over the United States is usually around FL350 in the winter. Climbing above the tropopause and into the stratosphere often results in being above the jet stream.

I recall one flight over the Pacific between Honolulu and Guam during which a climb from FL350 to FL410 in a Boeing 707 improved groundspeed by 110 knots.

This procedure usually cannot be used in the summer. This is because jet streams migrate north and seldom influence mid-latitude flights. Also, the tropopause rises to much higher altitudes over the United States during the summer and typically is above the ceiling of most jet aircraft.

But most jet pilots realize that no airplane can climb above all the weather, not even a Concorde. This was best summarized by a transmission made by one of the early astronauts (possibly John Glenn) upon reaching Earth orbit. "Houston," he said. "Another thousand feet and we'll be on top."

One of the highest fliers of them all, Francis Gary Powers, wrote in his book Operation Overflight about how he once looked up—way up—at the top of a Middle-Eastern thunderstorm while operating his Lockheed U-2 spyplane somewhere in the vicinity of 80,000 feet.

Although jets obviously cannot top all thunderstorms, they can top many of them. This, however, can be risky business. The top of a cell might represent the upper limit of visible moisture, but it does not necessarily represent the upper limit of the convection responsible for the development of the storm. Some of the worst turbulence I have ever encountered has been in the clear above a thunderstorm.

Most airlines recommend giving thunderstorms a margin of at least 5 nautical miles when the outside air temperature (OAT) is above freezing, 10 miles when the OAT is below freezing, and 20 miles when at or above 25,000 feet.

One reason to maintain a healthy distance from thunderstorms is to avoid hail that can be encountered while in clear air and many miles from the originating cell. Such an experience at jet speeds gives a new meaning to the word "loud." It is deafening. Nor is hail particularly good for leading edges, windows, compressor blades, and radomes.

Fortunately, deviating around thunderstorms at jet speeds does not take long and is not as penalizing as when flying slower aircraft. I have flown several nonstop, transcontinental flights involving widespread thunderstorm activity over the Midwest that necessitated deviating as far as the Canadian or Mexican border without adding more than 15 or 20 minutes to the flight plan.

Nor does enroute detouring consume much additional time. It usually is possible to find a clear and sufficiently wide gap through which high-flying aircraft can pick their way through a line of thunderstorms.

But not always.

Some years ago, I was flying a Boeing 707 through a line squall over the Oklahoma panhandle. The gap between two large cells was more than adequate, and we could see plenty of blue on the other side. So we banked left and headed for the chasm.

But as we approached the line, we could see a new cell rapidly filling the gap. Its growth was incredibly fast and reminded us of the time-lapse photography used to show, for example, the blooming of a flower in 10 seconds or less. We barely had enough time to turn away from the maturing menace before committing the aircraft to penetration.

High-speed flight in cloud near the freezing level increases the likelihood of another phenomenon—St. Elmo's fire, a visible form of static electricity.

And that reminds me of my most electrifying experience. We were holding at a fix 20 DME south of the Kansas City VOR in towering cumulus. As we rolled out of a turn inbound to the VOR, my first officer and I noticed a swirling mass of static electricity growing like Pinocchio's nose from the radome of our Boeing 727. It was about as long as a telephone pole and rapidly became brighter and more electrically active.

Then came what sounded like a muffled explosion and a blinding flash. Seconds later and while we were regaining our composure, the intercom chimed—a call from a flight attendant.

"What [expletive deleted] was that?"

"What do you mean?" I had no idea that the flash had been seen in the cabin.

"You mean you don't know?" she asked incredulously. "A huge, spinning ball of fire rolled down the aisle at about a hundred miles an hour. We're scared to death back here. What's going on?"

It was over, of course, almost as quickly as it had begun, but I had to spend several minutes on the public-address system explaining that we had just had a rendezvous with St. Elmo, which usually is as harmless as it is dramatic.

The intensity of static electricity and St. Elmo's fire can be reduced by climbing or descending away from the freezing level and reducing indicated airspeed, which reduces the friction generated by particles in the air.

Structural icing is seldom a serious problem for jets. This is because the supercooled water droplets needed to form ice on the structure cannot exist at such high, dry, and cold cruising altitudes. High-altitude clouds consist of ice crystals that aircraft simply brush aside.

For this and other reasons (including the compressional heating of air that occurs at high speed), modern jetliners are almost impervious to structural icing. Most pilots are surprised to learn, for example, that the Boeing 767 wings and tail are not protected by anti-ice or de-ice systems. Only the engine inlets, instrument probes, and three outboard, leading-edge slats on each wing are protected against the formation of ice.

Ice and snow that accumulate on an aircraft on the ground must, of course, be removed before departure. But the best way to do this was developed by the French.

When preparing for departure at Charles de Gaulle Airport in Paris, aircraft laden with ice are allowed to taxi toward the departure runway. Prior to taking off, the aircraft must stop under a gantry that looks like something constructed with an oversized Erector set. Once under the gantry, the aircraft is shot by glycol cannons that rapidly (and noisily) remove all ice and snow. The aircraft then takes off before additional ice can form.

Dense fog is not the problem that it used to be. Modern jets with the proper equipment and qualified crews are allowed to make Category IIIb ILS approaches and land with no ceiling and a runway visual range of only 300 feet. This means that the crew may not see anything until the aircraft is rolling along the runway.

Someday, we are told, we will be making CAT IIIc ILS approaches, which means that the ceiling and RVR will be absolutely zero. When that day arrives, I certainly hope they figure out a way for us to find the gate. Even in VFR conditions, this can be the most challenging part of a flight.

Chapter 25 **Deep Stalls**

A turbojet-powered airplane with a T-tail is being flown on a constant heading in level-flight attitude. Forward speed, however, is nil, and the aircraft is sinking vertically at an alarming rate. The flight controls are ineffective, and the earth continues to rise. The fate of the aircraft is sealed.

Impossible? A dream? It is neither. It can happen, especially when flying a swept-wing airplane with aft-mounted engines. It is a deep stall, one of a jet pilot's worst nightmares. It is an excursion beyond the envelope and from which return may be impossible. (Although rare, deep stalls also have occurred in T-tailed light airplanes and high-performance sailplanes.)

The T-tail became popular in general aviation design circles in the 1970s in part because it gives an airplane a jaunty, rakish appearance. It also is more effective than a conventional tail. This is because it operates in the free airstream above the disturbed air left in the wake of propellers and wings, allowing the use of smaller horizontal surfaces to do the same job. The result is less drag and an increase in performance, which makes T-tails particularly advantageous in the design of jet aircraft. Raising the horizontal tail surfaces high above the fuselage also makes it easier for the designer to accommodate aft-mounted turbofan engines. (In small aircraft, however, the use of a T-tail can reduce longitudinal stability and degrades handling quality about the pitch axis.)

In an airplane with a conventional tail, the pilot usually is warned of an impending stall when the horizontal tail surfaces are lowered into the wake of the wing. In most cases, the pilot feels and sometimes hears the buffeting that this creates. If he fails to take appropriate action, it is likely that the nose will fall and automatically begin the process of stall recovery. The pilot, of course, must continue the process by releasing back-pressure on the control wheel and reducing the wing's angle of attack.

Many pilots do not understand what causes the nose to drop. It has little to do with the stall and mostly to do with the tail. During normal flight, the horizontal tail surfaces produce a down load (negative lift, if you will) that prevents the nose from pitching down on its own. But when these surfaces are lowered into the low-energy wake of the wing, the tail loses effectiveness and can no longer produce the down load. As a result, the nose pitches downward. At the same time, the elevator also loses much of its authority, which prevents the pilot from forcing the aircraft into a deeper stall.

Things can happen differently with a T-tail. As the pilot applies back-pressure to raise the nose, the horizontal surfaces might still remain above the wake of the wing even after the wing has begun to stall. This is why the pilot might not feel any buffeting or natural stall warning. With the elevator still in the free airstream, it remains effective and allows the pilot to unwittingly drive the wing into a deeper stall at a much larger angle of attack.

Finally, the wing reaches an extreme angle of attack. The pilot continues to pull back on the wheel and buries the horizontal tail surfaces in the wing's wake as shown in Figure 23. The elevator rapidly loses effectiveness. Also, the disturbed, relatively slow air behind the wing might approach the tail at such a large angle that the tail itself stalls. The pilot loses all pitch control and is unable to lower the nose.

Figure 23. Horizontal tail surfaces are blanketed in the wake of the wing.

The fuselage is another factor to consider. This is because, at very large angles of attack, the fuselage acts like a fat, stubby wing and produces a modicum of lift. The trouble is that this "wing" has an extremely small aspect ratio (the ratio of span to chord). This means that when the fuselage is at a large angle of attack, it also creates induced drag in the form of "wing tip" vortices. These are shed from along both sides of the fuselage, which behave like the tips of an absurdly proportioned wing.

These fuselage-generated vortices attack and interfere with the horizontal tail surfaces. They also can exert a downward pressure along the top of the stabilizer. This forces the tail down further and deepens the stall.

Many pilots believe that aft-mounted engines contribute to the deep stall because of the additional and seemingly excessive weight that they add to the rear of the aircraft. But this weight has no direct influence on deep stalls. The designer maintains the aircraft in perfect balance simply by moving the wing aft. This results in a strikingly long fuselage section ahead of the wing and is quite noticeable on aircraft such as the McDonnell Douglas MD-80.

At large angles of attack, the lift produced by a lengthy, forward-fuselage section has substantial leverage. This tends to hold the nose high during a deep stall, which exacerbates the problem. Also, the fuselage—unlike a real wing and more like a barn door—does not stall. Instead, it produces increased effective lift with increasingly large angles of attack, even after the wings become fully stalled. Aft-mounted engines can contribute to a deep stall for a different reason: At large angles of attack, their nacelles generate vortices that can interfere with the tail surfaces.

Another factor is wing planform. It is characteristic of swept wings that—as angle of attack increases—the wing tips tend to stall first. And because the tips of a swept wing are on the aft part of the wing (behind the center of lift), it follows that a loss of lift near the tips causes the center of lift to move forward. This forces the nose farther up and the wing more deeply into the stall.

The designer, however, attempts to preclude the possibility of tip stalling, which, among other things, can affect the ailerons and erode roll control. There are some design tricks that help to ensure that the wing roots stall before the tips. These include washing out the wing tips (reducing their angles of incidence), adding stall fences, using a combination of airfoils, and so forth.

Even if the designer is successful in delaying the tip stall, however, it is possible for the tips to eventually stall more fully than other areas of the wing. The result is that—despite the designer's best efforts—the swept wing might still contribute to a deep stall.

Upon entering a deep stall, the tail surfaces become ineffective and the aircraft becomes locked in a nose-high attitude. At this point, there is little that can be done about it.

Assume that the pilot pulls back so far on the control wheel that the tail is somehow brought below the wing's wake and below the vortices spawned by the fuselage and the nacelles. Because the free airstream below the aircraft has much more velocity than the low-energy wing wake, it can force the tail to rise back up and into the disturbed air that caused the problem in the first place.

After the aircraft enters a deep stall, increasing drag reduces forward speed to well below normal stall speed. Sink rate increases to possibly thousands of feet per minute. The aircraft eventually stabilizes in a vertical descent. The angle of attack approaches 90 degrees, and indicated airspeed is virtually nil. The emergency ends when the aircraft pancakes into the ground in near-level attitude. The crash signature of a deeply stalled aircraft impacting the earth is unmistakable.

Some pilots speculate that they might break the stall by rolling in one direction and then kicking bottom rudder to get the nose down. Anything is worth a try, but this probably would not work. Flight controls are generally ineffective when the wing is at a 90-degree angle of attack no matter how aggressively the pilot moves the control wheel and rudder pedals (although this might have some aerobic value). If rudder alone is effective, the pilot might use it to yaw the aircraft and select the view that he will have while crashing.

This does not mean that a pilot should give up and accept the role of being a passenger in his own airplane. Anything is worth a try. Cycle the controls, the landing gear, the spoilers, the flaps. Try every possible combination. It might also be worthwhile to have the passengers move forward because an aft CG worsens the problem.

Can a pilot power his way out of a deep stall? Probably not. Air passing vertically in front of the engine inlets undoubtedly will result in severe compressor stalling and prevent the development of meaningful thrust.

Nor is the deep stall anything that a pilot can practice (not that he would want to). In this respect, it is like a flat spin. A pilot's first is likely to be his last.

Fortunately, deep stalls are easily avoided as long as published limitations are observed. Airframe manufacturers go to great lengths to provide sophisticated stall-warning systems such as stickshakers and pushers. A pilot does his part by heeding these warnings and not operating a flight when a required stall warning system is inoperative.

In addition to a deep stall, the pilot of an aircraft equipped with a variable-incidence (or trimmable) stabilizer might discover that it is possible for his aircraft to become "locked" at the other end of the speed spectrum. This is when it will become clear to him that he cannot recover from a high-speed dive.

A trimmable stabilizer is used on many jet aircraft because it creates less trim drag than a fixed horizontal stabilizer that requires deflecting the elevator to provide pitch trim. But there is one problem with the trimmable stabilizer. It usually is accompanied by a relatively small elevator. This is because all of the real work is done by moving the stabilizer. The elevator is used only to make small pitch changes to the trimmed attitude.

Assume that a pilot encounters turbulence that causes the nose to pitch up, and he (or the autopilot) reacts by applying significant nose-down trim. Immediately thereafter, however, the nature of the turbulence changes, and this—combined with the nose-down trim—forces the nose down sharply. The pilot hauls back on the yoke. The trouble is that the feeble elevator is unable to overcome the more aerodynamically powerful stabilizer. The pilot then jabs at the thumb switch on the yoke in an effort to apply nose-up trim. But the trim motor may not be strong enough to override the opposing force created by nose-up elevator, as shown in Figure 24.

The best and perhaps only way to recover from the resultant high-speed dive is to release back-pressure on the control wheel as if attempting to recover from a stall. This relieves the trim motor and allows the pilot to reposition the stabilizer.

It seems that no matter how sophisticated the airplane or how esoteric the maneuver, the control wheel does little more than control the size of houses below. Pull it back, and the houses on the ground get smaller; pull it back further, and the houses get bigger.

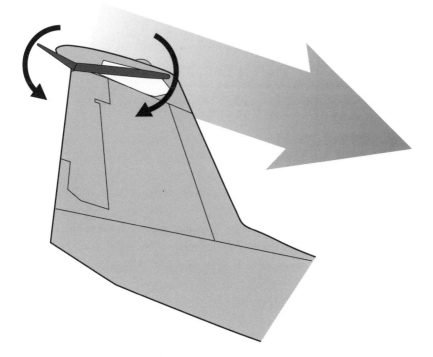

Figure 24. A trimmable stabilizer is an excellent way to provide pitch trim with minimal drag. During a nose-down mistrim, however, simultaneously applying nose-up elevator and nose-up trim results in opposing forces that can prevent the stabilizer from moving.

Chapter 26 **Maximum Range and Cruise Control**

The Lockheed L-1011 was soaring high above the Pacific Ocean en route from Los Angeles to Honolulu and was in the vicinity of the equi-time point. This meant that—should a diversion become necessary—it would take just as long to proceed to Hilo, Hawaii, as it would to turn around and divert to San Francisco, these being the two closest airports during most of the en-route phase of flight.

Somewhere in the cold, dark recesses of the fuel system, a fuel line had begun to chafe against an adjacent object until it could no longer contain the kerosene. The leak might have begun as a trickle, but it eventually developed into a gusher.

In the cabin, more than 200 passengers were watching a movie, and on the flight deck, the crew relaxed, enjoying the tranquillity of a Pacific crossing. The flight engineer made a periodic check of his panel, paying particular attention to the fuel system. (This is not a place to have a fuel problem.) The gauge for one of the three main tanks arrested his attention. It indicated a lower quantity than the other two at a time when all three tank quantities should have been equal. An instrument error, the engineer might have thought initially. But it did not take long to confirm that the quantity in that tank was falling with alarming rapidity, so much so that there was some doubt about whether enough fuel remained to reach what was then the near-est airport, Hilo.

The crew reprogrammed their inertial navigation computers with the new destination, declared an emergency, turned to a more southwesterly heading, and proceeded directly toward the Big Island of Hawaii. And what later proved to be a stroke of genius, they crossfed fuel from the leaking tank to all three engines. The crew reasoned that it was better to consume as much of this fuel as possible before it had a chance to evaporate into thin air.

For the duration of the flight, the crew used every means at their dis-posal to extend range. They and the flight attendants began to prepare for what appeared to be a likely ditching at sea. The Coast Guard in Honolulu had been alerted for an intercept and possible rescue operation.

Lady Luck smiled that day. A safe landing was eventually made, but there was not enough fuel remaining to allow so much as a go-around and one tight circle of the airport.

Although this is an extreme example, there are many occasions when pilots of turbofan airplanes need to extend range. Often, for example, maximum-range cruise (MRC) control comes in handy to avoid an enroute fuel stop or to safely divert to an unexpectedly distant alternate. (Long-range cruise, or LRC, is a compromise that provides increased airspeed with only a small sacrifice in range.)

In theory, maximum range is determined by the thrust vs. airspeed curve (Figure 25) for a given set of conditions. The low point on the curve represents the airspeed at which minimum thrust is required to maintain level flight. Consequently, this is the speed for maximum endurance because thrust—which is loosely analogous to fuel flow—is at a minimum.

Maximum range, on the other hand, is determined by a line that extends from the origin of the graph and is tangent to the curve. At this point of tangency, the ratio of speed to fuel flow is at a maximum. In other words, this is where the airplane gets its best mileage (for a given set of conditions and configuration).

For the technically oriented, it is worth noting a significant difference between propeller and turbofan airplanes. In a jet airplane, the speed for maximum endurance is the point at which the lift-to-drag ratio of the airplane is at a maximum. But in the case of a propeller-driven airplane, $[L/D]_{MAX}$ coincides with the speed for maximum range.

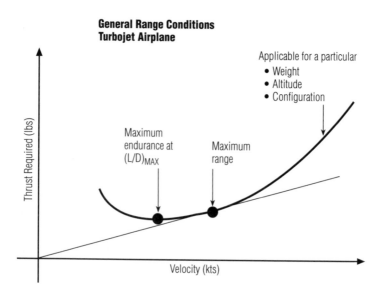

Figure 25. Thrust vs. airspeed

Range normally is discussed in terms of specific range. This is the number of nautical air miles that an airplane flies per unit of fuel consumed and allows a method of directly comparing range efficiency at various flight conditions.

For example, when a Learjet 35A weighing 16,000 pounds is in normal cruise at Flight Level 350, it consumes 1,248 pounds of kerosene per hour and has a true airspeed of 431 knots. This equates to a specific range of 34.5 NM per 100 pounds of fuel. But when in long-range cruise (LRC), the same airplane at the same altitude has a true airspeed of 386 knots while consuming only 1,019 pph. This equates to 37.9 NM per 100 pounds of fuel, which represents a 10 percent improvement in specific range.

Establishing flight at maximum-range cruise is normally a matter of referring to the appropriate MRC chart in the pilot's operating handbook, climbing to the recommended altitude, accelerating to the suggested cruise airspeed, and setting the thrust levers. The POH for some of the smaller turbofan airplanes, however, do not contain MRC charts. Instead, pilots must use long-range cruise data, which normally is quite close to MRC. In the case of the Learjet 36A, for example, LRC is within 1 percent of MRC.

Unlike propeller-driven airplanes, altitude has the greatest effect on the specific range of turbofan airplanes. At FL400 instead of at sea level, for example, airspeed and specific range increase by more than 100 percent while consuming the same amount of fuel.

To this can be added the beneficial effects of altitude on engine performance. As altitude increases, the rpm required to produce the required thrust increases, which in turn reduces specific fuel consumption (pounds per hour of fuel flow per pound of thrust). In other words, the fuel efficiency of a turbofan engine increases with rpm.

The higher the altitude, therefore, the better is the specific range, but only to the extent that maximum-allowable continuous thrust is capable of sustaining the necessary airspeed.

Aircraft weight also has a significant effect on range. When heavy, an airplane cannot climb as high as when it is light, which makes unavailable the beneficial effect of a higher altitude on range. And although a 10 percent increase in gross weight increases the MRC airspeed of a turbofan airplane by 5 percent, it requires a 10 percent increase in thrust and reduces specific range by 5 percent.

There are two lessons here. The first is that as the aircraft becomes lighter, pilots need to diligently consult their MRC charts and make periodic reductions of power and airspeed. Otherwise, range will decrease as the flight progresses. When the aircraft becomes sufficiently light, the pilot should request and obtain a higher cruise altitude to maximize range.

The second lesson is that carrying fuel beyond that needed to complete the flight safely—a procedure known as tankering—increases gross weight and the fuel required to execute a given flight. As a result, a portion of the additional fuel is consumed in the process of carrying it to the destination. This can be wasteful except when fuel at the destination or at an enroute stop is particularly expensive. In this case, it can be cost effective to burn additional, less expensive fuel to prevent from having to buy more of the costly kerosene than is necessary.

Ambient temperature also affects specific range but not to the extent that weight and altitude do. Unusually warm temperatures can reduce specific range by a few percentage points, and unusually cold temperatures can improve range somewhat. One reason for this is that colder-than-standard temperatures improve the specific fuel consumption (SFC), and warmer temperatures have a detrimental effect on the SFC. Unusually warm temperatures at altitude also can limit thrust availability.

Temperature, however, can have a substantial effect on performance. This is because maximum-range cruise normally is flown at a constant Mach number, which—at any given pressure altitude—is equivalent to a constant indicated airspeed irrespective of temperature. The effect on true airspeed, therefore, can be dramatic.

An L-1011 flying MRC at FL350 while tipping the scales at 360,000 pounds, for example, has a cruise airspeed of Mach 0.801 and an indicated airspeed of 272 knots irrespective of ambient temperature. True airspeed, however, varies from 480 knots at an ambient temperature of -35°C to 438 knots at -75°C. (Standard temperature at FL350 is -54°C.) Warmer temperatures obviously improve airspeed but have only a small effect on specific range. Under these conditions, the specific range of an L-1011 at FL350 varies from 3.1 NM per 100 pounds of fuel at -75°C to 3.0 NM/100 pounds at -35°C.

Until now, specific range has been discussed in terms of air miles per pound of fuel, not miles over the ground. Wind, therefore, plays a significant role in discussing actual range. A headwind always decreases range, and a tailwind always increases it.

This does not mean, however, that a pilot cannot take some action to partially offset the handicap of a headwind (and take additional advantage of a tailwind). At typical bizjet cruising speeds, a pilot can come close to optimizing range by increasing indicated airspeed 1 knot for each 20 knots of headwind component (within applicable airframe and powerplant limits). Similarly, he can come close to maximizing range by reducing indicated airspeed 1 knot for each 20 knots of tailwind component.

When at the cruising altitude recommended by the computer (or manual) flight plan, pilots often hear or obtain wind reports from other pilots in the area. Reports of less intense headwinds at lower altitudes, for example, often cause a pilot to consider descending. Although this might increase ground-speed appreciably, it could also erode range.

This inevitably causes a pilot to wonder how much less headwind component or additional tailwind component justifies the additional fuel flow that results from descending into more favorable conditions. A rough rule of thumb for a typical turbofan airplane (if there is such a thing) suggests that a 5-knot wind improvement is needed to justify descending 2,000 feet; 15 knots to descend 4,000 feet; 25 knots for 6,000 feet; 35 knots for 8,000 feet; 45 knots for a 10,000-foot descent; 60 knots for 12,000 feet; and 75 knots for a 14,000 change.

In other words, it takes a substantial change in head- or tailwind component to justify a significant departure from the target cruise altitude. Such is the beneficial effect of remaining high.

There is an interesting procedure that can be used to minimize fuel burn on very short legs. It results in what is loosely described as a parabolic climb/descent profile. The idea is to climb toward an altitude that is much higher than actually needed. While climbing, the pilot notes the point a which a power-off (engines idling) descent can be made to the final approach fix at the destination. He then retards the thrust levers and pushes the nose over into a gliding descent. This obviously requires some cooperation from air traffic control and is very gratifying when performed properly.

Although it is unlikely that many pilots will have to cope with the type of emergency described earlier, they nevertheless should be familiar with how to get the most out of every pound of fuel. One never knows when additional range might come in handy.

Chapter 27 **Spoilers and Speed Brakes**

Considering the amount of effort required to design an efficient airplane, the notion of adding spoilers to destroy lift would seem to be an anathema. But some aircraft are so well designed that spoilers are often needed.

Jet-powered airplanes are aerodynamically clean and do not have the drag of windmilling propellers to help slow them down. This is why they have glide performance that is double that of piston-powered airplanes. As a result, jet pilots often cannot comply with a request from a controller to go down and slow down at the same time.

Spoilers, however, change the rules of the game. Deploying them allows the aircraft to descend at a great rate without necessarily increasing airspeed. (Spoilers on piston-powered airplanes allow a pilot to descend rapidly without having to reduce power so much that he would risk shock-cooling the engine.)

Although there are various types of spoilers, the most common consists of one or more rectangular plates that lie flush with the upper surface of each wing. They are installed approximately parallel to the lateral axis of the airplane (depending on wing structure and geometry) and are hinged along their leading edges. When deployed, spoilers deflect up and against the relative wind, which interferes with the flow of air about the wing. This both spoils lift and adds drag. Spoilers usually are installed forward of the flaps. They are not placed ahead of the ailerons because this would interfere with roll control.

There is some confusion among pilots regarding the difference between spoilers and speed brakes. Perhaps this is because both devices look the same when installed on the upper surfaces of the wings.

The primary purpose of spoilers is to spoil lift even though some drag is created in the process. The purpose of speed brakes, however, is to produce drag even though some lift might be sacrificed in the process. The difference between them is their location along the chord of the wing. If the surfaces are relatively far forward, they are most effective at dumping lift and are called spoilers. When relatively far aft, they are most effective at creating drag and are called speed brakes. It all depends on the designer's intent.

There is a simple test that a pilot can perform to determine if his aircraft is equipped with spoilers or speed brakes. He needs only to note the effect of deploying the devices while holding a constant and approximately level attitude. If a significant sink rate develops and airspeed decay is minimal, they probably are spoilers. But if the results are initially the other way around, they most likely are speed brakes.

Despite what they are called, however, spoilers and speed brakes are used in the same manner and for the same purpose. When either are deployed, the descent profile can be steepened without the usual increase in airspeed, or they can be used to reduce airspeed by keeping the sink rate in check.

Raising spoilers against the force of the relative wind obviously requires muscle, which is why hydraulic power most often is used. Sailplane pilots obviously must deploy their spoilers manually. To assist these pilots, their aircraft often are equipped with balanced spoilers, conventional spoilers on the upper wing panels that operate in conjunction with speed brakes under the wings. These "air brakes," however, are hinged at their trailing edges and deploy backward as shown in Figure 26.

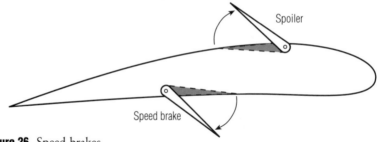

Figure 26. Speed brakes

When the sailplane pilot pulls the spoiler handle to begin a descent, the relative wind strikes against the rising spoilers (on top of the wing) as if attempting to push them back into their stowed position. At the same time, however, the wind pushes against the inner surface of the opening speed brakes (on the bottom of the wing), which assists in opening them further. Because the speed brakes are linked to the spoilers, the power of the relative wind is used to help raise the spoilers, which lightens operating forces.

Pure speed brakes are those installed on the fuselage of an airplane, similar to the dive brakes on military jets. Included, of course, is the landing gear, which often makes a splendid speed brake.

Many jet pilots do not like to use spoilers during descent. One reason for this is that spoilers often create a rumbling buffet that can be disconcerting to passengers. This is most noticeable in the rear of the cabin. Another reason for not wanting to "pop the boards" is that this might be interpreted to mean that a pilot did not plan his descent properly and that spoilers must be used to correct for not getting down soon enough.

There are, of course, several reasons for using spoilers, not the least of which are unexpected descent clearances from air traffic control. Another is the need to descend rapidly through a band of reportedly harsh turbulence without exceeding the turbulence-penetration speed. Because spoilers destroy some lift in their immediate vicinity, wing loading elsewhere on the wing necessarily increases. This has the effect of reducing gust-induced G loads, which softens the ride somewhat.

Spoilers also can be modulated to prevent gaining altitude in the powerful updrafts of strong mountain waves instead of shoving the nose down and risking excessive airspeed.

One of the most important roles for spoilers is to enhance a rapid descent from high altitude necessitated by a loss of cabin pressure. Training for such a maneuver often involves teaching pilots to react rapidly to the simulated emergency. Almost without thinking, we are expected to quickly don an oxygen mask, retard the thrust levers, deploy the spoilers, lower the nose, and maintain an airspeed somewhat shy of the barber pole (redline) all the way down.

But there has been a change of philosophy. Pilots now are taught to first evaluate the emergency instead of simply reacting to the decompression with a steep dive. If the pressure loss is caused by structural failure, descending at high airspeed could worsen the damage.

Because such a rapid descent can result in pegging the vertical speed indicator and descending at many thousands of feet per minute, it is not difficult to overshoot the target altitude. To prevent this, plan to raise the nose and reduce the sink rate when no less than 1,000 to 2,000 feet above the target. Spoilers should be fully retracted by the time there are only 500 feet to go.

Although spoiler deployment is allowed in some aircraft with the flaps extended, this procedure ordinarily should be avoided. This is because of the hazards associated with high sink rates near the ground while in a high-drag (and probably low-power) configuration.

On other aircraft, using spoilers and flaps together is prohibited. One reason for this is that the combination can result in significant buffeting, which eventually can lead to structural fatigue. This is particularly true of the tail, which usually is most susceptible to buffeting.

On the Boeing 727, simultaneous use of flaps and spoilers is banned because this would create such large openings in the wing that continued and controlled flight would be difficult at best.

Another problem with using spoilers during an approach is that—on some aircraft—there is so little buffeting that a pilot could forget that the boards had been deployed. This is something that I once observed from a cockpit jump seat and almost did not survive.

Deployed spoilers have curiously little effect on stall speed and seldom affect stall quality. They do, of course, make it more difficult to recover from a stall with a minimum loss of altitude.

Spoilers also are invaluable when deployed immediately after touchdown. They obviously add substantial drag to assist in slowing the airplane. They also kill a great deal of lift (as much as 80 percent in some cases). This immediately places more of the airplane weight on the wheels, which substantially improves braking performance.

While recently being "retreaded" at a recurrent-training class, my classmates and I were treated to a movie that showed the effect of spoiler deployment on a Boeing 747. The camera was mounted beneath a wing so as to frame one of the landing-gear struts. As the aircraft touched down, the oleo strut obviously compressed. But when the spoilers were deployed, strut compression doubled. This is very impressive to see and makes it easier to understand why spoilers should be deployed as soon after touchdown as possible. This also is why some aircraft are equipped with automatic spoilers that deploy as soon as the wheels are on the ground. Although spoilers are important because they contribute to the reduction of landing distance, they are more invaluable during an aborted takeoff when there often is less available distance within which to stop.

When landing some airplanes with an aft center of gravity, deploying spoilers (and possibly applying reverse thrust) can cause the nose to pitch up enough to cause a tail strike. This can be avoided by lowering the nose slightly and immediately after touchdown. Do not hold the nose high while raising the spoilers.

Although spoilers are used primarily to vary the descent profile, they also are used on some aircraft to control roll because some ailerons lose effectiveness during high-speed flight. A design advantage of using spoilers to supplement roll control is that this allows the use of smaller ailerons, which makes room for larger flaps. In the case of systems that use only spoilers for roll control—such as on the Mitsubishi MU-2—the trailing edge of the wing can be devoted entirely to full-span flaps. Roll-control spoilers are used differentially (on one wing at a time). Entering a right turn, for example, deploys the spoiler(s) on the right wing, and vice versa.

Another advantage of using spoilers for roll control is that they typically create less adverse yaw than ailerons do. There is a another use of spoilers that cannot be found in operating manuals and is seldom discussed by those who use this "special" procedure. (Please regard the following as confidential.)

It is common practice for captains to share landings with their copilots. This can lead to an element of competition between the two pilots, especially if the copilot is at least as skillful as the captain, which occasionally is the case. The idea, of course, is to see who can make the smoothest landings.

Sadly, some captains have egos the size of watermelons and cannot stand the thought of losing a landing contest to a "mere" copilot. So if it seems to the captain during the landing flare that his first officer is about to grease one on, he sneakily reaches for the spoiler handle and moves it slightly, just enough to force the airplane onto the runway with a thump. The captain wins again.

Chapter 28 **Jet Landing Techniques and Performance**

Worldwide, half of all jet accidents occur during the landing phase of flight, yet this typically represents only 4 percent of total flight time. The landing phase clearly is the most dangerous.

Many such accidents are the result of uncontrollable events such as poor weather, wind shear, contaminated runways, and system failures and malfunctions.

Many others, however, are caused by pilots who deviate from proper procedure. Common deviations include excessive approach speed, excessive or insufficient height over the runway threshold, excessive floating, and incorrect stopping technique.

It is axiomatic that the best landings usually are the result of stabilized approaches. This is especially true when flying jet airplanes. Such approaches are considered so critical to safe operation that some airlines require their pilots to pull up and go around if the aircraft is not stabilized when below 500 feet AGL.

A stabilized approach is one in which the aircraft is properly configured (gear and flaps down) and in trim while descending on the glideslope (visual or electronic) and maintaining target speed and sink rate. Cross-tracking the localizer is not allowed.

Target airspeed (V_{REF}) is 1.3 times V_{S0} plus half of any reported gust factor. This gust additive protects against transient airspeed losses and helps to maintain controllability.

The stabilized approach also allows a jet airplane to demonstrate its speed stability and frees the pilot from having to make continuous thrust and pitch changes. This enables him to better detect changing wind and weather conditions.

Maintaining the proper airspeed also helps the pilot to keep the engines spun up. This is important because jet engines typically accelerate and develop power well from high power settings but respond poorly when producing low or idle power (such as when the pilot reduces power to dissipate excess airspeed). Slow engine response is particularly hazardous when power is needed quickly to recover from a high sink rate or a wind-shear encounter at low altitude.

Compounding the problem is the lack of a propeller slipstream to increase wing lift (and lower stall speed) when the thrust levers are advanced.

Excessive approach speeds cannot be tolerated when available runway length is critical. This is because each surplus knot of touchdown speed typically increases the stopping distance of a jet aircraft by 50 feet. An extra 10 knots, for example, requires an additional 500 feet. Each knot of tailwind has a similar effect.

Pilots of narrow-body aircraft typically cross the runway boundary at 50 feet AGL while aiming for a touchdown target that is 1,000 feet beyond the threshold. (Pilots of widebody aircraft use a 1,500-foot touchdown target.)

Height above the threshold (HAT) must be controlled carefully. This is because each foot above the glideslope translates into an additional 20 feet of landing distance. An airplane crossing the boundary with an excess of 50 feet typically uses an additional 1,000 feet of runway.

Jet aircraft should be flown onto the runway. Full- or near-stall landings like those performed in lightplanes must be avoided. This is because a jet aircraft is so aerodynamically clean (even in the landing configuration) and its idling engines produce so much residual thrust that speed bleed while "holding it off" is agonizingly slow. Each knot of speed lost during a landing flare typically consumes 250 feet of runway. This means that deceleration on the runway is five times better than when flaring the aircraft above it. Consequently, a landing is made by raising the nose just enough to reduce sink rate to 100 to 200 fpm and gingerly flying the aircraft onto the concrete.

"Fly" the nosewheel onto the ground immediately after touchdown because a jet aircraft decelerates poorly when held in a nose-high attitude. Placing the nosewheel tire(s) on the ground also improves directional control, especially when deploying reverse thrust. It also reduces wing lift, which adds more weight to the main landing gear and increases braking effectiveness. (Landing-distance charts for jet aircraft assume that the nosewheel is lowered onto the runway within four seconds of touchdown.)

Spoilers can increase drag by 50 percent and kill enough wing lift to place 70 to 80 percent of the aircraft weight on the wheels. Because spoilers are most effective at high speed, do not hesitate to deploy them (if available) immediately after touchdown. If the aircraft is equipped with autospoilers, confirm that they have deployed. Never assume it. Failure to use spoilers typically increases stopping distance by 25 percent.

Some lateral (roll) control may be lost when spoilers are deployed during crosswind landings, so be sure to aggressively apply aileron to keep the wing down. It is much easier to hold a wing down than to replace it after a crosswind causes the wing to rise.

The thrust reversers of first-generation turbojet engines were noisier than they were effective. But those associated with turbofan engines are much more arresting. They are intended to be used only on the ground. One exception is the early edition Douglas DC-8. The reversers of the inboard engines (numbers two and three) of that aircraft can be used to help decelerate and descend. Otherwise, reversers usually are locked out so that they cannot operate in flight.

Like spoilers, thrust reversers are most effective at high speed and should be deployed quickly after touchdown, but do not command significant reverse thrust until the nosewheel is on the ground. This is because the reversers might deploy asymmetrically and force the aircraft to yaw uncontrollably toward the side on which the most reverse thrust is being developed. The sideways resistance of the nosewheel tire on the runway helps to contain such a yaw until the pilot has the presence of mind and the time to resolve the problem by reducing reverse thrust.

On some aircraft, applying reverse thrust causes the nose to pitch up, another reason not to apply full reverse until the nosewheel is on the ground and can be held there.

When the aircraft decelerates to below 80 knots or so, a jet engine may begin to inhale its own exhaust (depending on reverser design) and this explains why reverse thrust should be reduced when below this speed. Consider also that substantial reverse thrust at low speed in the winter can reduce visibility to near zero as the reversers blow clouds of snow ahead of the aircraft.

Pilots need to be cautious about coming out of reverse too rapidly. The engines might still be spun up and provide a spurt of forward thrust at a time when it cannot be tolerated (such as when turning off an icy runway).

So come out of reverse slowly but not completely. Use idle reverse to offset residual forward thrust until turning off the runway. Idle (residual) thrust is usually underestimated and can be sufficient to accelerate an aircraft to impressive taxi speeds.

Although reverse thrust can be highly effective in helping to stop a jet aircraft, it is noteworthy that landing-performance charts are conservative and do not take reverse thrust into consideration. One reason for this is that when a pilot makes a maximum-effort stop by braking heavily, he may not have enough time to deploy and use reverse thrust before reaching a speed below which the reversers lose most of their effectiveness.

If sufficient runway exists, avoid conventional wheel braking until below 80 to 100 knots because they are most effective at low speed. But if they are needed at high speed, apply them gingerly and increase brake pressure progressively as speed decreases. If a panic stop is required, use whatever braking is available.

Be particularly careful about braking if the aircraft is not equipped with an antiskid system. In such a case, heavy braking can cause the wheels to lock and the tires to skid (and possibly fail), which reduces braking effectiveness 15 to 40 percent.

An antiskid system prevents the wheels from locking even when a pilot stands on the brake pedals. The system allows the wheels to roll slowly. This results in a better coefficient of friction and much better braking than when the wheels lock and the tires skid.

Decelerating from a touchdown speed of, say, 130 knots to 70 knots or so gives the impression of a significant speed reduction. A pilot can be deceived into believing that the aircraft is moving slower than it really is. As a result, he tends to relax his stopping effort. But 70 knots is still a substantial speed. Do not relax until confident that the aircraft can be turned off the runway without shearing a tire from its rim.

Here are additional factors that affect landing distance:

• Each 1 percent increase in aircraft landing weight increases landing distance by 1 percent because of the increased resistance to deceleration (inertia).

• Each increase in ambient temperature of 10°F above standard increases landing distance by 3 percent because of the increase in true airspeed for a given indicated airspeed.

• An increase in elevation of 1,000 feet increases landing distance by 4 percent for the same reason.

• Each degree of downhill runway slope increases ground roll by at least 2 percent.

• Wet and icy runways can reduce tire traction by more than 75 percent and more than double required landing distance.

When landing on a contaminated runway, forget about trying to impress your passengers with a grease job. Instead, plant the aircraft on the runway quickly and firmly. This maximizes effective runway length and reduces the likelihood of hydroplaning. Employ aggressive stopping procedures as soon as the aircraft is on the ground. Consider, however, that reverse thrust and aircraft drag (including spoilers) can be more effective than conventional wheel brakes when the runway is wet or icy, as shown in Figure 27.

Relative Contribution of Stopping Forces			
	Brakes	Reverse thrust	Drag
Dry runway	55%	15%	30%
Wet runway	30%	30%	40%
Icy runway	20%	30%	50%

Figure 27

If reverse thrust is available when landing on a contaminated runway, consider delaying brake application until below 100 knots. High-speed braking on wet runways is a contributing factor in hydroplaning incidents.

Heavy braking also reduces the ability of the tires to maintain traction in the direction in which they are rolling. So if a significant angle develops between aircraft heading and track, it might be wise to release the brakes at least partially until directional control is restored. Conversely, if nothing seems to happen when brakes are applied on a wet runway, the tires are probably hydroplaning—but do not just wait for something to happen. You might still be waiting as the aircraft slides off the far end of the runway. Instead, release the brakes and try again. Continue to repeat the process until the brakes become effective (or the aircraft slides off the runway, whichever occurs first).

An unexpected and dangerous condition can develop when reversing heavily on a slippery runway when landing under the influence of a strong crosswind. At such a time, the aircraft can weathervane into the crosswind, as shown in Figure 28. When this occurs, a component of reverse thrust exacerbates the problem by pulling the aircraft toward the downwind edge of the runway. It is even possible for reverse thrust to pull the aircraft completely off the runway.

The only way to resolve such a dilemma is to come out of reverse until the aircraft can be returned to the runway centerline. In extreme cases, this might require the use of forward thrust. Once the aircraft is again under control and tracking properly, reapply reverse thrust and braking as needed.

Finally, it might be interesting to review Figure 27, which shows the relative contribution of brakes, reverse thrust, and drag in stopping an airplane in three different runway conditions.

Although water skiing and ice skating can be fun, attempting to do the same on a set of aircraft tires can produce thrills a pilot is unlikely to forget.

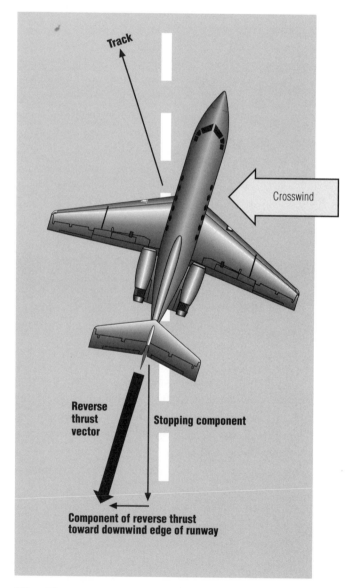

Figure 28

Chapter 29 **Crew Resource Management**

Some years ago, the crew of a United Airlines DC-8 cargo flight discovered an apparent landing-gear malfunction while on final approach to Portland, Oregon. Instead of landing on a possibly lame leg, the captain opted to execute a missed approach and attempted to rectify the problem while circling to the east.

Unfortunately, there was not an abundance of fuel on board, and it was not long before the first officer and the flight engineer began to express concern to the captain about the dwindling reserves. But the captain was preoccupied with the landing gear and appeared not to understand how little fuel remained in the tanks. By the time he finally began to head for the airport, it was too late. The engines flamed out, and the DC-8 crashed.

Although the captain took the brunt of the blame for this accident, the National Transportation Safety Board was highly critical of the other crewmembers because of their failure to be sufficiently assertive about the seriousness of the situation.

This was one of many accidents that eventually convinced safety experts of the need to improve the manner in which crewmembers interact. Thus was born the concept of crew resource management (CRM), which often is pronounced "cram." Its goal is to provide training that will help to avoid accidents attributable to poor group decision-making, ineffective cockpit communications, inadequate leadership, and poor resource management. Consequently, CRM has become a required phase of every airline pilot's initial and recurrent training and is becoming increasingly more prevalent in air-taxi and corporate flight training.

In the past, pilot training focused almost exclusively on developing and maintaining the technical skills and competence needed to master an aircraft. Little attention was paid to the human factors aspect of flight operations.

This is where CRM steps in. Its role is to prevent accidents by "improving crew performance though better crew coordination." It focuses on training crewmembers to function as a team. Captains learn to regard their crews as valuable assets, sources of advice, information, and assistance. I have learned much from my crewmembers, and foolish indeed is the commander—no matter how experienced—who does not think that he cannot learn from his crew—no matter how inexperienced.

It has not always been this way, and for many it never will be. An example of this occurred in 1965 during my second flight as a Boeing 707 first officer. We were enroute from JFK to LAX and had only been at cruise altitude for about 15 minutes. As was required by the airline, at top of climb I pulled out my whiz wheel and calculated our groundspeed.

I couldn't believe it—a 140-knot headwind! As a general aviation pilot, I had never even heard of such a monstrous wind. I double-checked my figures.

I did not realize it at the time, but the captain obviously was accustomed to such winds in the winter and probably already knew our groundspeed because the DME indicator had been moving so slowly.

Anxious to prove my worth, I said, "Captain, we've got a 140-knot headwind!"

He removed the pipe from his mouth, looked at it while shaking his head, blew a stream of smoke toward the ceiling, and turned toward me. "Tell me, son. Just what do you expect me to do about it?"

I shrank in my seat and swore not to volunteer another word for the rest of the flight. This captain flew solo and did not have the slightest interest in anything his subordinates might have to say. It is this type of behavior that CRM is designed to discourage.

On the flip side of this issue is the team leader. Such a captain shows respect for his crew and bolsters their self-esteem and effectiveness by encouraging them to participate in all facets of the operation.

Captain Frank Timoshik was such a leader. I shall never forget one dark and stormy night as we held over the Albany VOR because of weather and traffic delays in Boston, our destination. While holding at flight level 370 in the 707, he turned to me and the flight engineer and said, "I don't think I'd feel comfortable diverting from here to our alternate with less than 14,000 pounds in the tanks. How do you guys feel?"

I agreed and said so. The engineer gave his whiz wheel a studied look and said, "You know, Frank, I'd feel a whole lot better if we had 16,000 pounds."

Without hesitation, Timoshik agreed. He did everything possible to make everyone feel as though they were an integral part of a team. He solicited their input, considered their views, and tried to make certain that they did not feel uncomfortable about his decisions.

I have discovered during my career that captains willing to listen to their crewmembers and delegate responsibility are those who seem to have the greatest confidence in themselves.

It is possible, of course, to carry a good thing too far. The cockpit is not an altar of democracy. The captain cannot always be beneficent and take a vote when decisions need to be made. The FAA mandates autonomous command authority to the captain; he alone shoulders responsibility for the safety of his flight.

Consequently, there are times when the captain must make an immediate decision and take whatever action deemed appropriate at the moment. An example of this is when something goes awry during takeoff as the aircraft approaches V_1, the decision speed. It might be a strange vibration, a loud noise, or any of several other possibilities. At such a time, there is no time for discussion. The captain must decide immediately whether to abort or continue. There will be no consultation, and those on board may live or die by his decision. Literally.

Conversely, there are times when crewmembers must speak up and assert themselves when they believe that they can contribute to flight safety. The fuel-exhaustion tragedy cited at the beginning of this discussion is a classic example of when crewmembers must put tact aside and be somewhat forceful. A case can even be made for usurping the captain's command authority when a crewmember is convinced that such a drastic measure is necessary to protect the flight. (But he had better be certain.)

One aspect of airline training never ceases to amaze me. When reporting for a given flight, I might be meeting my crew for the first time. None of us might know anything about each other except the way in which we were trained. But once in our seats, we know exactly what to expect of each other. It is much like the surgeon who has only to open his hand and know that he will be handed the correct instrument and in precisely the prescribed manner. This is the technical aspect of flying, which is the easiest.

But each crew consists of unique and independent personalities thrust together into a confining and demanding environment with the expectation that they will perform as a team. Although we know the function of each and every switch and instrument, we do not know how each crewmember will interact with the other(s). We do not know how well we will operate as a team. This is where CRM training steps in. It is designed to help pilots develop as much appreciation for the human factors of a flight as they do for the technical aspects.

I was first introduced to a three-man crew (there were only men in the cockpit in those days) when I was hired by TWA in 1964 as a first officer on the last of the Lockheed Constellations. (A year or so later, TWA became the first all-jet airline and advertised that propellers were only for boats.)

Since then, I have flown several different types of transport aircraft that require two- or three-pilot crews. Everything else being equal, I much prefer having three pilots on the flight deck. This is because of the manner in which such a crew copes with emergencies.

When an emergency occurs on a flight with a three-pilot crew, two of the crewmembers can attend to handling the emergency. One reads the checklist while the other—under the watchful eye of the first—attends to the required actions. In the meantime, the third crewmember is free to concentrate on flying the airplane without becoming distracted by the problem.

The safe and efficient division of responsibility is more difficult with a two-pilot crew. This is because one pilot must cope with the emergency while the other concentrates on flying the airplane and attends to communications. This means that no one is available to back up and double-check the actions of the pilot handling the emergency. The pilot flying could (and usually does) divert his attention and assist with the emergency, but such distractions have been responsible for a number of disasters.

The single-pilot crew, however, often faces the greatest challenges and encounters the heaviest work loads. Except in rare circumstances, an airline or corporate crew of two or three does not operate under as much pressure or have as much potential for difficulty as the lone pilot flying a light, piston-powered twin in IFR conditions at night or in high-density airspace. An engine failure or other emergency that to a turbine crew is only an inconvenience can be overwhelming to a crew of one.

Those who fly business jets know that the captain must possess the applicable type rating. Also required is a second-in-command, except when flying certain Cessna Citations that are certified for single-pilot operation. Although such a copilot need not have a type rating, he must be trained in aircraft systems and have made at least three takeoffs and landings during the previous year (for most types of flights). Unfortunately, some bizjet operators ignore this requirement and allow any certificated pilot to sit in the right seat and fill the space with a warm body. Depriving a captain of a trained and qualified first officer, however, has led to a number of incidents—and accidents.

Although some rave about CRM's contributions to aviation safety, there are many who believe it serves little purpose other than to provide employment for the psychologists who develop the training programs. The critics tend to be the pilots who need it the most. They usually just tolerate the class and pay lip service to the lecture; the lights are on but nobody's home.

In this respect, CRM may be similar to safety seminars presented by the FAA as a part of its Accident Prevention Program. Those who need them the most never show up.

Chapter 30 **Principles of Turboprop Engines**

My sons and I were absorbing history through the National Air and Space Museum's impressive array of aeronautical lore and memorabilia. Brian and Michael studied many of the antique airplane exhibits with awe, wondering how pilots of the past could muster the courage apparently needed to fly such fragile, awkward machines.

We soon reached a display of aircraft engines that evoked fond memories. "Dad," Brian asked, "did you really use these engines?" I nodded.

"But how do they work?"

"Well," I began, "there's a coffee-can-shaped thingamabob that rapidly jerks back and forth within each of these metal sleeves." I continued to bewilder him with descriptions of valves, rings, pushrods, and other related paraphernalia. But he found it difficult to accept that such a contraption actually could produce power without thrashing itself to death, which the piston engine occasionally has done.

Fictional reverie? Of course, but it does dramatize the relative obsolescence of the piston engine. Compared to the turbine engine, it is an archaic way to turn a propeller. Piston power survives only because turbine power, the logical replacement, is so expensive to manufacture. In almost every other respect, turboprop engines are superior.

Consider, for example, the power-to-weight ratio of Pratt & Whitney's PT6A-36 gas turbine engine. It weighs only 303 pounds and produces 786 hp (2.59 hp per pound). On the other hand, Textron Lycoming's four-cylinder IO-360-AlB6 weighs a pound less but develops only a meek 200 hp (.66 hp per pound). Pound for pound, this turboprop engine is almost four times as powerful as the piston powerplant.

The turboprop engine also is more reliable, has fewer moving parts, and is less complex than the piston engine. It runs more smoothly, which results in greater passenger comfort, and reduces airframe and propeller fatigue because components do not suffer abuse from the impulse vibrations of a piston engine. Turbine engines also have less frontal area and do not require external cooling, which results in much less drag. They are easier to operate, have simplified ignition systems, and consume a trickle of oil (less than .01 quarts per hour).

Compared to piston engines, turboprops are reputed to be fuel guzzlers, but the accusation is unjustifiable. The average specific fuel consumption (SFC) of Garrett's TPE331 engine, for example, is .535 pounds of fuel per hour per horsepower (at maximum power). Because jet fuel (kerosene) weighs 6.7 pounds per gallon (compared to 6.0 pounds for avgas), this SFC equates to .080 gallons per hour per horsepower. By way of comparison, Teledyne Continental's IO-520-BB, 285-hp engine at maximum power consumes 24.2 gph, or .085 gallons per hour per horsepower. Turboprop and piston engines, therefore, have similar appetites for fuel. Also, both piston and turboprop engines achieve their greatest fuel efficiencies at higher altitudes. (Turboprop engines, however, are not very fuel efficient at the lower altitudes at which most piston-powered aircraft operate.)

Jet fuel is less volatile (safer) and costs less per gallon than 100LL avgas. Another turboprop plus is that these engines are mated with reversible-pitch propellers that contribute superior braking and controllability on wet or icy runways.

In principle, turboprops are little more than turbine engines with propellers attached. Figure 29 is a cross section of a simplified turbine or turbojet and is typical of those found on early model jet aircraft.

Such an engine is started by rotating the compressor section with an electrical starter (on small engines) or an air-driven starter (on large engines). As compressor rpm accelerates, it brings in air through the inlet duct, compresses it, and delivers it to the burner section, where fuel is injected by a fuel controller and ignited by two igniter plugs. (Not all of this compressed air is used to support combustion; some bypasses the burner section to provide

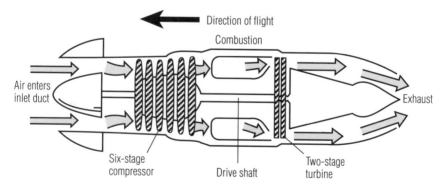

Turbojet Engine

Figure 29

internal cooling.) The mixture of hot air and gases then is directed to the turbine blades, which forces the turbine section to rotate like a high-speed water wheel.

Once the turbine section is powered by gases from the burner section, the starter is disengaged, and the igniters are turned off. Combustion continues until the engine either fails or is shut down by turning off the fuel supply.

The compressor section continues to rotate and pump air into the engine because it is physically connected to the turbine section by a long shaft. After powering the turbine section, the excess high-velocity exhaust exits the tailpipe and produces jet thrust. Turbojets—like piston engines—have four cycles: induction, compression, combustion, and exhaust (referred to colloquially as suck, squeeze, bang, and blow.) Turbojet engines, however, allow these phases of power to occur simultaneously and continuously instead of one cycle at a time.

Figure 30 shows how Pratt & Whitney uses the gas turbine engine to drive the propeller of its PT6A-series engines. An additional turbine is placed in the path of the jet exhaust, and this converts almost all of the jet thrust into torque, which, through reduction gears, powers the propeller.

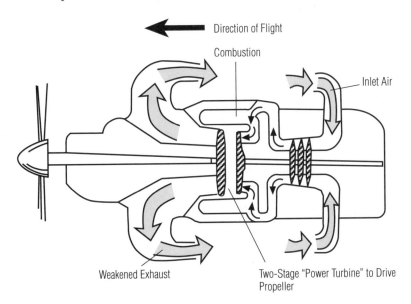

Direction of Flight

Combustion

Inlet Air

Weakened Exhaust

Two-Stage "Power Turbine" to Drive Propeller

Free-Turbine, Reverse-Flow Turboprop Engine

Figure 30

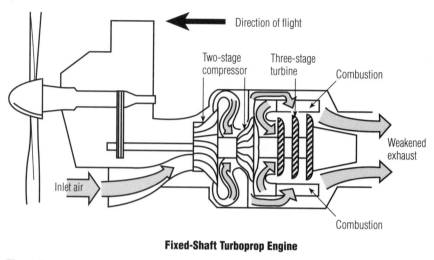

Fixed-Shaft Turboprop Engine

Figure 31

The propeller and its turbine are not connected physically to the gas turbine engine. Such a configuration is called a free turbine. Because the propeller is mounted behind the engine, the PT6A usually is installed backward (a reverse-flow engine). Inlet air enters the compressor section at the rear, and exhaust gases exit forward, immediately behind the propeller. Consequently, a Pratt & Whitney-powered general aviation airplane is easy to spot. Just look for the exhaust stubs (or horns) on the forward portion of the nacelle.

The only other turboprop engines presently used in significant numbers by manufacturers of U.S. general aviation airplanes are Garrett's TPE331-series engines. Garrett's approach to turboprop design is somewhat different.

Instead of employing a free turbine at the rear of the engine, Garrett uses a single, three-stage turbine that drives both the compressor section and the propeller with a single fixed shaft (as shown in Figure 31). Notice also that the propeller is mounted at the forward end of the engine. Exhaust leaves the Garrett powerplant through a conventional tailpipe.

Such a discussion inevitably prompts someone to ask why propellers are attached to gas turbine engines instead of simply mounting the engines on a general aviation airplane and using only jet exhaust to provide the necessary thrust (à la Learjet)?

Simply stated, a propeller is more efficient at generating thrust at relatively low airspeeds. Such a claim, although accurate, leaves many people scratching their heads and wanting more of an explanation. Characteristically, a turbojet engine ingests a relatively small amount of air and expels it from the tailpipe at a very high velocity. A propeller, on the other hand, has a larger diameter and can act upon much more air than can the turbine engine to which it is attached. The propeller, however, does not accelerate air to as high a velocity. Consequently, jet exhaust has much more kinetic energy (because of its velocity) than does the air flung rearward by a propeller.

Unfortunately, kinetic energy languishing behind an airplane is a waste of propulsive energy. If the airplane could move forward as rapidly as the exhaust leaves the tailpipe, this energy waste theoretically would be reduced to zero. Turbojet engines are most efficient at high speeds, but propellers, which generate less kinetic energy, are most efficient at slow and medium speeds (less than 400 knots).

Recognizing that propellers improve takeoff and climb performance, jet-engine manufacturers developed the turbofan engine (Figure 32).

Notice that not all of the air passing through the first and larger compressors is ingested by the engine. Much of it is accelerated rearward and flows outside the engine. These large compressors are called fans (or turbofans), and their outer portions are little more than high-speed propellers. Turbofans, or fanjets, are used on almost all modern jet airplanes because the multi-bladed fans, acting like propellers, improve performance during takeoff and climb. (Ducted-fan and bypass engines are variations on the same theme.)

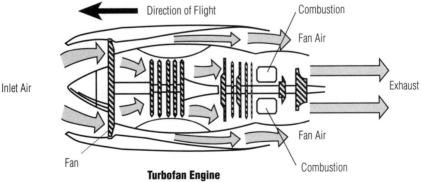

Turbofan Engine

Figure 32

The power output of a piston engine is measured in horsepower and is determined primarily by rpm and manifold pressure. The power of a turbo-prop engine, however, is measured in shaft horsepower (shp). This is essentially the same as conventional (brake) horsepower but is determined by rpm and the torque (or twisting power) applied to the propeller shaft (hence, shaft horsepower).

Because turboprop engines are driven by gas turbines, some jet thrust is produced by exhaust leaving the engine. This thrust is added to the shaft horsepower to determine total engine power, or equivalent shaft horsepower (eshp). Jet thrust usually accounts for less than 10 percent of the total engine power.

Operating a turboprop engine is child's play compared to managing the comparatively temperamental piston engine. Cockpit controls consist primarily of a throttle, called a power lever, and a propeller-pitch control, usually called an engine-rpm lever (Garrett) or propeller-rpm lever (Pratt & Whitney). Although Pratt & Whitney adds a condition lever that opens and closes a fuel valve, Garrett incorporates this as one function of its engine-rpm lever. (Manually feathering the propeller simultaneously shuts off the fuel.) Forget about leaning, carburetor heat, magnetos, and, with most turboprop engines, cowl flaps.

Engine instrumentation includes not only conventional fuel and oil gauges, but also a torque gauge that responds to movement of the power lever. Torque, like manifold pressure, indicates how hard the engine is working to power the propeller. It is measured by a device that determines the torsion (or twist) being applied to a drive shaft.

The tachometer is a bit unusual, too. Instead of displaying propeller speed in hundreds of rpm, it indicates the percentage of allowable rpm to save pilots from having to work with the large numbers associated with turbine engines. Assume that the Garrett engine is being operated at 100 percent rpm. This means that the engine is spinning at 41,730 rpm (maximum allowable). The propeller cannot be allowed to turn so rapidly without the risk of slinging the blades into orbit. In a typical installation, a 20.9:1 set of reduction gears limits the propeller to a maximum of 2,000 rpm. Because the propeller and its fixed-shaft engine always have the same relative rpm, a single tachometer is used for both.

Pratt & Whitney's free turbine engine justifies two tachometers. Because the propeller is not attached physically to the shaft of the gas turbine engine, a separate tachometer is used to indicate the rpm of each. The propeller's tach usually indicates hundreds of rpm, and the engine tach displays percentage of maximum-allowable rpm.

All turboprop engines have an engine temperature gauge. There are three popular types, depending on where the temperature-sensing probe is located. In the first, the probe is placed immediately in front of the turbine section, and the instrument indicates turbine inlet temperature (TIT); the second measures the temperature between any of the turbine stages, or interstage turbine temperature (ITT); and the third measures exhaust gas temperature (EGT).

Engine temperature (TIT, ITT, or EGT) is of critical importance. Excessive heat can weaken the turbine blades and result in metal particles being flung from their tips at high rpm. The result can be a catastrophic engine failure. Should engine temperatures become excessive, the power lever must be retarded. If this occurs during engine start (i.e., a hot start), the attempt must be aborted immediately by shutting off the fuel.

Starting a turboprop engine can be as simple as flicking a switch. The Cessna 441 Conquest, for example, requires only the push of a button. The rest of the normal start sequence is completely automatic. The pilot simply monitors the engine gauges, ready to shut down the engine in case of a hot start or a hung start. The latter occurs when engine rpm stagnates and fails to accelerate to idle speed. The most likely causes for this are low battery (cranking) power or some form of internal mechanical drag.

Manual starting procedures are a bit more complex. Typically, the pilot turns on the ignition, engages the starter, and turns on the fuel after the engine has reached a specified rpm.

Starting a turboprop engine that only recently has been shut down sometimes requires a procedure known as "motoring." With a typical manual system, the pilot uses the starter to turn the engine and purge it of hot air and gases before proceeding with the starting checklist.

Engine runup also is simple because none is required. Various systems checks, however, are needed. Because these engines contain much less oil than a piston engine, only a moment's worth of warm-up (usually accomplished while taxiing) is recommended before applying takeoff power.

Other than the smooth surge of seemingly excessive power, there is nothing unusual about flying a turboprop airplane. However, a pilot can close the throttle(s) at any time without worrying about cooling the engine too rapidly and warping valves. Consequently, rapid descents with the propeller(s) in low pitch can be dramatically steep. And at idle, the turboprop engine still pumps sufficient bleed air (from the compressor section) to keep the cabin pressurized. Hot bleed air also can be used to protect the engine inlet ducts from icing.

Landing some turboprop airplanes (as well as some piston twins) can result in a hard, premature touchdown if the engines are idled too soon. This is because large propellers spinning rapidly in low pitch create considerable drag. In such airplanes, it is wise to maintain power until the proper landing attitude has been established and the pilot is fully prepared to land.

Once the power levers have been retarded and the airplane is firmly on the ground, the levers (in most airplanes) then can be raised out of the idle detents and retarded even further. This simultaneously reverses propeller pitch and adds power (torque) to aid in braking. (When blade angles are decreased to less than their normal low-pitch limits, a propeller is said to be operating in its beta range.) After arriving at the tiedown area, the engines should be idled for a moment to allow internal engine temperatures to stabilize before shutdown.

Because U.S.-built, general aviation turboprop airplanes are powered mostly by Garrett or Pratt & Whitney gas turbines, it is noteworthy to compare these powerplants.

One substantial difference is the propeller feathering mechanism. When a P&W PT6A engine loses oil pressure during engine failure (or shutdown), a valve opens to expedite the flow of oil from the propeller dome, resulting in automatic and rapid feathering of the propeller blades. Consequently, the blades of a PT6A always are feathered when the engines are shut down.

Garrett's TPE331 uses a negative torque sensor (NTS). If an engine fails, it no longer applies positive torque to turn the propeller. At such a time, the windmilling propeller actually drives the engine and, in so doing, applies negative torsion (torque) to a drive shaft in the gear-reduction unit. When the NTS detects this negative torque, it causes most of the oil pressure in the propeller dome to be relieved, which drives the propeller blades to very large pitch angles. Although this reduces most of the propeller drag, it is up to the pilot to completely feather the propeller.

When the Garrett engine is shut down, pilots are advised to prevent the propellers from feathering by using a procedure that activates stop locks to keep propeller pitch from increasing and later causing undue stress on the starting mechanism. Consequently, the blades of a Garrett engine usually are in low pitch when the airplane is parked, another way to distinguish at a glance between Garrett and Pratt & Whitney gas turbine engines.

Starting a PT6A requires less electrical power because cranking the engine does not require turning the propeller. (The propeller of a free-turbine configuration is not connected physically to the engine.) A feathered prop does not unnecessarily burden the electrical system with excessive drag during engine start.

Cranking a TPE331, however, requires a healthier battery because the engine and the propeller are turned simultaneously, which is why this prop must not be feathered during engine start. For similar reasons, an air-start in a Garrett engine does not require cranking. An unfeathered, windmilling prop does the work of turning the compressor. The windmilling prop of a PT6A does nothing. An air-start usually requires starter engagement.

Fixed-shaft engines also are more responsive to throttle movement and have slightly thriftier fuel specifics. Free-turbine engines, however, are quieter on the ground. For ultraquiet ground operations, the free-turbine engine can be kept at idle with the propeller feathered and revolving very slowly. Also, free-turbine engines are well suited for helicopter operations.

Turboprop engines do not require maintenance as frequently as piston engines do, but each visit to the shop usually costs more. Although turbo-prop engine maintenance is more expensive per engine hour, including re-serve for overhaul, it probably is less expensive—on a per-horsepower basis—than maintaining a piston engine. Recommended time between over-hauls (TBO) for general aviation turboprop engines typically vary between 3,000 and 4,000 hours. Inspection of an engine's hot section (the combustion and turbine section), however, is required halfway to overhaul. Commuter operators can extend TBOs to 9,000 hours, with hot-section inspections re-quired each 3,000 hours.

Research is being conducted to find a way to produce an economical, low-horsepower turboprop for airplanes and automobiles that does not re-quire expensive and exotic metals (such as forged titanium). But until such research bears fruit, pilots of most general aviation airplanes will have to settle for the status quo.

Chapter 31 **Principles of Inertial Navigation**

Although inertial navigation has revolutionized long-range navigation, it's doubtful if many general aviation pilots will use it to span oceans and continents in their light singles or twins. The global positioning system (GPS) is much more practical for most aircraft. INS is much heavier, more expensive, and requires a 400-watt diet of AC and DC electrical power. But general aviation pilots would do well to understand the way it works.

In theory, inertial navigation is quite simple; in practice, simpler yet. Airline pilots use it routinely to fly the world's oceans without needing a computer, a plotter, a pencil, or even a chart. A reasonably bright person could just as competently use INS to go anywhere in the world. All you need to know is the point from where you're starting and where you want to go.

Inertial navigation operates on the principle of inertia, a property possessed by every object in the universe. Sir Isaac Newton probably best defined inertia with "...every object at rest tends to remain at rest and every object in motion to remain in motion unless acted upon by an exterior force."

Because every human being has mass—some of us have a bit too much—and a brain, each of us is a crude inertial navigator that can operate, in principle, the way INS does.

Assume, for example, that a man sitting blindfolded in the rear seat of a stationary automobile is told exactly where in the city he is located and in which direction the car is headed. In effect, his brain has been "loaded" or "initialized" with the necessary "preflight" information.

The driver starts the engine and accelerates the car to 60 mph. The passenger's body has mass (inertia), so the acceleration presses his back against the rear seat. Now assume that he can approximate the amount of this force and know that his body has been accelerated to about 60 mph. In the meantime, his internal clock counts the minutes and seconds during which time the driver maintains a constant speed. After 30 minutes, the driver slows to 20 mph, a deceleration detected by the passenger as his body pitches forward slightly. "Aha," he says, "I have traveled 60 mph for 30 minutes and therefore have traveled 30 miles. Now I am traveling at only 20 mph."

The car stops half an hour later. The man concludes that while traveling at 20 mph for 30 minutes, he has traveled an additional 10 miles, or a total of 40 miles. By carefully measuring acceleration and deceleration, the passenger has determined his speed at any given time and converted this to distance traveled.

Had the driver changed direction at any time, the passenger would have detected the centrifugal force resulting from the turn and could have computed the amount of turn and the new direction of travel.

The human brain, of course, cannot accurately measure acceleration, keep track of time, and account for the myriad velocity changes that occur during even a short ride. But an inertial navigation system can.

A major advantage of INS is that it's totally self-contained. It operates independently of radio transmitters, satellites, the Earth's magnetic field, and the positions of celestial bodies. Also it doesn't transmit energy as does radar and is accurate despite wind, sea, and atmospheric conditions.

Because INS is impervious to exterior influence, it found early military acceptance. An enemy cannot jam, intercept, or detect nonexistent signals to or from an inertially guided device.

The Germans made first use of INS in the V-2 missile during World War II. When the preset distance had been traveled (as measured by the crude inertial computer), a cutout signal was sent to the engine. The missile then fell onto its prey. The system admittedly was primitive. Had it been more accurate, its effects on London and environs would have been considerably more damaging.

The heart of INS consists of three extremely sensitive accelerometers that measure speed change (rates) in three planes or axes: longitudinal (fore and aft), lateral (right and left), and vertical. Any aircraft motion acts in one or more of these axes.

The accelerometers are so sensitive that they can typically measure any acceleration between 0.0008 and 10 Gs. This means that INS can measure the acceleration of an object from 0 to 2 knots during one hour or, at the other extreme, the huge acceleration of a missile that rockets from a standstill to 600 knots in a few seconds.

All aircraft speed and attitude changes—no matter how slight—are detected by the INS computer, which continuously converts this information into track and distance data. The computer knows at all times where it's been, where it is, where it's going, and at what speed.

Because INS accelerometers measure speed changes with respect to the Earth, they must be kept aligned with the Earth's surface. This is accomplished by placing them on a small platform held parallel to the Earth's surface with gyroscopes, in the same manner as an artificial horizon. The result is called an inertial platform or a "stable table."

Because these gyros keep the platform so perfectly aligned with the Earth, they can also serve as reference for the pilot's attitude and heading indicators. Compensation circuits within the INS prevent gyroscopic precession from affecting either the inertial platform or the attitude display.

Operating INS is only slightly more complicated than using a push-button telephone. Before departure, the pilot enters the exact latitude and longitude coordinates defining the aircraft's position and then the coordinates of the first nine waypoints along his route of flight. And that's about it.

Because INS senses the Earth's rotation, it determines during warm-up the direction of true north to the nearest tenth of a degree. This information can be fed to the directional gyros so that—as long as he elects to do so—the pilot can navigate with respect to true north. No longer must he be concerned with the magnetic compass.

En route, INS develops a slight error that increases with time. If he desires, the pilot can input actual aircraft position data obtained from radar, visual, or radio position fixes into the computer. The INS will digest the error, "think" about it a while, and remove a portion of the error. This has the effect of increasing accuracy with usage.

At flight's end, the INS computer may disagree with the actual aircraft position by a few miles. It makes you wonder if the airport is really where everyone thinks it is.

Considering that INS receives no enroute updating from ground- or satellite-based stations, it is very accurate. Tests conducted during 3,000 flights and 14,000 hours of flying reveal that 50 percent of the time, INS errs less than 0.41 NM per hour of flight. Ninety-five percent of the time, the error (two-sigma error, in engineering-ese) is less than 1.4 NM per hour. This means that at the end of a 10-hour flight, an inertially guided aircraft has a 95 percent chance of being within 14 NM of its destination. Now INS is being integrated with GPS so that the INS solution can be continually updated with the highly accurate GPS satellite inputs.

The first- and second-generation inertial systems, based on accelerometers and spinning mass gyroscopes representing 1960s technology, have been supplanted in the most recent air transport, military, and large business jets by inertial reference systems (IRS), which use far smaller, simpler, and more reliable ring laser gyros (RLGs).

RLGs actually are not gyros at all, in that they do not use rotating mass and in fact have virtually no moving parts. Instead, they measure the time two beams of light take to travel in opposite directions around a triangular path. Any component of aircraft motion, acceleration, or deceleration that acts along the plane in which the light beams travel makes one beam complete the circuit slightly faster, the other slower. From the difference, the IRS computer derives rates, speeds, and headings. An RLG (or two, for redundancy) is oriented to each of the three flight axes along which it senses aircraft motion. An IRS based on RLGs—or the even newer fiber optic gyro technology that uses the same principles—does not require a separate stabilized platform to isolate it from the aircraft structure. Hence, the IRS is referred to as a "strapdown inertial" system.

The weakest link in the INS chain is the flight crew, who might program the computer with the wrong coordinates. Evidence suggests that such a navigational error led Korean Air Lines Flight 007, a Boeing 747, into Soviet airspace where it was shot down on September 1, 1983, resulting in the loss of 269 lives.

Without the human factor, you could probably insert the coordinates of heaven and have every reason to believe that INS would guide you safely there (even though GPS will do it more accurately).

Section 4

Personal Observations

Becoming a proficient pilot requires blending skill, knowledge, and experience with judgment. Skill is the product of practice, and knowledge is derived from study. Although experience is the best teacher, it usually is the most difficult to obtain. My intent in this section is to share with you a series of vignettes that distill some of the most important lessons I have learned (sometimes the hard way) during a flying career that began in 1952 as a 14-year-old student pilot. I hope that you find them of value.

Chapter 32 **Getting More Ratings**

Several years ago, the captain of a Delta Airlines Lockheed L-1011 was startled to discover shortly after takeoff from San Diego that he had lost almost all pitch control. This was caused by what appeared to be a jammed stabilator. Such an occurrence is considered so unlikely by Lockheed that L-1011 crews are not trained to cope with such an emergency.

The captain of this flight, however, had flown the Boeing 707. His training for this type rating included a procedure designed to cope with a jammed stabilizer. It involved deactivating certain spoilers so that deploying the remaining spoilers would result in a strong pitching moment in the desired direction. (Deploying the aft/outboard spoilers on a swept wing moves the center of lift forward and causes the aircraft to pitch up, and vice versa.)

Would using such a procedure on the disabled Lockheed have the desired effect? The captain had nothing to lose by trying. Fortunately, his use of the Boeing procedure did restore enough pitch control to allow him to nurse the aircraft into nearby Los Angeles International Airport.

If the captain had not had a 707 type rating, the outcome of this flight probably would have been tragically different.

There are some who believe that earning additional category, class, and type ratings does not necessarily make a pilot better. But I disagree and cannot understand how a pilot would not benefit from the additional knowledge and skill, as the preceding example demonstrates.

When working for a seaplane rating, for example, transitioning pilots are taught a special procedure for landing on glassy water. This training is required because it is often difficult to judge height above such a smooth, reflective surface.

The maneuver requires maintaining a shallow (approximately 200 fpm), slow, nose-high, power-on approach. This configuration is held until the aircraft touches (splashes) down. In essence, the aircraft is not flared for landing because it is in a flared attitude during the approach. A conventional approach and last-minute flare could result in flaring prematurely and stalling too high; flaring too late or not at all can be equally catastrophic. A glassy-water approach and landing can be made entirely on instruments and without looking out the window.

Pilots can also use this procedure when landing on wheels during conditions when depth perception is in short supply (such as when landing at night without the benefit of landing or runway lights).

A glider rating also rewards a transitioning pilot with a wonderful assortment of additional skills and knowledge that can enhance the way airplanes are flown.

Sailplane pilots are so reliant on the movement of the atmosphere that they are compelled to develop an intimacy with wind and current that power pilots can only envy. They also master gliding techniques that can be extremely useful when sitting behind a stilled prop, such as how and when to use a minimum-sink glide and how to compensate for wind while attempting to maximize forward gliding distance.

The Air Canada captain who glided his fuel-exhausted Boeing 767 onto a drag strip at Gimli, Manitoba, credits the survival of his aircraft and passengers to his experience as a glider pilot.

Learning to fly helicopters teaches us how secure and comfortable it is to fly with fixed wings. I apologize to chopper pilots for saying what many of us consider to be a truism. Even though I am a rotorcraft instructor (in helicopters and gyroplanes), I have never become totally accustomed to a machine lacking visible means of support and seemingly bent on self destruction.

The airline transport pilot certificate is required of those who fly as pilot in command for the airlines. (No, copilots are not required to have an ATP.) Because scheduled airlines no longer operate single-engine aircraft, it might appear that only a masochist would endure the agony required to obtain a single-engine ATP.

Others argue that acquiring the skills necessary to earn an ATP—even in a single—brings them one step closer to being able to fly an airplane as well as it can be flown. When executing an ILS approach during the flight test for an instrument rating, for example, the localizer and glideslope needles may wander anywhere during the approach as long as neither reaches maximum deflection. But during the test for an ATP, the ILS needles must be kept within "one dot of the bull's eye." Mediocrity is unacceptable.

Obtaining a single-engine ATP gives a certain boost to the ego and allows the bearer to emblazon each sleeve of his pajamas with four gold stripes. Some insurance companies also pay tribute in the form of premium reductions.

On the other hand, an additional rating can be dangerous. Consider, for example, the newly rated multi-engine pilot who never again practices engine-out procedures (because there is no requirement to do so). This explains why such a pilot is more likely to bore a smoking hole in the ground following an engine failure in a twin than if he were to have had that failure while flying a single.

When a pilot obtains an additional rating, he effectively reverts to being a student pilot in that aircraft and must conduct himself appropriately.

In 1938, Prime Minister Neville Chamberlain returned to London after attending the Munich Conference, waving a document that he triumphantly claimed would "bring peace in our time." But when Adolf Hitler was asked by his staff why he would sign such an agreement, he commented that it was only a "scrap of paper." Hitler made his point by invading Poland and sweeping the world into war.

An additional rating also can be a mere scrap of paper, a word or two inscribed on a certificate. Or it can document a pilot's dedication to continuing education. It obviously depends on how it is used.

Chapter 33 **The Rule of Sixty**

The westbound progress of the 707 above the snow-covered plains of Kansas was more like that of the propeller-driven Connie I had recently flown. Our Mach 0.85 airspeed seemed feeble against the powerful jet stream that angled across our track as if challenging our right of passage.

"Look at that DME," I said, shaking my head slowly in disbelief. "We're hardly moving."

The winter sky seemed to hold us in suspension. Nothing was moving except the fuel gauges.

Perry Schreffler was seated to my left. He motioned toward the VOR needle on his panel. "Look at this," he said, "a 120-knot crosswind component."

How did he know that, I wondered.

Schreffler recognized my confusion and volunteered his secret. He told me that at our airspeed of 480 knots, each degree of drift (or crab) is caused by an 8-knot crosswind component. And because we were crabbing 15 degrees to keep the VOR needle centered, the crosswind component had to be 120 knots, the result of multiplying crab angle by 8.

Over the years, this formula has been at least as handy for impressing my copilots as it has been for estimating crosswind components. It is based on the "Rule of Sixty," which has other in-flight uses.

Most pilots were introduced to a variation of the rule during their early study of dead-reckoning navigation. The rule stated that for each 60 miles of flight, an airplane will be 1 mile off course for each degree of drift. Three degrees of drift during a 120-mile flight, therefore, would cause the aircraft to be 6 miles off course.

Determining the crosswind component is simply a variation of the theme. For each 60 knots of true airspeed, each degree of crab represents a 1-knot crosswind. For example, a 180-knot aircraft crabbing 4 degrees is under the influence of a 12-knot crosswind. To simplify the problem, multiply airspeed (expressed in nautical miles per minute) by crab angle to obtain the crosswind component. The 707 mentioned earlier had an airspeed of 480 knots, which is 8 NM per minute. Multiplying 8 by 15 (the crab angle) results in the crosswind component of 120 knots.

Calculating crosswind in this way is particularly useful when approaching an airport without a wind-reporting facility. A pilot crabbing 14 degrees while on short final at 90 knots (1.5 NM per minute), for example, might want to know that he is about to challenge a 21-knot crosswind.

The Rule of Sixty also has some interesting applications during vertical navigation. For example, an aircraft on a 1-degree descent profile loses 1 mile (approximately 6,000 feet) every 60 miles. In other words, it loses 100 feet of altitude per nautical mile.

The typical ILS approach has a 3-degree glideslope, which means that the aircraft descends 300 feet per mile.

This seemingly innocuous piece of information can be particularly helpful when making a straight-in, VFR approach at a time when conditions make it difficult to judge and maintain a normal approach slot. This can occur at night, for example, when making a so-called "black-hole" approach to a runway not equipped with either a glideslope or a VASI.

At such times, descending 300 feet per nautical mile assures a pilot that he is on a normal 3-degree approach slot. For example, altitude should be 1,800 feet AGL when 6 miles from the airport, 1,500 feet when 5 miles out, and so forth. With a little practice, a pilot can learn to accurately descend along a 3-degree glidepath without the approach aids and visual cues normally required to do so. Such altitude awareness can prevent a pilot from being lured by optical illusions into premature and untimely descents.

Speaking of descent planning, I used to fly with a captain who could intercept a glideslope by lowering the nose exactly the right amount. He would adjust attitude in one smooth move that always resulted in precisely the sink rate required to capture and initially remain on the glideslope. He did this without knowing groundspeed or consulting the sink-rate table published on the ILS approach plate.

He was the envy of the line, and it was only upon his retirement that he decided to reveal his secret.

"It's really no big deal," he said matter-of-factly, almost surprised that everybody didn't know how to do it. "All you have to do is approach glideslope intercept at the desired altitude, with airspeed stabilized and the aircraft in approach configuration. Then, when the glideslope needle is about to center, lower the nose exactly 3 degrees (or whatever the glideslope angle is supposed to be). Capture is automatic, guaranteed."

Everyone was dumbfounded. How could it be so simple? Well, it is. Try it.

A few months ago, I was trying to impress yet another copilot with my ability to compute crosswind by "resolving wind triangles in my head." But my reputation apparently had preceded me; he was ready with his own bag of tricks.

"I know all about your Rule of Sixty, Skipper. Been using it for years. But I'll bet you don't know how to do a 10-second groundspeed check."

A 10-second groundspeed check? I racked my brain. I had never heard of a 10-second check. I regularly used a 36-second check, a method by which a pilot observes the DME for 36 seconds and multiplies the distance traveled by 100 to arrive at the groundspeed. Works pretty well. But a 10-second check? Never heard of it. Nor would it work very well.

"Nope, never heard of a 10-second check. I'll have to call your bluff."

The copilot smiled, picked up his mike, and said, "Chicago Center, this is TWA 702. Request a groundspeed check."

"Roger, 702. We show you doing 520."

And it took only 10 seconds.

Chapter 34 **The Preflight Inspection**

The preflight inspection is one of a pilot's most important responsibilities, but it also is one of the most mundane. As a result, many take the walkaround for granted and overlook potential problems.

I once had an instructor who ensured that none of his students performed a perfunctory preflight. He did this by cleverly sabotaging the airplane before each student would arrive for his lesson. One of his favorite tricks, for example, was to place a small piece of Scotch tape over one of the static ports. Others included disconnecting a spark-plug lead, plugging a fuel vent with a small and easily removable piece of paper, removing the bolt that held a control stick in place, and so forth. Whether or not the student discovered the flaw, a few minutes of the preflight briefing were devoted to discussing the potential consequences of such a problem. He taught us well but, in my case, perhaps not well enough.

Many years later, on January 22, 1975, my close friend Hal Fishman and I were about to assault two world speed records (for Class C-1.d, piston-powered airplanes) held by the Soviet Union. I had just flown the 500-kilometer, closed-circuit course, and it was Fishman's turn to fly the 1,000-kilometer course. We climbed into the turbocharged, slightly modified Aerostar 601 prior to the second flight and were ready to start when Ted R. Smith, the Aerostar's designer, and a photographer walked in front of the airplane to take a few publicity photos. The photographer framed the brand-new twin and was preparing to take the picture when Smith told us to center the rudder. After all, he wanted his creation to look as sleek as possible. Fishman neutralized the rudder pedals and motioned for the photographer to proceed. Smith shook his head and walked over to the open clam-shell door. "Perhaps you didn't understand what I meant," he said. "Neutralize the rudder."

"But Ted," Fishman replied, "the rudder is centered. Look at the pedals."

Smith was puzzled. "Something's wrong." He removed his jacket, loosened his tie, rolled up his sleeves, and proceeded to climb through the baggage compartment and into the tailcone.

He returned a few minutes later and declared that the rudder was not connected to the push-pull tubes. Nor, he said, had it ever been. Somewhat embarrassed, he said that "it looks like the airplane left the factory this way."

I briefly reviewed what might have happened if we had had an engine failure during our previous flights in the airplane. Without a rudder, there would have been no way to maintain directional control without throttling the good engine and making a forced landing.

Not offering an excuse, it is difficult to verify rudder operation of an Aerostar because the control surface cannot be seen from the cockpit. Nor is this unusual. The rudders and elevators of many airplanes cannot be seen from the cockpit.

Many large airplanes are equipped with surface-position indicators to verify before takeoff that all flight controls are operating normally. Because lightplanes are not so equipped, these pilots must take greater care. (One way to confirm proper control surface movement is to observe their shadows with the sun on the right.)

Pilots need to be particularly vigilant during preflight inspections conducted after any maintenance or inspections have been performed. Things might not have been put back together properly, a mechanic might have left a tool or rag where it does not belong, or perhaps something has been reinstalled or reassembled incorrectly.

Larry Shapiro, for example, took off from Big Bear City Airport in California, which is surrounded by mountains. Shortly after liftoff in his Beech Travel Air, which had just had major maintenance, the left engine failed. Moments later, the right engine failed. Fortunately, Shapiro had gained enough altitude to glide over a low ridge to a low-elevation airport near San Bernardino, where it was discovered that the fuel-selector valves had been reinstalled backward.

Shortly after takeoff in a Cessna 210 that had just had an annual inspection, I heard a loud banging noise that came from under the cowling. I was convinced that the engine was about to come apart, declared an emergency, and returned to the airport for an immediate landing. After removing the cowling, the mechanic who had performed the inspection found his missing vice grips, which I got to keep.

And then there was the accident caused by a pilot taking off with a loose exhaust stack, which led to an engine fire and the demise of his family.

There is nothing about a preflight inspection that can be taken lightly. A problem discovered on the ground is usually only an inconvenience but, when taken aloft, has the potential for tragedy.

By the way, Fishman and I did capture those Soviet-held speed records for the United States. Our performance during the second flight, however, could have been slightly better. We were in such a hurry after reconnecting the rudder that we inadvertently took off with the ignition switch of the left engine selected to the left magneto instead of both, which proves that checking for problems should be a never-ending process.

Chapter 35 **Destinationitis**

I am fascinated by how a comment made in casual conversation can have a profound and lifelong effect on how we regard and value the events in our lives. At least that is how Jim Taylor's remark affected me.

Jim and I were on a flying safari in East Africa using a rented Piper Arrow. On the day in question, we were heading from Arusha, Tanzania, to Nanyuki, Kenya. We were to spend a couple of days there lounging at William Holden's Mount Kenya Safari Club and raising "sundowners" in honor of whatever suited the moment.

While en route, we were confronted by a line of thunderstorms that challenged our right of passage. There appeared to be some clear spots in the line, so I advised our wives in back to tighten their seat belts in anticipation of a rough ride.

Jim was riding shotgun and knew how excited we were about getting to Nanyuki. We had been planning this vacation for months, and our expensive accommodations had been paid in advance (without possibility of a refund).

But Jim looked ahead at the ominous cells and put a father-like hand on my shoulder. "Barry," he said, "in a few years, it won't make any difference whether we get there or not."

That was in 1969. And Jim was right. It eventually didn't matter at all. But it might have made a great difference had we continued.

Jim's profound observation has served me well since then and probably has saved my life more than once.

A year later, my closest friend, Hal Fishman, and I were ferrying a turbocharged Piper Aztec C to Europe. Hal was and still is a news anchor for KTLA-TV in Los Angeles. The primary purpose of our flight was to produce a documentary film about the safety and reliability of general aviation airplanes. We had even made extensive arrangements with AT&T for Hal to transmit a live broadcast via high-frequency relay from the aircraft to his southern California audience.

And because the flight was to originate in Los Angeles and terminate in its sister city of West Berlin, Mayor Sam Yorty had given us an official proclamation to be presented to West Berlin Mayor Klaus Shutz at a banquet to be held in our honor. Much depended on the timely completion of this mission.

The flight to Gander, Newfoundland, in N6649Y had been routine except for the automatic direction finder, which failed over the Gulf of St. Lawrence. Fortunately, Eastern Provincial Airlines had a first-class radio shop at Gander, where the faulty ADF could be repaired.

But the ADF could not be repaired and was declared a lemon. We called Piper and were promised that a new unit would be shipped to us "as soon as possible."

In the meantime, a forecaster at the Gander Weather Bureau gave us the bad news about the meandering isobars on the constant-pressure charts. An intense low-pressure system was moving northeastward along the coast of Nova Scotia. We were advised that unless we intended to log some serious sightseeing time in Gander (not recommended), we should leave soon.

This was before the advent of the global positioning system and satellite navigation. The only checkpoints between Gander and Shannon were a pair of low-frequency radiobeacons aboard two enroute weather ships: Ocean Stations Charlie and Juliett. But an ADF was needed to find these waypoints. The approaching low also would create a net headwind along the direct route to Ireland and require using some of our fuel reserves.

The only other options were to take one of two longer routes to Europe. The first involved heading southeast to the Azores. But the first half of such a flight would be plagued by that deepening low-pressure system. It would produce the kind of strong crosswinds that hinder pilots from finding little islands in the middle of big oceans.

The other alternative was to head northeast and use Greenland and Iceland as stepping stones across the Atlantic. But the approaching low was pumping warm, moist air across southern Greenland. Widespread icing conditions were in the forecast.

Our plans, however, could not tolerate lengthy delays. Consequently, we decided to leave without the ADF and before the arrival of the low-pressure system.

But then I began to remember Jim Taylor's avuncular admonishment from our flight over the Serengeti Plain: "In a few years, it won't matter whether we get there or not."

It has been more than 20 years since Hal and I congratulated ourselves for postponing the ferry flight and allowing our plans to fall by the wayside. And as traumatic as that decision might have been at the time, it never did make any difference.

Thanks again, Jim.

When a pilot focuses so intently on reaching a destination that he loses his safety perspective, he is suffering from a syndrome known as "destinationitis." Although seldom cited in accident reports as a probable cause, it undoubtedly is an underlying reason for a great number of general aviation tragedies.

This is one reason why airline flights are typically safer than private operations. Airline pilots seldom are personally involved with the destination and do not become emotional or irrational when confronted by conditions that could delay or cancel a flight.

But general aviation pilots can develop an equally safe philosophy about any flight simply by recognizing that "in few years, it won't matter whether you get there or not."

What does matter is whether or not you survive to think about it.

Chapter 36 **Survival**

Recurrent training gives airline pilots an annual opportunity to practice emergency procedures not required during the normal course of events. It also allows us to review the use of emergency equipment.

So it was no surprise when my fellow pilots and I returned to the training center after lunch some years ago and found our assigned classroom filled with fire extinguishers, personal breathing equipment, smoke goggles, oxygen masks and bottles, and other paraphernalia. Each of us got our turn putting out a fire in a wastepaper basket, donning a smoke hood, and so forth. When we were through with these drills, the instructor reached into a large carton at the head of the classroom and tossed a neatly packaged life jacket to each of us. Another boring drill. How many times had we practiced putting on a Mae West? The room filled with muffled groans and mild expletives.

As we began to open the plastic wrapping, the instructor said, "Hold it guys. Not so fast. Don't do anything with those jackets until I give the word."

We stopped—and were puzzled.

"Wait until I count to five. Then put on the jackets and inflate them as quickly as possible. Pretend that your aircraft is sinking. Every second counts."

Big deal, we thought.

"One...two...three...four...five...go!"

As we once again began to rip open the pouches, the lights went out. The room turned pitch black—no light leaking through the windows. There were sounds of confusion. More expletives. But these were louder than before.

Moments later, the lights came back on. Freeze frame. We stopped dead in our tracks and felt the stinging embarrassment of failure. If it were not so deadly serious, it would have been comical. Not one of 20 veteran airline pilots had come close to properly donning his life jacket.

Having emergency and survival equipment aboard the aircraft is one thing, being able to use it is another.

A few years ago, I was giving an instrument competency check to a pilot in a single-engine airplane. While en route to Catalina Island for a VOR approach (and buffalo burgers for lunch), I retarded the throttle to simulate an engine failure. We obviously were beyond gliding distance of land, but the life jackets were in the baggage compartment and beyond reach.

Even airline passengers take survival equipment and training for granted. Have you ever noticed how so many of them seem to intentionally ignore the safety demonstration before departure? They busy themselves with a newspaper or magazine as if to show that they know all of that stuff and do not need to pay attention.

But actual emergencies prove that they do not "know all that stuff." During an evacuation, passengers tend to rush toward the door through which they entered. They either pass up emergency exits along the way or fail to use closer exits that are in the opposite direction. (One of the first things an airline pilot does when boarding an airliner as a passenger is to locate the nearest emergency exit.)

During a loss of cabin pressure, passengers demonstrate again that they ignore safety briefings by failing to pull down on the oxygen mask (to start the flow of oxygen) before attempting to use it.

General aviation pilots also have the legal and moral obligation to brief passengers before departure. We must ensure that they understand how and when to use seat belts and shoulder harnesses. It also is imperative that we demonstrate how to use the doors, windows, and emergency exits in case the pilot is incapacitated and not available to lead the way during an accident.

Some years ago, for example, two passengers were entombed in a fiery Piper Arrow because they did not know about the top latch and were unable to open the door.

I am not sure which is more sinful, having emergency equipment and not being able to use it, or not having it available in the first place. For whatever reason, pilots are reluctant to equip their aircraft with such necessities as fire extinguishers, survival kits, and first-aid kits. (In some countries, these are required aboard all powered aircraft.)

The least expensive and most easily obtainable survival equipment is water, but only a few pilots bother to carry a supply on cross-country flights. I have been able to change the errant habits of some of these pilots by describing to them what it is like to die of dehydration in a desert climate (such as that of the southwestern United States).

The temperature in the sun can reach more than 150°F. In an attempt to remain cool, the body perspires and loses up to 2.5 pints of water per hour. After a day or so, however, sweating ceases because the body has no more water to give. The tongue swells, and speaking becomes impossible.

Crash survivors develop such a raging, overwhelming urge to drink that they resort to drinking urine, fuel, and oil. Delirium sets in, and people imagine that the sand or dirt is a lake and begin to "drink" it, but the throat is so swollen that swallowing is impossible.

Water can no longer save such a person. A cut does not bleed because the blood is too thick. Body temperature rises. And just before this gruesome, agonizing death, some may discover that they have just enough water left to cry tears of pain.

What is particularly sad about such a death is how easy it is to prevent.

Chapter 37 **Ham-Fisted Pilots**

When FAA-designated examiners congregate at their required annual meetings, they have a rare opportunity to compare notes. One popular and entertaining discussion involves relating unusual experiences that each of us has had with our applicants.

Inevitably, an examiner claims that he can tell whether an applicant will pass or fail during the first 10 minutes of a flight test. Right or wrong, heads nod and there are murmurs of agreement. When asked what he means, the examiner usually replies by saying that he can judge a pilot by the smoothness with which he controls the aircraft.

There is an element of truth to this. The best pilots do caress the control wheel with a velvet hand and minimize their passengers' awareness of attitude, power, and configuration changes. They fly as if their mother were in the back seat.

This is not meant to imply that smooth pilots do not make mistakes. They do. It is how they recover that sets them apart.

Consider, for example, a VFR pilot who suddenly realizes during descent that he is about to overshoot his target altitude. To avoid this, he hauls back on the yoke, adds a G or two, and arrests the altimeter hands at exactly the right place.

A pilot who flies with finesse, however, momentarily accepts the error, smoothly raises the nose, and climbs back to altitude without it being noticed by his passengers. (This is not meant to imply that those flying IFR can similarly develop a tolerance for altitude busts.)

The same is true during a turn. When a pilot who flies mechanically suddenly recognizes that he is about to overshoot a desired heading, he jerks the ailerons and snap-rolls the aircraft into level flight. Someone with more consideration for his passengers accepts the overshoot and makes a smooth, gradual correction.

A source of constant amazement, by the way, are those who steadfastly maintain altitude and heading—the wrong altitude and heading. When assigned 7,500 feet or 270 degrees, for example, they hold 7,300 or 260 degrees. And they do so precisely.

It is easy to help them break such a habit. I simply compliment the pilot on his precision and ask if it would be any more difficult for him to hold the correct heading or altitude.

A pet peeve is the pilot who taxies with excess power and keeps ground-speed in check by riding the brakes. Go ahead, scoff. This is more common than you might imagine.

Speaking of braking, you can tell much about a pilot by how he brakes the aircraft to a stop in the runup area. If he clamps on the binders and forces the nose to bob down and compress the oleo strut, the odds are that he is equally thoughtless about how he operates the aircraft in flight.

An airplane should be brought to a halt in a way that cannot be felt by those inside. This is done by releasing some brake pressure just as the aircraft is about to stop. The technique can and should be practiced in an automobile.

Ham-fisted pilots are at their worst when demonstrating stalls. This is when I surreptitiously tighten my seat belt.

Such pilots seem to be in a hurry to complete the maneuver. Rather than allowing the speed to bleed slowly, they haul back on the wheel and yank the aircraft into an outrageously nose-high attitude. And when the stall occurs, they shove the nose down vigorously. Negative Gs pull me out of my seat, and the aircraft pitches over until the ground fills the windshield.

Upon realizing that he has pitched over so steeply, the startled pilot yanks back on the yoke with even greater enthusiasm. The result? Positive Gs and a secondary stall. No wonder so many pilots have an aversion to practicing stalls.

More often than not, the applicant's instructor is as much to blame because of his failure to teach proper stall recovery. The nose must be lowered smoothly and positively to a safe attitude. Dumping the nose excessively or too rapidly increases the probability of a secondary stall or results in an unacceptable altitude loss.

Being rough on the controls can be especially hazardous in turbulence. The loads imposed by maneuvering compound the problem by adding to those created by gusts. When in turbulence, it is both safer and more comfortable to apply control pressures carefully and smoothly.

Pilots with a feel for their aircraft learn to anticipate pitch changes caused by gear and flap extension and compensate for these as they occur. For example, lowering the wheels of a Cessna 310 causes the nose to pitch one way, but deploying the flaps results in an equal and opposite pitch change. An adroit pilot learns to deploy first the gear and then the flaps in a way that neutralizes these strong opposite and uncomfortable pitching moments.

Is a smooth pilot better than one who is not? Yes, but only in the sense that he probably is more skillful. This does not mean that he is necessarily a safer pilot. Aircraft handling is only one element of airmanship. At least as important are experience, knowledge, and judgment. This includes a healthy respect for our limitations and those of the aircraft we fly.

Possessing these critical elements, however, does not give our ham-fisted pilot an excuse to slam the nose down and paste me against the ceiling during stall recovery.

I just hate that.

Chapter 38 **Distractions**

The Eastern Air Lines L-1011 circled low over the Everglades while the three-man crew attempted to resolve an apparent landing-gear malfunction prior to a scheduled landing in Miami.

But the pilots were so preoccupied with the problem that none of them noticed when the altitude-hold function of the autopilot tripped off, the result of one pilot inadvertently bumping a control wheel. Nor did anyone notice the shallow descent that followed. Moments later, the big Lockheed made an uncontrolled crashlanding in the night-shrouded swamp.

From this tragedy comes the lesson that one pilot of a three-man crew should be delegated to concentrate on flying the airplane during the resolution of a mechanical problem. He should effectively ignore the difficulty and leave it to the remaining crewmembers to resolve.

In the case of a two-pilot crew, one pilot flies while the other deals with the emergency. The problem with a two-man crew is that such a division of responsibility makes it difficult for one pilot to check on the progress of the other without risking a fatal distraction.

Worse off, however, is the lone general aviation pilot who must both fly the aircraft and cope with operational demands as they occur. There seldom is anyone upon whom he can call for assistance.

Passengers also can be distracting. A classic case is the midair collision that occurred over downtown San Diego on September 25, 1978. This is when Pacific Southwest Airlines Flight 182, a Boeing 727, overran a Cessna 172. The recovered cockpit voice recorder revealed that laughter and irrelevant conversation took place between the pilots and a deadheading captain prior to impact.

Based on this and other factors, investigators concluded that this accident probably would not have occurred had it not been for this distraction. This tragedy eventually led to the evolution of the "sterile cockpit," which was created by Federal Aviation Regulation 121.542. This prohibits "nonessential conversation" on the flight deck of an airliner while taxiing and during critical phases of flight, which includes all operations below 10,000 feet.

There is a lesson here for general aviation pilots, too. Because passengers can be dangerously distracting, they should be reminded not to unnecessarily interrupt a pilot during critical phases of flight. These typically occur within the first three minutes after takeoff and within eight minutes of landing. This plus-three, minus-eight concept was developed by the airlines after discovering that this is when the majority of accidents occur.

It is impossible to determine how many general aviation accidents have been caused directly or indirectly by distractions in the cockpit. But it probably is safe to conclude that they are more of a contributing factor than we realize.

Inadvertent gear-up landings, for example, often are the result of a distraction that interrupts a pilot's routine. His attention is diverted so that he either forgets to lower the gear or fails to verify gear position after it presumably has been extended. (This is why a pilot should keep his hand on the switch or handle as a reminder until confirming that the gear really is down and locked.)

The FAA believes that many stall/spin accidents also are caused by distraction, which leads to inattentiveness to airspeed and faulty stick-and-rudder coordination (skidding) during low-altitude maneuvering. This is why flight instructors are encouraged to be creative about distracting students during training that involves slow flight and maneuvering at minimum-controllable airspeeds.

Those who read Ernie Gann's masterpiece, *Fate Is The Hunter,* probably will never forget how Captain Ross lit matches under Copilot Gann's nose as he attempted to shoot a low-frequency range approach to minimums in a Douglas DC-2 using only needle, ball, and airspeed. (The artificial horizon had gone belly up while doing battle with a thunderstorm on an earlier approach.) As soon as Gann would blow out one match, Ross would quickly strike another, which made it difficult to see the instruments beyond the flame. This infuriated Gann, but he completed the approach despite the sadistic distraction.

Although none of my captains were ever this outrageous in their training tactics, a few were at least as inconsiderate. I recall flying with one cigar-smoking tyrant who kept the air in front of him clear by blowing his smoke in my direction.

It was true, though. If you could shoot a manual approach under such trying conditions, it was indeed much easier when all of the clouds were kept outside the cockpit.

This probably is not the kind of training the FAA has in mind. Nevertheless, it apparently was effective. Gann later said, "Nearly four years would pass before I would again see Ross's matches flaming before me. Then, even though distracted by the drumming of my heart, I would know their incalculable worth."

Sometimes technological advancements designed to reduce pilot work load also create insidious and dangerous distractions. Such is the case with the global positioning system. GPS databases are so extensive and their computers provide so much data that pilots often are intrigued and incessantly attracted to their displays, which increases the potential for a midair collision.

Captain Ross's solution to this might be to light matches in the faces of such pilots. His purpose would not be to make it more difficult to see the displays but to remind them that they would be well advised to spend more time looking elsewhere.

Chapter 39 **Keeping Up With the Airplane**

At one time or another, every pilot has been "behind the airplane." This describes a situation where the airplane arrives at the destination before the pilot is mentally prepared. It most often occurs to those transitioning to high-performance aircraft and results in frustration and a sense of having lost control.

I became a victim early in my career after learning to fly in an Aeronca 7AC Champion. For those not familiar with this wonderfully docile, fabric-covered taildragger, it had an engine little larger than that in a power mower and sipped fuel at only 3 gph. It ripped through the sky at a blistering 70 knots and had climb and glide speeds of only 52 knots. A flight around the pattern seemed like a cross-country flight.

Shortly after I had become accustomed to the little Champ, my instructor offered me a chance to check out in a Cessna 180. It was a huge airplane with 225 horses under the cowl. It even had metal skin, an electrical system, a starter, toe brakes, control wheels, side-by-side seating, humongous flaps, and an instrument panel filled with a bewildering array of instruments, switches, and gadgets.

So this is what it would be like to fly an airliner, I thought. So vast was the difference between the Cessna and the "Airknocker."

I was delighted with the 180. It was so stable and responsive. Performance was outstanding, perhaps too much so for someone being weaned from a trainer that only flew a mile a minute. My biggest problem was keeping up with the airplane. I had difficulty getting it down and slowing it in time to land. As a result, it kept arriving before I did.

All the while, I could peripherally see my instructor shaking his head in silent and obvious disappointment. After the flight, he offered advice that has served me well. He said that pilots get caught "behind the mental power curve" because they tend to prepare for arrival at certain fixed distances from the airport.

"Look, Barry," he said. "You probably didn't realize it, but you were flying the 180 as if it were a Champ. You descended and made speed reductions at the same places and distances from the airport that you had become accustomed to using when flying at lesser speeds.

"The key to staying ahead of a faster airplane is to use common times from the destination, not common distances."

Applying this advice does help to prevent getting caught behind the airplane. It certainly makes it easier for me to make the mental transition between flying widebody jetliners one day and lightplanes the next. No matter what I am flying at the time, a Beechcraft or a Boeing, I usually plan to begin descent and prepare for landing when 20 minutes (based on cruise groundspeed) from the destination. It is a reliable rule of thumb (except when in helicopters, balloons, and sailplanes). Adjustments obviously must be made for unusual cruise altitudes and circumstances.

Students and newly rated instrument pilots also are susceptible to being caught behind the airplane. This is not because of aircraft performance as much as it is a matter of seemingly having too much to do and not enough time in which to do it.

Until developing the experience needed to cope with the challenge of instrument approaches, for example, pilots should reduce speed as soon as they arrive in the terminal area. This gives them more time to accomplish the necessary chores. There is nothing wrong or unacceptable about taking your time if this is what is needed to get everything done in a timely fashion. I have seen professional pilots doing this while flying heavy jets, so there is no reason that general aviation cannot do the same.

But the most common reason for getting behind during an IFR flight is that the pilot simply fails to think ahead. He often does have the time to prepare for an approach but fails to take advantage of it. Instead, he waits until something needs to be done before doing it.

I had a wonderful instructor who cured me of that habit with a memorable and valuable piece of philosophy. He said to me, "Barry, if you're not doing something all of the time, then you're just not doing it right." Think about it.

And is it possible for a pilot to get ahead of the airplane, a situation where a pilot is ready to go but the airplane is not? You bet. It happens all the time.

Consider the pilot about to embark on important flight. He taxies into the runup area, performs an ignition check and—oops, a bad mag. All plans must be set aside until appropriate repairs are made.

Such disappointment often can be avoided by borrowing a procedure from the airlines: the post-flight inspection. By inspecting an airplane and performing an abbreviated power check after a flight, discrepancies can be discovered and repaired in time to avoid delaying a subsequent departure.

When you think about it, it just does not make sense to wait until ready for departure to discover a mechanical discrepancy. Maintenance should be conducted when you plan for the airplane to be on the ground, not when you need it to be taking you somewhere.

This does not mean, however, that a post-flight inspection should replace the vital preflight inspection. It is intended only as another way for a pilot to stay ahead of the airplane.

Chapter 40 **Procedure Versus Technique**

The argument was so loud and intense that I could hear them through the cockpit door while I was still in the cabin, returning from a short break.

After closing the door behind me, I found my first officer and flight engineer in the heat of verbal battle. Both general aviation pilots, they were involved in that seemingly ageless controversy about when to raise the landing gear after taking off in a single-engine airplane.

The first officer, an ex-military pilot, argued that the gear should be raised immediately after liftoff to improve initial climb performance and gain altitude as rapidly as possible in case of engine failure. The flight engineer, who had learned to fly in a Cessna 150, insisted that the gear not be raised until reaching a point beyond which a straight-ahead landing could not be made on the runway in case of engine failure.

Each presented sound arguments to support his view, but it was obvious that neither would emerge victorious or unscathed from this animated debate. This is because such a discussion often reflects a comparison of preference rather than what is absolutely right or wrong. It is the difference between procedure and technique, a concept many pilots fail to consider.

A procedure is a course of action with a specific objective. The tasks published in pilot's operating handbooks, FAA regulations, and so forth are procedures. Examples include retracting the landing gear after takeoff, performing a crosswind takeoff, leaning the engine at cruise altitude, and conducting a preflight inspection. But the method by which a pilot achieves these objectives is a matter of technique.

For example, a procedure is to select the fullest fuel tank for takeoff. Just when the pilot accomplishes this, however, is a matter of technique. Most make or verify tank selection in the runup area because this is where the before-takeoff checklist usually is reviewed. But this might not allow enough time to verify fuel flow and system integrity. There might only be enough fuel in the lines to allow a takeoff and climb to a few hundred feet before fuel starvation occurs.

Other pilots select the tank to be used before engine start. This provides additional time to operate on the selected tank and determine system integrity and reliability.

242 Flying Wisdom: Proficient Pilot Volume 3

In this case, one technique has a decided advantage over the other.

Some techniques are clearly dangerous. Consider the procedure of complying with the before-takeoff checklist. Although most pilots perform this procedure in the runup area, others impatiently perform their checks while taxiing for takeoff. Some even go to the extreme of checking mags and propeller operation while on the go. Dividing attention in this manner is a primary cause of taxi accidents.

At other times, techniques are a matter of efficiency. One example is the manner in which too many pilots level off and establish cruise flight after climb. Upon reaching altitude, they lower the nose and almost simultaneously reduce power. This deprives the airplane of the power needed to accelerate, and it winds up mushing along at less-than-normal cruise speed.

A more efficient technique suggests being patient about reducing power. Upon reaching cruise altitude, leave the throttle and propeller-pitch control alone. Don't touch a thing. Allow climb power to accelerate the airplane until indicated airspeed reaches some maximum value. Then reduce power. The airplane will decelerate somewhat, but the result is noticeably more speed than when power is reduced prematurely.

A third technique is appealing to some but yields to mythology. This involves climbing few hundred feet above the target altitude and then establishing a shallow dive (while still using climb power) to return to cruise altitude. In theory, this puts the aircraft "on the step" and results in slightly more cruise speed.

Wrong—flight tests fail to validate this wives' tale. The resultant airspeed is the same as when using climb power to accelerate in level flight.

Technique often is a matter of taste or preference. For example, concert pianists Vladimir Horowitz and Artur Rubenstein strike the keys in the exact sequence specified by Mozart when he wrote his "Piano Concerto No. 21." This is the procedure. But each uses a different technique, a statement of individual flair and style that proves the obvious: There is more than one way to get the job done.

When learning to fly or getting a new rating, pilots are first introduced to the procedures that must be mastered. But the techniques used to perform those procedures often reflect the bias of the instructor and might or might not be the most suitable. Lacking comparisons, students loyally adhere to what they have been taught. You've heard it before: "But my instructor told me to do it this way."

The thinking pilot is open-minded and flexible. He recognizes that there are many ways to perform a procedure and is constantly on the lookout for new and better techniques. He spends his career learning, appraising, adopting, and rejecting new ways to get the job done.

Just remember, though: When you fly with me, there are only two ways to do things: my way and the wrong... never mind.

Chapter 41 **Instructors: Good and Bad**

A month seldom passes without someone asking me to recommend a flight school for a friend. My response is always the same. I advise that the school is not nearly as important as the instructor.

I am then asked to recommend a good instructor. I usually cannot do this either. Although I am acquainted with many CFIs, I have not flown with them as a student and cannot judge them as instructors.

One way to find a good instructor is to ask other students. Another is to ask designated pilot examiners. They can rate local instructors on the basis of how well or poorly their students are trained.

What is the difference between a good instructor and a bad one? The most significant difference, I believe, is that an ineffective instructor is simply a commander who issues orders. He demonstrates a maneuver and then has the student repeat it over and over until he gets it right.

The best instructors, however, analyze the needs of each student and modify their teaching methods accordingly.

Consider, for example, the student who has difficulty judging height above the runway when learning to land. Some instructors simply have the student conduct "circuits and bumps" until he finally gets it right. For some, such learning by rote can take a long time.

An innovative instructor, however, knows that a student gets only 5 or 10 seconds of flare practice during each landing attempt. He recognizes that a student may need more than this and creates an exercise to accelerate the learning process. He has the student attempt to fly the aircraft in slow flight along the entire length of the runway with the tires only inches above the surface. With the instructor controlling power, the student has substantially more time to develop a sense of flare height. And rather than being regarded as mistakes, each inadvertent touchdown serves to improve the student's perception of aircraft height above the runway.

Some instructors teach stalls in the time-honored tradition of having the student raise the nose until it points toward the sun at high noon. The predictable result is a student who develops an almost justifiable fear of practicing stalls.

The instructor's job is to teach stall recovery, not stall entry. Recognizing that steep entries can be frightening to new pilots, the enterprising instructor simply requests his student to retard the throttle and bleed off airspeed by maintaining altitude. The aircraft eventually will stall, but in a more realistic manner.

A pet peeve is an instructor who seems more interested in having the airplane flown perfectly than in having the student learn to fly it. He does not allow the student to make and profit from mistakes, which often is the only way one can learn.

Any student—whether pre-solo or preparing for an airline transport pilot certificate—should realize that it is his job to learn and the instructor's job to teach. If the student is frustrated by a lack of progress, he should speak up and request that the CFI adopt a new approach to the problem. If he does not, then it might be time to switch.

As an 18-year-old instructor in 1956, I also tried to be innovative, but my creative efforts were not always appreciated.

Although I do not think that he knew it, Tom Paris was my first student. Because of some innate ability, he had made remarkable progress and was ready to solo after only seven hours of dual in a taildragger. His landings were squeakers. The problem was that Tom never demonstrated that he could recover from a bounce. That's because he never bounced.

Before I could let him solo, I had to determine that Tom could recover from a botched landing. So I told him that I would bounce the Aeronca Champ during the next few landings, and he was to execute the recoveries. As I had expected, he recovered easily from each aberration.

I advised the tower controller that I was releasing a student for solo and climbed out of the airplane. This apparently got the controller's attention. He later said that he had never before seen such horrendous landings by someone about to solo. This is why he alerted the crash crew (really) and called out the local FAA inspector after Tom had been cleared for takeoff.

The familiar gray Ford with the federal markings pulled up just as Tom made his first solo landing. It was a greaser. So was the second. And the third.

I learned to fly in the same kind of tandem taildragger where the instructor sat behind the student. My first instructor, Mike Walters, had created his own method of teaching. He would express displeasure with my performance by whacking me on the back of the head with a rolled-up sectional chart. At the end of every painful lesson, he would throw away the limp chart and replace it with a new one in preparation for his next student. (A new chart cost only 25 cents in those days.)

Mike's students measured their progress not by his praise (there was none) but by how long his chart would last before having to be replaced. The reward was not so much the joy of solo as it was an escape from the dreaded sectional.

Chapter 42 **Eavesdropping on the Radio**

When pulling contrails over the oceans of the world, airline pilots monitor a pair of VHF frequencies. One is the emergency frequency, 121.5 MHz. The other is an air-to-air frequency used to exchange pilot reports and information with other flights.

These frequencies usually are quiet. It is possible to cross the Atlantic or the Pacific without hearing a word on either channel. Once in a while though, a pilot yields to the boredom of routine operations and broadcasts a joke "in the blind" or starts a conversation about the latest rumors. (In the airline industry, a rumor is something started by a pilot who has not heard one by noon.)

An intriguing abuse of the air-to-air frequency occurs with some regularity about halfway between Hawaii and California. Someone seems to take delight in breaking radio silence by playing an eerie rendition of "The High and the Mighty" on an instrument that sounds like a nose flute. It is as if the ghost of Dan Roman (played by John Wayne in the movie) were paying homage to fellow aviators passing in the night. Older pilots usually respond with an appropriately nostalgic comment, but most of the younger pilots apparently do not recognize the haunting melody.

Attempts to identify the mystery pilot have been fruitless.

The emergency frequency usually is quieter. But once in a while a voice of desperation arrests attention. I recall when the pilot of a light twin was en route from Iceland to Newfoundland. He was low on fuel and frightened that he might not make landfall. Using high-frequency communications, we relayed his predicament to Gander Radio, which alerted the Canadian search-and-rescue facilities.

After landing in Boston, we learned that the pilot had ditched 100 miles from shore and was plucked from the icy water with little time to spare.

General aviation pilots typically do not monitor the emergency frequency even though they usually have a spare receiver. Perhaps this is because they believe that anyone calling for help over the contiguous United States will always be within earshot of someone. This is partially true. An aircraft usually is within range of an FAA or military facility. But this does not necessarily mean that someone is listening.

I have conducted experiments by making short transmissions on 121.5. Most of the time, no one ever replies (including the time I made such a transmission while over Los Angeles). Controllers explain that FAA facilities are supposed to monitor "guard" but often do not. Others have the volume turned down so low that a call for help cannot be heard.

Lengthier emergency transmissions (such as those emitted by ELTs [emergency locator transmitters]) often are detected by search-and-rescue satellites. Using triangulation, SARSATs also compute the location of an emergency signal and issue an alert to search-and-rescue facilities.

This is why normal communications on 121.5 must be avoided. SARSAT interprets any broadcast on 121.5 in excess of 30 seconds or so as a plea for assistance.

Shorter voice transmissions on 121.5, however, might not be heard by anyone. As a result, all pilots are encouraged to monitor the emergency frequency whenever a spare receiver is available, especially when over desolate and rugged terrain.

One of my favorite pastimes when on long cross-country flights in lightplanes is to eavesdrop on other frequencies, too. This can be both educational and entertaining. For example, I often tune in the ATIS (automatic terminal information service) at nearby airports, even though I have no intention of landing there. It is a handy way to pick up the current altimeter setting and gives me information about possibly changing weather conditions. This can be important even when the sky is severe-clear. A knowledge of surface wind, for example, can be invaluable in case of an emergency or forced landing.

An ATIS broadcast also can be amusing. Last Christmas, the recorded voice at Carlsbad (CRQ) Airport told pilots to advise that they had Information Yuletide. (I was flying Cessna N210JB and could not resist calling in as "Cessna Two-One-Zero Jingle Bells.")

Enroute eavesdropping also has taught me to be skeptical about AWOS, the automated weather observing system. I have heard that impish android, R2D2 (or a voice synthesizer that sounds like him), transmit data that completely misrepresents actual conditions. A passing cloud was reported as an overcast and little things like approaching thunderstorms and fog banks were undetected.

I also enjoy tuning in approach control at airports in Class B and C airspace. There seems to be no end to the number of original ways that air traffic control finds to ban VFR pilots from penetrating their precious perimeters.

One can learn much by listening to the pilots, too. I often can tell whether a pilot will gain admittance just by listening to the tone, confidence, and professionalism of his transmission. Those who need to improve their communication skills can learn much by listening to these busy facilities.

It also can be interesting to eavesdrop on airline pilots alerting their ground stations of maintenance that will be required upon arrival. I will never forget the response to a pilot who complained vigorously that the autoland system in his airplane resulted in hard landings.

"But Captain," came the confused reply. "Your ship is not equipped with autoland."

Chapter 43 **Using Checklists**

Although the captain of an airliner is responsible for the safe operation of his aircraft, he is not necessarily the one flying it at any given time. This is because he usually shares the flying with his first officer. (Some cynics believe that is done to provide the captain with a scapegoat for his occasionally "firm" touchdown.)

Years ago on a flight out of Cairo, it was my copilot's turn to fly. I was reading the "Before Starting Engines Checklist," and he was responding. Such a procedure would impress a visitor with the ease and rapid-fire staccato with which the items are covered. The lengthy and complex checklist of a Lockheed L-1011 or a Boeing 747 can be completed in half a minute. But this proves only that a pilot is adept at responding to the challenges of the checklist. It does not necessarily mean that he has confirmed that all of the items have been readied for flight.

My copilot on this flight was extraordinarily skilled at responding by rote. He even seemed to take pride in the speed with which he could rattle off the correct responses to the checklist. But after the list had been completed, I noticed that two important switches remained improperly positioned.

"Bob," I said. "I'd like to try a little experiment. Would you mind if we run through the list again?"

Apparently not suspecting anything, he said, "Sure, Skipper. Go ahead."

I picked up the checklist and began reading. But this time, I started at the bottom. This interrupted Bob's routine and prevented him from responding rapidly and by rote. Instead, it forced him to actually check each item and respond accordingly. It also allowed him to discover that both of the stall-warning switches were in the off position.

Complacency and familiarity not only breed contempt; they encourage taking things for granted, errors for which aviation can be mercilessly intolerant. Numerous fatal accidents—involving both airline and general aviation aircraft—have been the result of pilots not spending enough time with each checklist item to confirm that things really are as they should be.

Some years ago, the captain of a Boeing 727 was about to depart Runway 8 at Albuquerque, New Mexico. But as soon as he advanced the thrust levers, the takeoff-warning horn blared intrusively. Something was wrong. He immediately retarded the throttles and taxied off the runway. The crew checked to ensure that the spoilers were stowed, the stabilizer trim was positioned in the green band, and the flaps were deflected properly for takeoff (5 degrees, in this case). Everything appeared normal.

After explaining to his passengers that the takeoff had been aborted because of "rabbits on the runway," the captain began another takeoff. The warning horn sounded again, which was followed by another rejected takeoff and another announcement about "those pesky rabbits." The three crewmembers confirmed again that all controls were properly positioned and agreed that the problem obviously was a faulty warning system. To prevent another so-called false alarm and get the flight under way, the captain asked the flight engineer to deactivate the takeoff warning system.

As the 727 approached 100 knots during the third takeoff roll, the first officer yelled, "My god; it's the flaps. Abort! Abort!"

After the aircraft had again been pulled off the runway (this time with smoking tires and overheated brakes), the cockpit crew finally saw that the flaps had been extended only 2 degrees instead of the required five (which also meant that some of the leading-edge devices were still retracted). What makes this incident so remarkable is that all three pilots had looked at but did not see the 2-degree indication. They instead "saw" a 5-degree indication because that is what they had been conditioned to expect. Had this takeoff been continued, the heavily loaded aircraft probably could not have become safely airborne in the distance available. The passengers and crew (and possibly a few of the rabbits that really do live around the airport) would have been sacrificed on the altar of checklist complacency.

A pet peeve of mine involves those who use the before-takeoff checklist as if it were a set of instructions. They use each item on the list as a reminder of what needs to be done. Someone who uses a checklist in this manner, however, often ignores items that might not be included (such as turning on pitot heat for an IFR departure).

The proper way to use a checklist is to initially not use it at all. Instead, use a visual flow pattern, an organized method of attending to every switch, control, and instrument in the cockpit. Touch each item and spend enough time with it to ensure that it either indicates, operates, or is positioned as desired. After everything is checked in this manner, then use the checklist for its intended purpose: to verify that a critical item has not been overlooked.

To save time, some pilots run through a checklist while taxiing. This also is a great way to bend metal.

Chapter 44 **Logging Time**

When I was an FAA-designated examiner, I had the opportunity to review a lot of logbooks. These varied from illegible to veritable works of art. One in particular was a masterpiece.

The pilot/artist was a woman of 47 who took great pride in her logbook. Every entry was painstakingly written in black calligraphy. But there were some exceptions to her use of black. Whenever she flew an aircraft type or landed at an airport for the first time, the aircraft and airport names were written in green and blue, respectively.

When I asked why she did this, she told me that this system allowed her to most easily keep track of how many airplane types she had flown and how many airports she had visited (each of which she collected the way some people save stamps). This also made it easier for her to find particular highlights without having to scan every line of every page.

Most important, however, were the comments she wrote in red on the far right side of each page. Every such entry serves to remind her of interesting and unusual experiences, and of lessons learned.

For this pilot, the logbook was as much a diary as it was a record of flight.

Although pilots are required only to log the flight time needed for an additional rating or advanced certificate and to show currency, this pilot claimed to have logged every flight she had ever made, no matter how brief or inconsequential it might have been. To her, every flight was important and warranted an entry.

It would be an understatement to say that I was impressed. Since that time, I have attempted to employ the same system. Although I have always highlighted noteworthy comments, I began to use color coding the way she did.

In some ways, I've gone a step or two further. Whenever I land in a new country, for example, I save a piece of low-denomination currency and later paste it under the logbook entry reflecting that visit. This explains why I recently glued a one-half-dinar note from Jordan on page 36 of my current logbook, which has become valuable to me for a number of reasons. Such use of a logbook does waste a few lines here and there, but no regulation requires that each and every line be used to record a flight.

The manner in which a pilot's log can be made more interesting is limited only by a pilot's imagination, and it is never too late to start. Unfortunately, such logbook artistry is not as applicable to computerized logs, which—in my opinion—are much too sterile and deny the pilot of creating his own books of memorabilia.

The most valuable and entertaining aspects of my logbooks, however, are the comments written after each flight.

For example, a remark in one of my books vividly reminds me of a late-afternoon flight when I was returning from Palm Springs to Santa Monica, California, in a VFR-only Luscombe 8E. The destination ATIS gave the bad news: a 100-foot overcast with visibility to match.

Nevertheless, I continued toward SMO hoping that the shifting layer of advection fog would move off the airport by the time I got there. No such luck.

The sun had just begun to snuggle behind the fluffy horizon as I turned toward my VFR alternate, Van Nuys. But as I rolled wings level, a reflection of light from the cotton-candy undercast caught my attention. I turned my head in time to see the Angel Moroni standing on the clouds. No, I was not hallucinating. The height of the clouds was at exactly the right height to obscure the Mormon Temple, which supported the gilded statue of Moroni.

I simultaneously wracked the little Luscombe into a steep turn and grabbed for my camera, which was behind the right front seat. Such a photograph would be invaluable, I thought. But the clouds were rising, and through my lens I could see only a ghostly image of what had been. A moment later, the statue of Moroni was totally shrouded, as if shy of exposure.

Although not captured on film, the image is indelibly recorded in memory and shall never be forgotten because of a few well-chosen words in my log-book: "Saw Moroni walking on the clouds. Honest."

Other comments are not so ethereal. After the first leg of my first solo cross-country flight, I wrote "Encountered Rain!" To this day, it reminds me of the terror I felt as raindrops began to fall on the windshield of the Aeronca Champ. After all, no one had cautioned me about what to expect when flying a fabric-covered airplane, held together by glue and nails, in rain. Because my only aviation experience in precipitation had been with paper models (which did not fly well when wet), I was genuinely concerned about the structural integrity of the airplane. As a result, I made a precautionary landing at an enroute airport. The old-timers there must have had a good laugh after advising in a patronly manner that—because of the high ceiling and unlimited visibility—it really was safe for me to continue my flight.

Another, albeit less entertaining entry, consists of the simple command, "Don't do that again!" Although I cannot recall exactly what I did to warrant that comment, it does not matter. The words remind me not to repeat any number of the mistakes I have made.

Chapter 45 **Midair Collisions**

My flight instructor, Mike Walters, leveled the Aeronca Champ at 2,000 feet MSL as we flew along the southern California shoreline during my first flying lesson.

"Pay attention, kid," he bellowed from the back seat of the trainer, "because you're about to learn the most important thing there is to know about flying."

I sat bolt upright, straining to hear every word above the snarl of the 65-hp engine. "Take a good look around," he barked, "and show me the nearest airplane."

Like any new student, I was anxious to please and scanned the sky diligently. But there was nothing to be seen. I told Mike that we were alone.

"Oh, yeah? Then tell me what this is." Mike threw the control stick to the right and told me to look up and to my left. A bright red Stinson passed within feet of our wing tip. This had the desired—and startling—effect. I was certain that we had narrowly missed colliding in midair.

"Just remember, kid. It's the airplane you don't see that'll kill you."

Yes, Mike had set me up, but I'll always be grateful for his unorthodox methods. He taught me about the need to "rubberneck" in a way that I shall never forget. And that was more than 40 years ago.

Four years later and while still a teenager, I had been scheduled to fly a short charter across the Los Angeles basin to Orange County Airport in a brand-new Cessna 180. But I couldn't take the flight because I was still recovering from minor surgery. This is why my employer, mentor, and cherished friend Paul N. Bell, owner of Bell Air Service, wound up taking my flight.

But I never saw Paul again. It was the airplane he never saw that killed him. He had descended into a Piper Tri-Pacer that had been maintaining the same track.

Some believe that I would have died in that collision had I taken the flight, but I don't think so. I would not have been in exactly the same place at exactly the same time because I would not have flown the airplane in exactly the same way. It seems that the sky is sinister to some and protective of others. Fate is like that.

Several years ago, a poll was taken of airline pilots that asked about their greatest safety concerns. At the top of the list was the threat of midair collision. It is an event over which a pilot has so little control. Given the same opportunity, I am certain that general aviation pilots would agree.

The threat of a midair collision is my greatest fear. And recent technological advances seem to be increasing the potential for this hazard.

A few years ago, I was in the rear seat of a Cessna 182 en route to Santa Barbara to pick up a Cessna 414 that had to be ferried back to Santa Monica, California. Shortly after takeoff, I noticed that both pilots had buried their heads in the cockpit and were teaching each other about the features of the recently installed GPS receiver. They became so mesmerized and entertained by the magic of GPS that neither of them bothered to look for traffic. It was nervous time.

In discussing this problem with other pilots, I have concluded that even though such systems ease the burden of navigation, they often distract pilots from rubbernecking as much as they should. Pilots should learn to use these systems on the ground, where distractions are acceptable.

Fate works in strange ways. Assume that two pilots are flying under the hood in different aircraft. They navigate so as to pass over a given VOR at the same time and altitude but in opposite directions as if attempting to collide. The odds are, however, that no matter how meticulous the planning, the two aircraft will not come anywhere near each other.

And yet—without trying—a predictable number of midair collisions occur every year. Each is the result of pilots unwittingly attempting to occupy the same chunk of airspace at the same time. Although such disasters occur under a variety of circumstances, statistics show that a midair collision is most likely to occur while flying in the traffic pattern of an uncontrolled airport on a clear summer Sunday afternoon.

Vigilance is the best way to avoid a midair collision. After all, the see-and-be-seen concept of traffic avoidance works only when somebody is looking.

There is a simple method that can be used to quickly determine if another aircraft poses a midair threat. Because you can only hit an airplane that is at your altitude, be most concerned with traffic that appears to be at or near the horizon. Aircraft above or below the horizon are above or below your altitude, respectively.

If an airplane appears to remain in a fixed position on your windshield, this means that you are approaching each other on a line of constant bearing. To a fighter pilot, this means that he will intercept the enemy. To a civilian, it means that a collision is possible. At such a time, turn so that the "enemy" appears to move across your windshield.

Remember, however, that the airplane about which to worry most is the one you don't see. Find it before it finds you.

Although I enjoy bumping into pilots wherever in the world I wander, I pray that no one takes me literally.

Chapter 46 **How to Escape a Killer Downdraft**

In 1985, a 7,000-hour flight instructor was flying in the Gorman Pass north of Los Angeles when his Piper Warrior was grabbed from the sky by a powerful downdraft.

According to the subsequent accident report, the pilot conformed to conventional wisdom by commanding maximum power from the engine and entering a climb at the best-rate-of-climb airspeed, V_Y. But this was not enough because the airplane had insufficient performance to overcome the inexorable pull. It impacted the terrain while descending at an alarming rate.

This was not a particularly unusual accident. During a recent eight-year period, there were 365 accidents attributable to strong up- and downdrafts. Fifty-nine of these were fatal.

Too bad, some might say, that the Warrior mentioned above was unable to outclimb the downdraft. Those who know more about coping with downdrafts, however, might say that it is too bad that the pilot had not had any glider training because this might have provided him with the tools needed to save his life.

Downdrafts, of course, are the bane of sailplane flying. To minimize their effect, pilots are taught to increase airspeed when flying in sinking air. The stronger the downdraft, the greater should be the airspeed. The purpose of this is to reduce the angle of descent.

This may seem counterintuitive. After all, lowering the nose to increase airspeed further increases sink rate, which would seem to compound the problem. But it can be shown (mathematically or with vectors) that the increased forward speed of the glider has the effect of reducing the angle of descent. This is so fundamental to glider operation that variometers (a form of vertical speed indicator used in gliders) often are marked with recommended "speeds to fly" that are to be used when operating in downdrafts. The greater the sink rate, the greater is the recommended airspeed. Conversely, sailplane pilots reduce airspeed when operating in rising air.

Steven H. Philipson, an experienced glider and airplane flight instructor who proselytizes sailplane training for power pilots, was a close friend of the pilot discussed earlier. He recognized that the fatal accident could have been avoided by using soaring principles. These, however, were not available in a form that could be directly applied to airplanes. The loss of his friend, however, inspired Philipson to use his knowledge of computational analysis to develop a set of specific rules that would enable power pilots to better cope with strong and threatening downdrafts.

His research led him to conclude that V_Y is a valid airspeed target when downdrafts are relatively benign. But if the aircraft is being flown at V_Y and is sinking faster than it should be climbing, the pilot should accelerate to maximum-cruise airspeed. That's right; he should resist the temptation to climb.

In other words, if the anticipated climb rate for a given set of conditions is 400 fpm, for example, discontinue attempting to outclimb the downdraft if the aircraft instead is sinking at or more than 400 fpm. (The greater the headwind, by the way, the sooner a pilot should consider accelerating to cruise.)

Complying with this advice, however, may be more difficult than it seems. How many of us would have the courage to lower the nose as the earth rises to meet the airplane? But it must be done to increase the probability of survival. In this respect, the maneuver is much like stall recovery. The pilot must lower the nose so that he can later raise it.

A fringe benefit of accelerating to cruise airspeed is that the increase in groundspeed might result in a more expeditious escape from the lateral dimensions of the downdraft.

Philipson's second rule states that when flying with a tailwind, the pilot should not give up on V_Y unless the aircraft is sinking at least three times as rapidly as it should be climbing.

Other recommended procedures to use when encountering strong downdrafts at low altitude are more obvious and include turning away from rising terrain and turning tail on the wind. (Headwinds increase descent angles relative to the ground, and tailwinds decrease them.)

Philipson, by the way, has demonstrated that when it comes to sailplane operations, he knows of what he speaks. Using a Grob 102 near Minden, Nevada, he has soared to a confirmed altitude of 32,000 feet. To a turbine pilot, that's Flight Level 320. Philipson's bigger challenge, however, is to convince the National Transportation Safety Board and the FAA that power pilots could benefit from some of the techniques and procedures used routinely by sailplane pilots. Although he has begun to receive a few receptive comments from the NTSB, his efforts generally have fallen on deaf ears. Judging by most of the responses that he has received thus far, it appears that many of our aviation servants in Washington, D.C., do not understand much about sailplanes and the principles of soaring.

They are apparently more interested in the principles of power.

Chapter 47 **The Maximum-Trim Technique**

At a recent AOPA Expo, I had the pleasure of chatting with Dr. Ian Blair Fries, who seems to spend more time spreading the gospel of aviation safety than he does practicing orthopedic surgery. He also has a pocketfull of ratings and is the chairman of AOPA's Medical Advisory Board.

During a lull in the conversation, Fries asked for my opinion about the "max-trim" technique. Having never heard of it, I confessed ignorance. His eyes lit up in a way that immediately told me I was in for something new.

"Well, Barry," he began. "It's a way to establish a glide following an engine failure in single-engine airplane."

My expression went from sincere curiosity to disappointment, but I continued listening nevertheless.

"It involves simply maintaining altitude to bleed airspeed and slowly applying nose-up trim until the trim wheel reaches its full aft limit. All the pilot has to do then is control bank and allow the aircraft to sink at its trimmed airspeed. He can forget about pitch control and maintaining a specific airspeed. The airplane will take care of pitch and speed by itself."

This raised all sorts of skeptical questions. "But Ian, surely this won't result in the best glide speed: it's bound to result in something less efficient."

This is when he began to drive home his most important point. "Look, Barry. Most pilots don't have a clue about their best glide speed; they only think they do. One of the first things to do following an engine failure is to establish the minimum sink speed [discussed later]. He should accelerate to the best glide speed only after selecting a distant landing site. Trouble is, this speed is affected by aircraft weight and wind velocity. Following an engine failure, who knows how to figure all this out? And if they did, would they have the time and presence of mind to do so? I sure wouldn't."

In this respect, I agreed with his assessment of coping with an engine failure. There often is too much for a pilot to do at such a time, not the least of which includes attempting a restart (time and altitude permitting) and briefing his passengers."

Recognizing that he had piqued my interest, Fries shifted into a higher gear. "So what I suggest in my seminars is that the pilot accept whatever airspeed results from maximum aft trim. Although somewhat less than the best [published] glide speed, it works almost as well and often yields better results than failing to take the variables into consideration."

Fries has performed "max-trim" glides in a number of aircraft and claims that this typically results in flying about 10 knots below the published glide speed. I have subsequently done the same in a handful of lightplanes and had the same experience.

Although we are taught to establish the published glide speed following an engine failure (and adjusting for wind and weight), this advice assumes that the pilot wants to maximize glide range. Often, however, this is not in his best interest because the selected landing site is nearby. At such a time, the pilot is better off using the minimum sink speed, which, alas, seems to be an unpublished secret, but is less than the best glide speed.

When using the minimum sink speed, glide range usually does decrease somewhat, but—more importantly—sink rate also decreases. This prolongs the descent and affords the pilot more time to assess his difficulty and formulate a plan of action. (In a manner of speaking, minimum sink is to best glide as best angle of climb is to best rate of climb.)

An advantage of the "max-trim" technique is that it usually results in an airspeed that approximates the minimum sink speed.

When using "max-trim," pilots should be cautious about rolling in aft trim too rapidly following an engine failure during cruise flight, unless he intends to perform a hammerhead turn.

This raises an interesting point. Following an engine failure during cruise, should the pilot rapidly convert airspeed into altitude and quickly decelerate to the glide speed of choice, or should he allow the airplane to decelerate more slowly while maintaining altitude? It is most efficient to decelerate slowly. Increasing the G load by hauling back on the wheel increases drag and decreases glide range.

Fries added another interesting point: "Max trim precludes the possibility of undertrimming and descending at too high an airspeed and sink rate, which is what many pilots tend to do during an emergency. The beauty of this technique is that it is a 'no-brainer.' It can be done blindfolded. And once the aircraft is fully trimmed, the pilot can take his hand off the control wheel and keep the aircraft pointed straight ahead using only the rudder."

There is one item that I would add to this technique. When nearing the ground, accelerate and retrim to the published glide speed. This assures more glide path flexibility during the approach and sufficient flare capability during landing.

There is considerable merit to the maximum-trim technique. It warrants consideration by any pilot who recognizes that learning to fly is an incessant process.

Chapter 48 **Oxygen**

It was a rare day in Anchorage. I could see 120-mile-distant Mt. McKinley from my room at the Holiday Inn. Highest peak in North America, the 20,000-foot sentinel stood beckoning against the northern horizon.

My friend Bob Cleaves and I rushed to the airport and departed northbound in our rented Piper Archer.

Mt. McKinley, like Kilimanjaro in Tanzania, is shy and elusive, frequently hiding behind a shroud of cloud, but not on this day. The majestic mountain grew large in the windshield and seemed willing to pose for the photographs we had been waiting to take. The Archer struggled toward the summit. Finally, when it would climb no more, Cleaves suggested that I hop into the back seat and take a wide-angle shot that would include him in the foreground and "Big Mack" in the background.

It wasn't easy, but I finally made it—and then promptly collapsed for what seemed like an eternity, but was only a few seconds. I hurriedly framed Cleaves and the mountain in my viewfinder, snapped the picture, and yelled for him to go down. At 18,500 feet, my chest was pounding, and I was having difficulty recovering from the exertion.

Cleaves quickly lowered the nose and began singing "Jingle Bells," even though it was July and he too was having trouble breathing. Moments later, we returned to that very thin layer of the atmosphere where pilots can function normally without the aid of supplemental oxygen.

I used to think that this was my first experience with hypoxia (a shortage of oxygen), but I was wrong. I have since learned that pilots can suffer from low-grade hypoxia as soon as they leave the ground. In this sense, a pilot is a normally aspirated engine and loses performance with altitude.

It is interesting that we readily accept the concept of an engine losing power during climb but are less willing to acknowledge an individual loss of performance. This is because the effects of hypoxia develop so insidiously. The most common symptoms include visual disturbances, loss of muscular coordination, an impairment in judgment, lightheadedness, dizziness, apprehension, and a bluish discoloration of extremities. Although it might seem that pilots would recognize these symptoms, they usually cannot because of what might be hypoxia's most dangerous effect: euphoria, a strong sense of well-being that camouflages the other symptoms. This should put a lie to any notion that a pilot can wait to recognize the symptoms of hypoxia before taking corrective action.

Although most pilots would never risk flying under the influence of drugs and alcohol, many of them expose themselves to similar dysfunctions by unwittingly operating under the influence of hypoxia.

Most of what I read about hypoxia usually involves a discussion of hemoglobin, erythrocytes, alveoli, red corpuscles, permeable membranes, and other terms that only remind me about how I struggled through Physiology 101.

There are only two things that a pilot needs to understand about hypoxia. The first is that he usually cannot recognize the disabling effects of hypoxia (particularly during periods of stress). The second is that there is only one instrument that can warn of hypoxia: the altimeter. Although the use of supplementary oxygen is not required until above 12,500 feet for more than 30 minutes and whenever above 14,000 feet for any period of time, these rules seem too liberal. The instructors at the FAA's Physiological Training Course in Oklahoma City teach that oxygen should be used when above 5,000 feet at night and when above 10,000 feet during the day (military and air-carrier requirements are similarly conservative). One pilot—who also is a flight surgeon—is so understandably conscientious about avoiding hypoxia that he has printed in bold red the word OXYGEN on his high-altitude, power-setting charts as a reminder to use oxygen at the appropriate altitude. He regards his supplemental oxygen system as a "turbocharger" that allows him to recapture the personal performance lost during climb.

Over the years, I have purchased a number of safety-related items to take on appropriate flights. These include a first-aid kit, a well-stocked survival kit, a fire extinguisher, and—most recently—a portable oxygen system that goes along on all night cross-countries and those daylight flights that could wind up above 10,000 feet. (I would love to have had the bottle available during my one flight into La Paz. The elevation of the main airport there is 13,300 feet MSL, and I could have used oxygen just to perform a walkaround inspection.)

There have been many accidents that can be at least partially attributed to hypoxia. Perhaps this is why many airline pilots don a mask and breathe oxygen prior to a night approach or when tired. Does this do any good when flying an aircraft pressurized to several thousand feet above sea level? I believe that it does. On the other hand, oxygen may be a little like chicken soup. According to my mother, it can't hurt.

Chapter 49 **Judgment**

My son, Brian, a first officer for TWA, is part owner of a magnificently re-stored Aeronca 7AC that is hangared at Creve Coeur Airport on the out-skirts of St. Louis. (At least, it was hangared there until the Missouri River got too big for its banks.) He derives a great deal of joy from the fabric-cov-ered taildragger and often calls to wax and bubble about his flights of fancy.

"Dad," he began not long ago. "I really had a great flight today. One of the best. The wind was sweeping across the grass runway and offered a per-fect opportunity for me to practice crosswind takeoffs and landings.

"It was a little rough taxiing out, though. The wind kept shoving the Champ in one direction while I struggled to go in another. Just as I was about to add power for takeoff, a strong gust side-swiped the Airknocker and began to lift a wing. When things settled down, I turned to my passenger, shook my head, and taxied slowly back to the barn."

"I don't get it," I said. "What did I miss? I thought you told me that you had a great flight."

"I did, Dad. It was great. It was great because it left me feeling so good about not going. It could have been a bad flight, a really bad flight."

Had I taught him that kind of wisdom? Probably not, I concluded. Ei-ther a pilot is blessed with good judgment or he is not. In aviation, judgment is the ability to assess a series of variables, weigh them against possible risk, and determine the safest and most practical course of action. It is the stuff of which good pilots are made.

Famed aviation author Ernest K. Gann once told me that he regarded sound judgment as the ability of a pilot to maintain options. This, he claimed, is because a given situation becomes more critical as the number of options declines. "Accidents most often occur," he said, "when options dwindle and a pilot is left without choice."

According to regulation, the "exercise of sound judgment" also is the stuff that pilots are supposed to demonstrate when taking an FAA flight test. This seems logical. After all, those incapable of exercising sound judgment should not be allowed to fly as pilot in command.

Unfortunately, determining a pilot's ability to exercise judgment is easier said than done. This is because a pilot under observation is on his best be-havior. He knows that questions involving judgment during a flight test are largely theoretical, and he responds to them with conservatism and relative ease. He takes no chance with an answer that might jeopardize his passing a flight test.

This makes it almost impossible for an examiner to appraise the applicant's ability to exercise judgment. He has no way of knowing how a newly rated pilot will behave when beyond scrutiny and confronted with real-world imperatives.

It is noteworthy that pilots often are more concerned about not doing something wrong during a flight test than they are about not doing something dangerous during a normal flight.

Anyone who doubts this should consider that pilots taking a flight test never overload the aircraft; they never scud-run; they never run low or out of fuel; they never buzz their boy- or girlfriend's house. Some will, however, commit these same potentially lethal acts during the course of a normal flight. They do it because they think they can get away with it. But the annual report of accidents published by the National Transportation Safety Board clearly proves that many do not get away with these lapses of judgment.

One of the best pilots I know is not a particularly skillful pilot. This may seem paradoxical, but is not. Although not unusually adroit with "stick and rudder," she is acutely aware of her limitations and stringently abides by them. As a result, she is one of the safest and, therefore, one of the best pilots I know. I would rather trust my family to her care than to a more skillful pilot who lacks her judgment.

A technique that almost assures the exercise of sound judgment and enhances safety is for a pilot to operate his flight as if there were an FAA inspector in the right seat watching his every move, grading his every decision. This attitude alone would probably prevent most accidents.

A fellow TWA pilot, Robert Pastore, claims that it is almost impossible to operate a flight exactly by the book. He challenges those who disagree to prove him wrong. It rarely takes them long to learn that Pastore is correct. They also discover—thanks to Pastore's incredible knowledge of the Federal Aviation Regulations—that it is almost impossible to conduct a flight without violating at least one regulation or another.

General aviation pilots who believe that they can conduct a flawless operation should hire an instructor and ask him to point out all errors (however small they might be). It can be a humbling, educational experience.

Finally, perhaps we can all benefit from the philosophy that my son taught me: Some of the best flights are those that never get off the ground.

Chapter 50 **Complacency**

One job of an airline captain is to supervise his first officer, who often is regarded as a captain in training. The less experienced the copilot, the more alert the captain must be.

On one particular flight, my first officer was a captain who had recently opted to move from the left seat of a McDonnell Douglas MD-80 to the right seat of a Lockheed L-1011. He gave up being a junior captain to improve the working conditions he would have as a senior first officer.

Flying with a captain in the right seat of my airplane would make this flight more relaxing because there would be little or no supervision required. "Larry," I said, "it's your leg. You fly it to New York, and I'll fly the return leg tomorrow night."

We landed in New York after an uneventful red-eye from Los Angeles and pulled into the gate. Larry shut down the engines and called for the checklist. It had been another routine flight. They should all be so pleasant, I thought. Minutes later, we were standing in front of the terminal building waiting for the hotel van.

One of our flight attendants waiting with us walked over to me and asked, "It's not even 6 o'clock. Why are they running an engine so early in the morning?" I shrugged, not paying any attention to the screaming turbine. One advantage to the hearing loss caused by years of flying is that loud noises are not as annoying as they used to be.

My flight engineer overheard the question and began a slow walk toward our airplane, which we could see parked nearby and on the other side of a chain-link fence. He spun around and yelled while pointing at the TriStar, "It's our airplane. We left an engine running!"

We ran madly into the terminal building where—you guessed it—we were delayed by a security check. By the time we reached the jetway, we could hear the engine winding down. A mechanic walked out wearing a sadistic grin. "You guys forget something?"

How did this happen? It's easy when you think about it. My first officer, an MD-80 pilot, was accustomed to shutting down two engines, not three, and this is exactly what he did. Second, the checklist does not require us to verify that the engines have been shut down at the end of a flight. After all, what kind of idiot needs to be reminded about that? Third, we cannot hear an engine from the flight deck of an L-1011 (or most other jetliners). If the sound of an engine were to attract our attention while deplaning, we probably would take it for granted and attribute the noise to an aircraft parked nearby.

The culprit responsible for this embarrassing incident is complacency, a factor responsible for many more accidents than is generally appreciated. An insidious aspect of complacency is that it most affects those with the greatest experience.

Guarding against one's own complacency is only half the battle; guarding against someone else's is the other half.

Many years ago, I flew a Twin Beech on a charter flight from Los Angeles to Acapulco, Mexico. Our first stop was at Hermosillo, an airport of entry, and the second was at Mazatlán. After refueling the D-18 and paying a host of annoying fees, I walked to the dilapidated shack for the obligatory weather briefing.

I entered the shack expecting to see at least a few weather charts, a teletype machine, and other familiar trappings, but there were none of these. Instead, there was only a black, old-fashioned, stand-up telephone caked with dust blown through the broken glass windows by the winds of time. It obviously had not seen recent use. The briefer was snoring in a chair that leaned at a perilous angle against a stained wall. His feet were propped up by a desk of such scarred antiquity that either of my ex-wives would have gladly emptied our bank account for the privilege of owning it.

I allowed the screen door to slam behind me, and it had the desired effect. The startled briefer sat upright and politely asked what he could do for me. I handed him the receipt proving that I had paid the requisite number of pesos.

"Where are you going?" he asked, wiping the sleep from his eyes.

"Acapulco."

"This is your lucky day, Señor. The weather to Acapulco is beautiful."

I again looked around for weather documents. Nothing. I must have missed something. "How do you know what the weather is like to Acapulco?"

"That is easy, Señor. The weather to Acapulco is always beautiful."

The briefer was right. The weather to Acapulco was beautiful, but only to those who behold beauty as having to deviate around and between thunderstorms at night without storm-detection equipment.

There is a tired but accurate adage in aviation. It reminds us that flying is hours and hours of boredom punctuated by moments of stark terror. Pilots need to remind themselves that complacency is one factor that can lead to such unexpected and undesirable excitement.

Chapter 51 **Aerobatics**

My first exposure to aerobatics was in 1956. I was checking out in a Ryan STA, a low-wing monoplane with tandem, open cockpits. It also had a narrow, inverted, in-line engine that contributed to the sleekness of the pre-World War II trainer.

I was in the rear cockpit and my instructor sat up front. We communicated using a gosport, a system of hollow rubber tubes that was the forerunner of the electronic intercom. The idea was to yell into a funnel at one end of a tube. The other end split into a Y such that the ends terminated at holes in the other pilot's helmet near where earphones would normally be. The instructor had a similar system for screaming at the student. This scheme even made it possible for pilots to occasionally hear and understand one another. It depended on how loud one yelled and how well the other listened.

On one particular flight, I should have been a better listener.

"Hey, Barry," came the barely audible voice. "Okay if I do an outside loop?"

I heard only that the instructor wanted to do a loop, a mild aerobatic maneuver. I never heard the word, "outside." Nor would it have mattered. I had never heard of an outside loop.

"Sure," I yelled into the gosport. "Why not."

I had expected the throttle to advance and the stick to come back, but everything happened bass-ackwards. The instructor shoved the nose down, and I came out of my seat to once again validate one of Newton's Laws of Motion. I was thankfully restrained by a gaggle of straps and belts. But considering what was to follow, it might have been more merciful to have fallen out and ended everything right then and there.

The negative Gs increased, and—as the blood rushed to my head—I began to see red, literally and figuratively. Redout, I later learned, is the opposite of blackout and can occur during negative Gs. The victim apparently sees red as a result of blood vessels in the lower eyelids becoming congested.

The loop did not last very long, but its aftereffects did. In the short term, I had difficulty climbing out of the airplane and walking without a wobble. I was violently nauseated and had a headache that lasted until the next day.

In the long run, it discouraged me from developing any enthusiasm for aerobatics. (It also taught me the importance of being considerate to passengers.) I eventually began to feel like an outcast because it seemed that I was alone in my dislike for aerobatics.

Aerobatics affects different pilots in different ways. Short people, for example, have more tolerance for G loads than tall people. This is because the heart of a tall person needs to pump blood a greater distance to the brain. During aerobatics involving positive Gs, the effect can be like stretching a pilot's neck to a giraffe-like length.

I recently decided that I had hidden my feelings about aerobatics long enough and began to come out of the closet (so to speak). What surprised me, however, was discovering how many others felt the same way. During an informal survey of 42 pilots, I found that 25 did not care for the discomfort resulting from aerobatic flight. Some thought that aerobatics was an expression of masochistic self-flagellation. A psychologist suggested, however, that many do not openly admit these feelings because of a fear that they might be interpreted as a certain lack of machismo. Okay, I admit it. I am not a macho pilot. (I have discovered that confessions come easier with age.)

Flying is multidimensional and is different things to different people. Some prefer dizzying snap rolls and hammerhead turns, and others find it more challenging and gratifying to keep the cross-pointers centered during an ILS approach in a turbulent crosswind. It obviously is up to each pilot to pursue that which he considers the most satisfying aspects of flight.

Is it necessary to learn aerobatics to become a proficient pilot? Some would argue that a pilot should be capable of flying an airplane to and within every corner of its operating envelope. Others claim also that a pilot should know how to roll an airplane because the maneuver might be needed to recover from a low-altitude upset caused by wake turbulence.

I disagree. Even if a pilot did know how to roll, would he have the instinct to do so at low altitude? It probably is more likely that he would react the way the rest of us would, by attempting to counter any rolling tendency caused by wake turbulence with opposite aileron.

None of this should be interpreted to mean, however, that I oppose some form of spin training. Pilots should know how to both avoid and recover from spins. But this does not necessitate first winding up an airplane into a 5- or a 10-turn spin. It requires only learning to recognize an incipient spin and then initiating timely recovery.

In the meantime, it really is okay not to love a loop or a lomcovàk (even though I envy those who do).

Chapter 52 **Trimming During Steep Turns**

It has been said that the 180-degree turn is one of aviation's most difficult maneuvers. This is because turning around is contrary to plan and forces a pilot to admit defeat in the face of adversity.

If this is so, then the steep turn may run a close second. Also called the steep power turn, it typically requires a 50- to 60-degree bank angle (a 45-degree bank angle in large aircraft) and is a maneuver that many pilots would rather not have to do.

Considering the elementary nature of the steep turn, it is interesting that it is the source of some controversy, especially among flight instructors. Many of them claim that students should be taught to use pitch trim when executing a steep turn, while others are adamantly opposed. (The FAA does not appear to take a stand on this issue.)

According to the FAA's *Flight Training Handbook*, the purpose of the steep turn as a training and proficiency maneuver is "to develop [and maintain] smoothness, coordination, orientation, division of attention, and control techniques." The maneuver is used during instrument training to help develop and maintain a scan pattern of the basic instruments.

In my opinion, trimming during the steep turn makes the maneuver much easier to perform and defeats its purpose as a training exercise. After all, if stick or wheel forces are trimmed away and the pilot can maintain control with his fingertips, the exercise becomes little more challenging than straight-and-level flight. Trimming also defeats the purpose of steep turns during instrument training, which is why airline instructors do not allow it.

Another reason for not trimming becomes obvious when having to roll out in a hurry. If the pilot cannot retrim quickly enough or forgets to add considerable forward pressure to the yoke, he might find himself making an involuntary entry to a hammerhead turn.

For similar reasons, pilots should avoid trimming during the landing flare, a practice that I have observed when administering biennial flight reviews to pilots flying airplanes equipped with electric trim. A rejected landing at such a time could result in a powerful nose-up pitching moment and the unsightly mess that results from stalling at low altitude.

The purpose of elevator trim is to relieve control pressures when maintaining a prolonged condition or attitude such as when climbing or descending. It is not intended for relieving transitory control pressures that occur during a brief maneuver.

When a pilot needs to make a steep turn during normal flight (and not for training purposes), it usually is of such short duration that there is not enough time or advantage to justify trimming. As a result, using trim when practicing steep turns is a form of negative training.

But I have saved the best for last. Aircraft designers make it difficult for pilots to inadvertently develop excessive and destructive G loads. They do this by ensuring that stick forces become heavy enough to warn a pilot when he might be doing something wrong.

For example, the straight-tail Beech Bonanza has a designed stick force of approximately 25 pounds per G. This means that a pilot must exert 25 pounds of pull on the control wheel to increase the load by 1 G. To achieve a load factor of 5 Gs (an increase of four), for example, requires a 100-pound pull, and so forth.

To eliminate these stick forces with elevator trim negates the effort of the designer and makes it easier for a pilot to overstress the airplane. Such excessive G loads most commonly occur when a pilot hauls back on the control wheel when attempting to recover from a developing spiral. (Although aerobatic aircraft are designed with light stick forces, these aircraft are designed also to withstand significant loads.)

The stick forces associated with the V-tail Bonanza are unusually light and that is one reason for its popularity. It is simply a delight to fly. But when loaded with an excessively aft center of gravity (which is surprisingly easy to do in that airplane without realizing it), the stick forces per G become too light. In this condition, it is relatively easy to haul back on the yoke and create enough of a load to break something, which is exactly what has happened in a number of cases.

In any event, steep turns should be performed at or below the maneuvering speed to prevent the possibility of overloading the aircraft, whether or not elevator trim is used.

Irv Siegel, a highly respected instructor with whom I enjoy debating such things, says that trimming during steep turns can be justified because it helps to prevent a pilot from inadvertently entering a high-speed spiral.

A good point, but pilots should be taught and know how to recover from a steep turn that gets out of hand. It requires no more than rolling the wings level and then gently raising the nose (and reducing power, if necessary).

Hauling back on the wheel during a spiral in an attempt to salvage a steep turn inevitably leads to a bust, which can mean either a busted flight test or a busted airplane, take your choice.

Chapter 53 **Expectations**

The vagaries of airline crew scheduling are such that two pilots working for the same company may frequently, rarely, or never share a cockpit during their careers. As a result, there is a reasonably good chance that I will never have to fly with Roger again.

In most respects, he is a bright, capable, and conscientious flight engineer. But he has one habit that makes me nervous. Roger operates the switches, levers, and buttons on his panel with such a flurry that I occasionally cannot keep track of what he is doing. His hands move in a blur like Vladimir Horowitz playing "Flight of the Bumble Bee" on piano.

Roger is quite proficient at operating the jumbo jet's complex systems. The trouble is that he often does not take the time needed to verify that the movement of a switch or control actually produces the desired result. He gets away with this most of the time because the systems are so reliable; they seldom fail. But every once in a while, Roger's speed backfires, such as when he inadvertently deployed the passenger oxygen masks just before departure. (The flight was delayed for hours while the masks were repacked.)

Many general aviation pilots fly with the expectation that all systems will operate normally. Consider, for example, those who think they have lowered the landing gear only to discover during the noisy and abbreviated landing roll that they have not.

Experience increases proficiency, but it also breeds complacency. When a pilot moves a switch a thousand times and gets the desired result each time, he develops the expectation that the action will continue to produce the same result. This is when that sadistic finger of fate is most likely to point his way.

When using any system, a pilot should attempt to verify that it is operating normally before diverting attention elsewhere. When lowering the landing gear, for example, he should keep his hand on the switch until verifying that the gear is down and locked. Otherwise, he can become distracted and forget to check on the actual status of the landing gear.

Other systems require similar attention, because things do not always work the way they are supposed to. When turning on an auxiliary fuel pump, simultaneously look for a momentary fluctuation in fuel pressure. This verifies that moving the switch actually turns on the pump. You similarly should check for an ammeter (or load meter) fluctuation when turning on the pitot heat. How else are we to know that flipping the switch will provide anti-ice protection prior to entering visible moisture?

The closest I ever came to losing control of an airplane and making a messy hole in the ground occurred when I was a victim of expectancy. I was executing an ILS approach to Gander, Newfoundland, in a Cessna 310 that I was ferrying to Manchester, England. The weather was abysmal, almost zero-zero in blowing snow. But because the wind was blowing straight down the runway and I had plenty of fuel, I opted to execute a look-see approach before diverting to my alternate, St. John's. Conditions were as advertised, however, and nothing of the ground was visible at decision height.

Within seconds of beginning the missed approach, the cockpit speaker boomed with an unexpected clearance to Goose Bay. This was necessary, I was told matter-of-factly, because the weather at St. John's had also become "zero-zero" and the airport was closed. I suddenly found myself rearranging charts, changing frequencies, spinning course selectors, and attending to a flurry of communications. I failed to recognize until it was almost too late that the twin Cessna had begun a left spiral dive. My initial reaction was that the left engine had failed. But the problem actually was caused by a throttle that had slowly crept aft. I had assumed that the throttles would stay where I had put them, but this assumption was almost my last.

Throttle creep is particularly dangerous during takeoff when a loss of power cannot be tolerated. This type of accident, however, is easy to prevent by keeping your hand on the throttle(s) during takeoff and low-altitude climb. (You would be surprised how many pilots do not.)

A related and disastrous accident occurred in 1982 when an Air Florida captain made the fatal mistake of assuming that his power gauges were indicating correctly.

If he had considered the possibility that the anemic takeoff and initial climb performance of the Boeing 737 was caused by erroneous engine pressure ratio readings (the result of structural ice blocking instrument probes in the engine inlets), he could have simply moved the throttles farther forward to obtain the additional and available power. But he did not, and 78 lives were lost when the Boeing slammed into the icy Potomac River within seconds after lifting off from Washington National Airport.

This accident and many others serve as grim reminders that pilots must never take anything for granted. The only thing we have a right to expect is the unexpected.

An acquaintance certainly never expected the aileron cables of his Twin Beech to have been reversed while his aircraft was in the shop for major maintenance. Perhaps this is why he did not pay much attention to the direction of aileron deflection before departure. The discovery was made shortly after liftoff, and only extraordinary airmanship enabled him to nurse the aircraft around the pattern and back onto the runway.

Somebody once said correctly that a superior pilot uses superior care to prevent having to use or demonstrate his superior skill.

The Twin Beech pilot could have had it worse. A few years earlier, an airplane had come out of a shop with only one aileron connected in reverse. Moving the control wheel left caused both ailerons to move downward, like a pair of flaps; moving the control to the right caused them to move up, like a pair of spoilers. The pilot never survived to describe what it was like to fly such an aircraft.

Although not necessarily dangerous, the unexpected behavior of other items can also be traumatic. Well-known educator and humorist Rod Machado says that his greatest fear is a runaway Hobbs meter.

Chapter 54 **Seat-of-the-Pants Flying**

Like other instrument students, I had my share of difficulty learning "blind flying." But one particular admonishment from beyond the plywood walls of the Link Trainer helped me to turn the corner.

"Think of the artificial horizon as a hole in your instrument panel, a hole through which you can see the outside world and the natural horizon. If you continue trying to fly by the seat of your pants, you'll wind up on your ass." Charlie Gress knew how to make an impression.

Years later, a friend heard me mention Gress' warning about trying to control an airplane while relying only on the seat of one's pants for guidance. That is all that Tom Sullivan had to hear. He regarded the statement as a challenge and asked if I would allow him to try flying blind without using an artificial or natural horizon.

Sullivan was not being whimsical. He had spent most of his life accepting challenge. He also believed that he would be better at blind flying than others. This is because he was blind and had been since birth.

Despite or because of his disability, Sullivan graduated from Harvard with honors, competed against sighted students to become an amateur U.S. wrestling champion, and became a professional musician and composer. Nor did being blind prevent him from sky diving.

Sky diving?

"Sure," he quips. "Why not? Sighted people are often frightened by what they see. I obviously don't suffer from that."

Sullivan did pose a problem at the jump school. How could a blind jumper steer toward the jump zone and judge his height above the ground in preparation for landing? The solution consisted of a small, portable VHF receiver that was placed in Sullivan's helmet. An observer on the ground would transmit instructions and call out critical heights.

Everything worked well until Sullivan's 37th jump. After bailing out and savoring the euphoria of free fall, he noticed that his earphones were silent. No static. No instructions. Nothing. The radio had failed. He quickly located and tugged at the D-ring attached to the rip cord. Seconds later, his body jerked convulsively in response to the blossoming chute.

He dangled helplessly, drifting and sinking into the black abyss. Terrified, he had no idea when, what, or how he would hit. The agonizing seconds passed slowly as he and his fate converged.

Miraculously, Sullivan landed in a tree and escaped with only a few broken bones. But this setback did nothing to dampen his zest for life, which ultimately led him to the cockpit of a Piper Cherokee Six. We believed that if anyone could fly an airplane by the seat of his pants, he could. This is because sightless people partially compensate for their disability by sharpening their other senses. Sullivan's senses would be superior to those of ordinary pilots.

I was particularly impressed with Tom's interaction with the airplane during our preflight inspection. He used his hands to familiarize himself with the various surfaces, nodding to himself as if understanding the function of each. His grasp of these fundamentals stemmed from his familiarity with model airplanes.

Following my instructions, Sullivan started the engine, called for a clearance, and learned to taxi by following my commands: "left rudder...right rudder...more power...less power."

We made the takeoff together and headed for the practice area, where I trimmed the aircraft for level flight.

"Okay, Tom. It's all yours."

Here is where Sullivan's heightened sense of hearing was of value. He could detect airspeed changes on the basis of sound changes long before I could. He actually did a reasonable job of holding altitude. But there was no way that he could keep the aircraft on an even keel. The wings remained level only as long as aircraft stability would allow.

At the end of the flight, Sullivan agreed that an aircraft could not be flown using only one's senses for guidance and was typically philosophical. "It's not so important to master something," he claimed, "as much as it is to try."

I concealed my disagreement. In aviation, it is important to master the airplane. Trying is not enough.

Sullivan and I obviously didn't prove anything. Most pilots know that an airplane cannot be controlled without the proper instruments and the proficiency to use them. But if this is true, why do so many accidents result from plunging headlong into worsening weather? Perhaps it is because it occurs inadvertently or at night when clouds can be difficult to see and avoid. Or perhaps it is because we overestimate our ability.

Some of these pilots might be better off resorting to the advice offered in a 1918 book titled *Flying and How To Do It*. The author, Assen Jordanoff, suggests that a pilot foolish enough to venture into cloud should take the safest course of action, which is to bail out.

Hmmm. Jump, eh? It would seem that the sky-diving Sullivan might be better prepared to cope with inadvertent flight into instrument conditions than those who otherwise fail to survive their transgressions.

Chapter 55 **Wire Strikes**

On September 31, 1962, my friend Bob Franks and I were ferrying a factory-new Cessna 172 (N2128Y) from Wichita to the Cessna dealer in Santa Monica, California. It had been a magnificent, low-level flight that had followed the contours of the land like a cartographer's pen.

As we approached the Colorado River from western Arizona, Bob suggested that we descend lower and follow the river as it snaked through an enticing, red-rock canyon near Parker, Arizona. The temptation was overwhelming, and we soon leveled off at 200 feet above the water. The increased sensation of speed and the beauty of the panorama created a grand exhilaration.

The first sign that something was amiss was a loud "twang" followed by a rasping sound as a telephone wire strung across the canyon burned through the leading edge of the left wing and wrapped itself around the tail. We thankfully still had control of the airplane and hobbled to a landing at nearby Parker Airport.

An aircraft mechanic there covered the superficial damage with high-speed tape and declared that the 172 was sufficiently airworthy to ferry to Santa Monica where permanent repairs could be made.

"You know," he said. "you guys are luckier than you realize. There are some 50,000-volt, high-tension lines right above those phone lines you flew through." (To add insult to injury, I later received an invoice from the Parker Valley Telephone Company demanding that I pay for the damage done to the telephone line.)

This was not an unusual accident. According to the National Transportation Safety Board, wire strikes are the cause of approximately one out of every 20 general aviation accidents. Most wire strikes occur in VFR conditions and below 200 feet AGL. (Obstructions below 200 feet AGL are typically not shown on sectional charts.)

In California alone, 59 aircraft were downed by wires during a recent 10-year period, and almost half of these were fatal. (Helicopter occupants are most vulnerable to injury.)

Pilots should consider that a typical power line cannot be seen during daylight hours until within 150 feet of the wire. This distance is flown in less than two seconds and is insufficient time to react and avoid the wire. Telephone lines are smaller and often cannot be seen at all.

A wire strike does not befall only those who foolishly choose to fly at such low altitudes. Wires at the end of a short runway often lie in wait to snatch aircraft lacking the performance (especially at high density altitudes) to clear them. Also, a significant number of accidents do not involve pilot error. These are the result of off-airport emergency landings.

A case in point involves Harold Ballatin, a retired United Airlines captain, and his pilot-passenger, Ginette Aelony. The two had departed Torrance, California, for Porterville in Ballatin's Glasair I. While climbing through 7,500 feet, Ballatin smelled fuel in the cockpit and switched tanks. The engine then failed and could not be restarted even though there was plenty of fuel in each tank.

Although there were no airports nearby, Ballatin and Aelony spotted an immense, vacant parking lot adjacent to the Six Flags Magic Mountain amusement park north of Los Angeles. It appeared to be within gliding range and suitable for a safe landing.

As the experimental airplane approached the edge of the parking lot, the couple began to relax. They had it made as long as Ballatin kept the wheels in the wells and the flaps retracted. He was willing to trade some belly damage for the assurance of gliding to a safe haven.

They had it made, that is, until the left wing snagged a 90-foot-high, 40,000-volt power line at the approach edge of the parking lot. (Neither occupant recalls having seeing it.) The airplane flipped over, landed on its back (in the parking lot) and skidded to a stop. Although Ballatin escaped the wreckage, Aelony was trapped inside for 1.5 hours with critical injuries. Rescue workers eventually placed inflatable bags under the wings, lifted the aircraft gently, and extricated her.

Aelony considers herself lucky to be alive and believes that she was spared so that she might begin a national campaign to (1) increase pilot awareness of the wire-strike problem, and (2) encourage the installation of bright orange balls on all wires that pose "an invisible threat" to unsuspecting pilots. This led her to inaugurate a program called "Adopt-A-Wire," which is similar to the "Adopt-A-Highway" plan. But instead of corporations committing to keeping a stretch of highway clear of debris, she is encouraging pilots to identify potentially dangerous wires and volunteer to work toward getting them marked. "An orange ball," she says, "costs little." (Ballatin is convinced that had the wires at Magic Mountain been so marked, he could have flown under them and made a safe landing.)

Aelony speaks about her crusade with evangelical fervor and is determined that her efforts will make flying safer. "In the 1950s," she reminded me, "the battle cry was 'bury the wires, or bury the pilot.' Trouble is, we're still burying pilots."

Chapter 56 **Hazardous Airports**

When they gather in ramp and dispatch offices, airline pilots often pass the time hangar flying. A favorite subject involves unusual and challenging airports into which they have flown. At such a time, someone is bound to mention Hong Kong's Cheung Chau approach, where the crew mushes along with landing gear and flaps extended at only 780 feet above the wind-swept waters of the South China Sea. After passing a nondirectional beacon, they descend while aiming for a 400-foot hill adorned with a pair of large, illuminated, orange-and-white checkerboards. When these warning signs fill the windshield, and one of the pilots begin to squirm, the other makes a sharp right turn to avoid the obstacle and align the aircraft on short final approach.

This is a thrill, but general aviation pilots often cope with airport-related hazards that are totally unacceptable to their airline brethren. Lightplane pilots routinely deal with one-way strips, unimproved surfaces, threatening obstacles, and so forth. (I am reminded of an airport in Africa for which this permanent NOTAM is published: "Caution: braking action nil [because of] worms on the runway."

I thought I had heard it all until I picked up a book with the seemingly innocuous title, *Fly Idaho!* by Galen L. Hanselman. It is filled with beautiful color photographs of and details about the airports of Idaho's Backcountry.

It takes an active imagination to call some of these minuscule patches of real estate airports. It is difficult to believe that pilots really fly into these places. At one airport, there is not enough room to make a go-around after crossing the runway threshold. Another has a blind approach, and others have runways where one end cannot be seen from the other.

A note regarding the Simonds Airport (which is 900 feet long and at an elevation of 5,243 feet MSL) cautions the pilot that when the grass is wet, the steep sideslope of the runway can cause an airplane to slide sideways.

A pilot must be particularly cautious when taking off from the 1,100-foot-long runway at Vines. This is because "the morning sun [will blind the] pilot" during his climbout into the steep and narrow canyon in which the airport is situated.

The runway at Elk City is shaped like a macaroni noodle yet is numbered 16/34. According to the diagram, it should be numbered 16/02 or the like. The pilot would then be warned to expect his magnetic heading to increase substantially while taking off in one direction and decrease when departing in the other.

According to Hanselman, the most hazardous airport in the Backcountry is Mile Hi. This natural clearing is on the side of a mountain. The runway—if you can call it that—has an elevation of 5,831 feet MSL and is 1,100 feet long (of which the first 540 feet of this one-way strip is unusable for landing). Not to worry though. The usable end of the "runway" has a 20-degree upslope to aid deceleration, and by veering 45 degrees right after landing, the pilot is afforded 500 feet of overrun that parallels a steep uphill ridge.

Some of these airports contain notes warning that they should be used only by experienced mountain pilots flying Super Cub-type aircraft. But this does not discourage some pilots from overrating their proficiency and aircraft performance. An almost predictable number of airplanes are converted annually into crumpled sheet metal.

Even if a pilot never plans to fly into Idaho's Backcountry, the book is worth perusing for its entertainment value.

Hanselman also has devised and describes a clever Relative Hazard Index that numerically rates every airport in the book. This RHI takes into consideration runway length, elevation, proximity of mountains and other obstacles, abrupt turns required before landing or after takeoff, runway surface conditions (such as the lack of markings, no wind sock, and deterioration due to animals), and so forth. Handy tables are provided so that a pilot can use this system to similarly rate any airport into which he contemplates operating.

Mile Hi Airport receives Hanselman's highest hazard rating, a 50. Most normal airports have indices between 0 and 5.

John Deakin, a friend and 747 captain for Japan Air Lines, owns an immaculate Bonanza bedecked with a Robertson STOL conversion that includes full-span flaps and spoilers for roll control. Deakin is challenged by Mile Hi and has been studying physics and performance to see if it would be feasible for him to land there. I pray that his motivation is theoretical. Otherwise, Deakin's historic landing at Mile Hi could provide fascinating grist for this writer's mill, especially the part about how a large truck was maneuvered into the area to extricate him and his machine. (May I have the exclusive, John?)

Unfortunately, many pilots do not pay sufficient attention to airport conditions (Deakin is not one of them) and tread where others fear to go. Some pay the piper for their lack of planning.

Perhaps cemeteries should be built adjacent to these hazardous airports, which is the case at Yurimaguas, Peru. According to local legend, the cemetery at the end of the runway there is for the convenience of pilots who fail to survive their own foolishness.

Chapter 57 **The Sterile Cockpit**

On September 25, 1978, a Pacific Southwest Airlines' Boeing 727 was on a visual approach to San Diego's Lindbergh Field, when it collided with a Cessna 172. The cockpit voice recorder recovered from the wreckage of PSA Flight 182 revealed that there had been substantial, nonessential conversation on the flight deck between the three crewmembers and a deadheading PSA captain during critical moments preceding the accident. Although there were a number of factors responsible for this loss of 144 lives (including seven on the ground), the National Transportation Safety Board concluded that distractions caused by extraneous cockpit conversation probably were a contributing factor.

From this tragedy was born what is known in the airline industry as the "sterile cockpit rule." Part 121.542, which applies to air carrier operations, makes it illegal for flight crewmembers to engage in nonessential conversation during critical phases of flight (which includes taxi, takeoff and landing, and all other flight operations conducted below 10,000 feet, except cruise flight).

This regulation was initially met with resistance, but most airline pilots now concede that the sterile cockpit does contribute to safety. Consequently, there are many who believe that a quiet cockpit during certain terminal operations could also benefit general aviation. No, they are not suggesting that the FAA create another regulation. (Lacking a cockpit voice recorder, there would be no way to detect non-compliance.) Rather, it is suggested that general aviation pilots voluntarily apply a similar concept during high-workload operations.

Some years ago, for example, a pilot was executing an instrument (VOR/DME) approach to a northern California airport at night in a non-radar environment. The reported weather included a 500-foot overcast and a visibility of 2 miles. The airplane impacted a hill that was a mile to the left of the final approach course.

An analysis of the communications recorded by ATC revealed the sound of passengers laughing and joking in the background as the pilot of the Piper Cherokee Six reported passing the final approach fix. Was this accident caused by a cockpit contaminated with noise pollution? We shall never know.

Nor can we know or even guess at the number of general aviation accidents might have been the result of pilots distracted by extraneous and nonessential cockpit conversation. But it is reasonable to conclude that there have been some and perhaps many.

For example, pilots are taught that distraction is a primary cause of accidents resulting from an inadvertent stall/spin. This is why FAA designated examiners are encouraged to be creative about distracting applicants while they maneuver at minimum-controllable airspeed during flight tests. Many of these examiners have discovered that intrusive conversation is all that is necessary to distract the pilot and precipitate an inadvertent event.

Might not similar distractions cause pilots to miss important transmissions from air traffic control? How many gear-up accidents can be attributed to similar distractions?

A pilot can prevent being distracted by passengers during critical phases of flight simply by briefing them before departure. All he has to do is say something like, "Look, Joe [or Jane]. I'm going to be busy talking with traffic controllers during the first few minutes of flight, and it is important that I don't miss any of their calls. So I'd appreciate it if you would contain your enthusiasm until after we've cleared the local area (unless you notice something about which I need to know)."

Such a briefing should be conducted tactfully so as not to alarm a nervous passenger. Consider keeping him occupied with "traffic-watch." Make him feel important by asking him to silently point out nearby aircraft. The idea is to keep the passenger busy, so that he does not interrupt departure and arrival duties.

The sterile cockpit is particularly desirable during instrument and tower-controlled departures, low visibility, special-VFR and night departures, and all similar arrivals. It obviously is not as important when departing an uncontrolled airport on a severely clear day.

The idea is to take command of and control the cockpit environment during all critical phases of flight. Some pilots go so far as to advise their right-seat passengers that the intercom will be turned off until the departure workload has been reduced. After all, it is important for a pilot to monitor and digest all communications, not just those directed at him. Conversations to and from other aircraft help a pilot to remain aware of other traffic and better understand the conditions in which he is operating.

Consider, too, that the majority of accidents occur during the "11 critical minutes of flight." These consist of the 3 minutes that begin with initial power application and the 8 minutes ending with the landing roll.

One pilot I know claims with a grin that he takes advantage of the sterile-cockpit concept as an excuse to silence a loquacious mate—for the entire flight.

Chapter 58 **Skill Versus Experience**

There are times when I prefer being professionally incognito. I especially feel this way when at a party or other social gathering attended by non-aviation people. As soon as someone discovers that I am an airline pilot, I get bombarded by the same tiring questions: "Have you ever had a real emergency?" "What is the most dangerous thing that's ever happened to you?" Ad nauseam.

Most people seem disappointed to learn that I have so little to report. My career has not been highlighted by the dramatic events of which movies are made.

This is why, when asked what I do for a living, I often sidestep the subject by claiming that I am a heavy-equipment operator, which contains an element of truth. The conversation usually turns quickly in a different direction.

Recently, however, a friend asked a much more provocative question about my experiences as an airline pilot.

She began with the premise that a professional pilot invests years accruing knowledge, skill, and experience the way a financial expert invests in stocks and bonds. Each does it for a payoff: the latter to walk away with a fortune now and then, and the former just to walk away—always.

My friend wanted me to describe my proudest moment, the time when I best utilized my accrued assets to save the day.

This was not an easy question to answer, but I eventually concluded that I passed my most difficult test about 20 years ago. A strong cold front had just marched through Philadelphia and left a blanket of ice and strong northerly winds in its wake.

We were on final approach to Runway 27 when the tower reported a 29-knot, direct crosswind (maximum allowable for our Boeing 727), and that braking action had been reported nil by the pilot of a Convair 880.

Turbulence increased as we approached the runway threshold and it took all my concentration to hold the glideslope and remain within the lateral limits of the runway. The gusts and buffeting crosswind seemed to conspire in an attempt to prevent a landing. But we hung in there.

Touchdown. It wasn't a pretty landing, but it connected us with the ground. Firmly. But there was no traction. The trijet slid in a crab and seemed intent on leaving the runway. We were on the ground but had to use the flight controls to prevent an excursion. Reverse thrust seemed to worsen directional control, and the brakes were essentially useless.

We finally heaved a collective sigh of relief after taxiing off the runway and onto the parallel taxiway. (Sailing might be a better description of how we maneuvered the aircraft on such a slippery, wind-blown surface). It was a masterful display of airmanship that really did require mustering all of my experience, skill, and knowledge. My copilot and flight engineer also massaged my ego with enthusiastic accolades.

And then we watched an Eastern Airlines 727 land on the same runway and under the same conditions. But he didn't make it. The "three-holer" slid off the end of the runway and almost 100 passengers had to evacuate into the Arctic-like blast.

Moments later the airport was closed and the runway was sanded.

Suddenly, I was not so proud of what I had done. Suddenly, I realized that it could have been me parked in the weeds. Suddenly, I realized that the Eastern captain might not have attempted that landing had he not been encouraged by my success. He had no way of knowing that I was just plain lucky and that the fickle finger of fate would opt to point in his direction.

As my experience, skill, and knowledge continued to build, I became convinced that the extraordinary pilot uses his extraordinary experience and his extraordinary knowledge to anticipate and avoid that which might require using his extraordinary skill. Any planning or in-flight decision that eventually requires a heroic effort usually reflects the poor judgment used to make that decision.

My landing in Philadelphia? It should not have been attempted. We should have instead headed for our alternate, Boston, and rewarded our wisdom with a lobster dinner. As captain of the flight, it was my fault that we did not.

Superior skills should be required only when the ordinary becomes extraordinary, when an unavoidable situation develops. Such events typically are the result of unforeseen mechanical or system failures. Some remarkable examples include the crew that managed to fly their crippled and controlless DC-10 into Sioux City, Iowa. And the crew that hobbled back to Honolulu on only two engines after the cargo door had blown off their Boeing 747. And the crew that miraculously landed their "convertible" at Kahului, Maui, after the Boeing 737 had literally blown its top.

Most of us will fly through our aeronautical lives without ever needing to perform so heroically because of the reliability of our equipment. General aviation aircraft, however, often are not as well maintained or as reliable as heavy turbine equipment. This explains why lightplane pilots benefit at least as much from training and experience.

A stunning example of the need for extraordinary skill was demonstrated a few years ago by an air show performer in Europe. While or shortly after performing his aerobatic routine, the pilot noticed that a spar had been damaged and the wing was in imminent danger of bending up and breaking off.

After quickly appraising his dilemma, the pilot rolled inverted to reverse the lift vector and held the wing in place. Immediately prior to touchdown, he rolled upright so that the landing could be made on the wheels instead of on the canopy. As he did so, the wing failed. But the aircraft was so close to the ground that the landing could be completed without further incident.

True story.

Chapter 59 **Fatigue**

It was during the night of the summer solstice, 1967. We were seemingly in suspension over Greenland at Flight Level 370 in a Boeing 707 on the great circle route from Los Angeles to London. Although it was past midnight (local time), the sun refused to die. The northern horizon was a muted band of orange twilight and the ice below an eerie, pale purple luminescence.

We had endured a lengthy departure delay and were hours behind schedule. The captain seemed especially tired and was restless in his seat as if trying to find a comfortable position. But he finally gave in to the fatigue and tilted the back of his seat aft.

His head fell onto a pillow propped behind his neck and then turned in my direction. "I know it's not legal to sleep in the cockpit, but there's nothing in the book that says I can't faint."

And faint he did. Moments later, he was gone. Out. Unconscious. The oiler (flight engineer) and I were alone on the flight deck and only an occasional snore-whistle broke the silence.

But at least this captain was direct about his need for rest. Others, I discovered, preferred a different approach. They would, for example, close their eyes and claim to be studying an emergency checklist or system diagram tattooed to the insides of their eyelids. I was at first amused by such an obvious deception. That is, I was amused until discovering for myself what an efficient method of study this can be.

Although some might choose to criticize these pilots, others recognize that catnapping during the calm of cruise is preferable to fading out on final.

No kidding. I have flown with first officers who fell asleep during the approach after particularly grueling night flights. I recall one first officer actually being asleep until my landing woke him up. (Some of the landings I have made when tired were sufficient to register on the seismograph at Cal Tech.)

I also recall landing at JFK directly into a blinding, rising sun after having been on duty for almost 16 hours. We were numb, literally and figuratively.

After turning off the runway, my first officer called ground control for a taxi clearance. But instead of being cleared via the usual inner or outer taxiway, we were advised to return to the tower frequency. Puzzled, we complied. The tower controller could hardly contain himself as he asked if we would now like to have our landing clearance. We were not amused.

Some 20 years ago, the crew of a Boeing 727 cargo flight overflew Los Angeles, their destination, at cruise altitude. Clearances from traffic controllers to descend fell on deaf ears. Why? All three pilots had inadvertently fallen asleep.

They emerged from their stupor when about 100 miles out to sea and returned to land without further incident. The crew, however, was required to do a "rug dance" in their chief pilot's office and spend some "vacation" time on the "beach."

Such fatigue often is the result of airline pilots being scheduled by computers that do not comprehend human weaknesses and cannot sense when pilots have had enough.

The FAA apparently will be coming to the rescue of airline pilots who endure lengthy duty periods on the "backside of the clock" by offering pilots permission (and possibly encouragement) to nap enroute. This federal beneficence, however, probably will apply only to a three-pilot crew so that two pilots will be awake while the third is allowed to rest. In other words, the FAA is about to make honest pilots out of those who have always regarded a cruise snooze as a time-honored tradition.

But what about the lone general aviation pilot? When tired, his only (and best) option is to land and get his rest on the ground. Unfortunately, many of us feel compelled to push on at times when we should be in bed. According to the National Transportation Safety Board, pilots who drive themselves in this manner are involved in many more accidents than can be proven. This is because the physiological evidence often fails to survive the crash.

Accidents resulting from pilots falling asleep at the controls typically occur between 1800 and 0600. Unless accident investigators can somehow determine that the pilots were fatigued, the accidents usually are attributable to such otherwise mundane causes as "spatial disorientation" or "uncontrolled descent and flight into terrain." Investigators know intuitively but cannot prove that many inexplicable accidents are caused by pilots flying beyond their personal endurance limits.

Several years ago, a friend and I were flying a Beechcraft Debonair from New York to Los Angeles. We reluctantly opted to fly throughout the night because he had to be in L.A. the next evening for an important business meeting. Weather forced us to the southern route, and we found ourselves westbound over the Mississippi swamps at three hours past midnight.

We were between layers, and the world beyond the cockpit was black and featureless. I do not recall whose idea it was, but we turned off all aircraft lighting to see just how dark it really was.

It was as black as black can be. We saw nothing and lost all visual reference to time and space. But then something strange happened. Both of us began to hallucinate, a reaction, I was later told, that probably was the result of fatigue.

The cockpit was quickly full of hands grabbing for switches. We could not turn the lights back on soon enough.

Tired writers, I understand, also need to recognize when it is time to quit.

Section 5

Flying for Fun and Profit

There are many ways for a relatively new pilot to simultaneously build flying time and earn an income. The most common is to obtain a flight instructor certificate and pass on to others the joy of flight. Three enjoyable ways not often considered are banner towing, glider towing, and flying on skis. The following three chapters provide an introduction to these challenging activities.

Chapter 60 **Banner Towing**

Descending toward the poles and making an aerial pickup of the banner is the most challenging aspect of banner towing. And it is the most fun.

Banner towing is also hard work. A pilot flies for hours at a time at the low end of the speed spectrum and spends much of that time searching below for the shadows of nearby aircraft.

But for Linda J. Cannon, a banner-tow pilot from Palm Springs, California, and others like her, it is a labor of love. She says, however, that "banner towing is not for everyone." A tow pilot must be comfortable flying low and slow. It is a seat-of-the-pants operation that demands the willingness to work long and sometimes boring hours.

The banner-tow procedure begins with a normal takeoff (without the banner).

Shortly after liftoff, the pilot tosses a three-pronged grappling hook out the window. This hook is reminiscent of that used by knights of old to scale castle walls, and is attached to the end of a 30-foot cable. The other end of the cable is connected to a tow hitch installed at the bottom of the aircraft tailcone. (This hitch is the same as those used for towing gliders).

During the subsequent climb, the hook dangles behind and about 8 feet below the aircraft.

The pilot then heads for the clearing where the banner has been carefully laid out. He aims for a pair of poles that are 15 to 20 feet apart and resemble diminutive goalposts from a football field (except that there is no crossbar). These poles are used to elevate the loop of a nylon towline that is attached to the banner.

The idea is to descend toward the poles and grab the loop with the grappling hook. The descent and approach to the poles should be made in a stable attitude to maintain the hook in a fixed position relative to the aircraft. (If the nose of the aircraft bobs up, centrifugal force causes the hook to rotate farther below the aircraft; if the nose bobs down, the hook rises.) Airspeed during the approach to the pickup point typically is 10 to 20 percent greater than the best-rate-of-climb airspeed.

When only a few feet from and above the poles, the pilot applies full power and pulls up sharply into a very steep, maximum-effort climb. Rotation of the aircraft swings the hook down and into the pickup loop.

As the aircraft climbs, the hook engages the loop, pulls up on the tow-line, and peels the banner off the ground in the manner that one would normally remove a long Band-Aid. The aircraft nose is simultaneously lowered to maintain a safe airspeed as the drag of the banner is added to that of the aircraft.

If the banner is picked up properly, the pilot will not notice the addition of the banner and will have to look back to make sure that he did not miss the pickup. (The pilot usually does feel a tug or a jerk, however, if the initial climb is not sufficiently steep.)

A typical banner weighs 23 pounds, has 30 letters, and is more than 100 feet long. This includes a lead pole, or mast, that is weighted at the bottom to help keep the banner upright. A tail unit, which is essentially a small, vertical drogue chute, is attached to the end of the banner to prevent fluttering. The entire assembly usually trails 250 feet behind and 50 to 75 feet below the aircraft.

An important part of banner towing can be getting to a specific location at the right time. You cannot, however, get there very quickly.

A banner creates so much drag that an early edition Cessna 182, for example, which normally cruises at 135 knots, can barely achieve 80 knots in level flight with a banner in tow. (What a drag!) Nor would you want to go much faster. Gasser Banners of Nashville, Tennessee, the world's largest manufacturer and supplier of banner-tow equipment, says that the maximum recommended tow speed is 70 knots. Going faster can tear the nylon letters.

Towing typically is done at 55 to 60 knots. This is slow enough to prevent damaging the letters and usually fast enough to provide adequate engine cooling, positive control of the aircraft, and a comfortable margin above stall. Flying slowly also better exposes the banner's message to the intended audience.

Cannon uses 10 degrees of flaps while towing. This reduces stall speed and lowers the nose somewhat, which improves engine cooling and forward visibility.

She tows banners using a 180-hp Cessna 150 equipped with a STOL kit consisting of wing fences, leading-edge cuffs, and aileron gap seals. The aircraft also is equipped with an oil cooler (because so much time is spent at high power settings and low airspeed) and a pair of 20-gallon fuel tanks to extend range and accommodate the thirstier engine.

With a few exceptions, aircraft handling characteristics are not altered much by the addition of a banner. When you turn such an aircraft for the first time, however, you discover that the additional drag on the tail resists yaw and tries to keep the aircraft flying straight ahead. As a result, turn entry and recovery requires noticeably more rudder than usual to prevent slipping. The increase in drag also makes it easier to get behind the power curve. And stall recovery requires being more aggressive with power and pitch.

Cannon points out that "having to fly slowly with the nose up and with large power settings for an hour or two at a time can cause your right leg to throb from having to hold so much right rudder for so long."

Banner-tow pilots have to abide by the same minimum safe altitudes as do the rest of us. When towing along a shoreline, they usually fly 200 to 300 feet above the water (but at least 500 feet from people and property).

The banner is towed so that those on the left side of the aircraft can read the message. Those on the other side see the reverse image. "But this," says Cannon, "can be at least as effective. That's because those on the 'flip side' of a banner seem challenged and try harder to read the message.

"If you really want to learn the effect of aerial advertising," Cannon adds, "just make a spelling mistake."

Banners are normally towed so that the target viewer looks up at a 45-degree angle. Furthermore, an adjustable trim tab on the lead pole at the beginning of the banner tilts the banner 15 to 30 degrees toward the viewer, which makes the message easier to read.

The letters usually are 5 feet tall, but are also available in 3- and 7-foot sizes as well. The smaller ones create less drag and are used when flying low-powered aircraft. Although 7-foot letters create the most drag and require the most power, they also are the most legible. These are used when tow aircraft must remain farther than usual from the viewing area (such as when a NOTAM raises the minimum altitude over a Super Bowl game or a popular concert).

Although most aerial advertising consists of a single banner, lengthier messages can be flown using two or more aircraft flying in trail.

The substantial drag created by a banner in tow explains the need to jettison the banner in case of engine failure. Not to do so would result in a dramatic reduction in glide performance.

But if an engine failure occurs over water and a ditching is imminent, it probably would be wise to land with the banner attached. This is because dragging the banner through the water will help to prevent the aircraft from skipping on the water or flipping over. The banner should be detached, however, by pulling the tow-release handle in the cockpit before coming to a stop so that a sinking banner cannot drag the aircraft down.

Every once in a while, a banner-tow pilot picks up the banner with his landing gear instead of with the grappling hook. This usually is more embarrassing than dangerous. Although the assigned flight can be completed in this configuration, it would not be prudent to do so, because it would be impossible to jettison the banner in case of engine failure. With so much drag, the resultant forced landing could be hazardous.

Consequently, the aircraft should be landed as soon as practical. The approach should be relatively steep to keep the banner above the aircraft. Also, the flare should be delayed until very close to the ground because an aircraft decelerates quickly with a banner in tow. Finally, maximum braking is applied to minimize dragging and damaging the banner.

Normally, however, the pilot does not land with the banner attached. Instead, he passes 100 to 200 feet above the drop zone and detaches the banner (including the grappling hook) by pulling the tow-hitch release handle.

If the banner is released from too high an altitude, it will drift in a crosswind and possibly miss the drop zone. If the pilot flies too low and forgets that the banner normally trails well below the aircraft, he might drag the banner and damage the equipment.

The trick is to release with just enough altitude so that the banner slows and touches down without forward motion.

Dropping the banner and relieving the aircraft of its aerodynamic shackles causes the aircraft to surge forward with a sudden burst of energy. The improvement in performance is like being catapulted into the sky (especially when 180 horses are rocketing a lightly loaded Cessna 150 to pattern altitude).

Learning to tow requires instruction and a check-out by an experienced banner-tow pilot and a Certificate of Waiver from the FAA. According to the Federal Aviation Regulations, this certificate, which must be renewed annually, allows the pilot to tow something other than a glider, and must be renewed annually. Also, towing is allowed only between sunrise and sunset.

It is estimated that the average person in the United States is inundated by 625 advertisements every day. Banner-tow messages, however, generally are among the most pleasant, and are remnants of aviation's heritage.

Chapter 61 **Towing Gliders**

For all of recorded history, man has envied and aspired to emulate the birds. The closest he has come is to soar among them on the quiet wings of a sailplane.

Flying gliders has been a personal passion ever since I first flew a Pratt-Reed PR-G1 in 1957. If it were practical, and if I were appointed czar of aviation, I would mandate that all pilots take their first lessons in a sailplane. Without the masking effects of power, there is no better way to learn the fundamentals.

Most sailplane flights in the United States begin with an aero tow. This involves attaching one end of an approximately 200-foot-long polypropylene towline to the nose of the sailplane and the other end to an approved hitch on the tail of a tow plane. After that, the sailplane is towed aloft and flown in formation behind the tug, until the glider pilot opts to pull the release knob and free himself from the umbilical cord.

After almost 40 years of soaring, I began to realize that I had always taken the tow plane and its pilot for granted. It was time, I thought, to see what life was like at the front end of a towline. This was during one of my frequent visits to Soar Hawaii, the largest soaring school in the state and the only one that rents modern gliders. It is located at Dillingham Airfield on the northwest tip of Oahu, where ridge soaring conditions are so reliable (because of the trade winds) that soaring enthusiasts are attracted from all over the world.

Elmer Udd, a 37,000-hour, retired Northwest Airlines' Boeing 747 captain, owns and operates Soar Hawaii and consented to teach me the ropes (no pun intended) of being a tow pilot. He has made "tens of thousands of glider tows" (as many as 85 in one day) and was superbly qualified for the job at hand. (A tow pilot obviously gets to make lots of takeoffs and landings.)

Most tow planes are taildraggers. They are more maneuverable on the ground and cope best with the rough strips from which glider operations often are conducted. Also, the rudder of a taildragger usually is more effective than the rudders of other airplanes. This makes it easier to maintain heading when the glider slides toward one side of the in-trail formation and pulls the tail of the tow plane in the same direction. One disadvantage of a taildragger is that it is possible for the towline to become entangled in the tailwheel during ground operations.

Soar Hawaii's tow planes are 1951 Cessna L-19 Bird Dogs powered by Teledyne Continental O-470-11, 213-hp engines.

Udd began my training by emphasizing that the tow pilot is in command of the formation as long as the two aircraft are tied together. He also is responsible for the condition of the towline.

When taxiing toward a sailplane, the tow pilot must remember that he is dragging a long towline and be careful not to snag something with it.

After the line has been attached to the sailplane, the tow pilot taxis slowly away to remove the slack and straighten the rope. If he taxis too far or too fast, however, he risks jerking the sailplane.

Traffic approaching to land is a greater hazard than usual. This is because once the tow pilot is lined up on the runway for takeoff, he cannot easily look behind for aircraft on final approach. The best procedure is have a ground crewman available to signal the tow pilot when it is safe to depart.

Before takeoff and to avoid disaster, the tow pilot should look aft and determine that the spoilers on the sailplane are retracted (in most cases), that the glider's canopy is closed, that no one is in front of the glider, and that the glider pilot signals his readiness for flight by fanning his rudder. (This purposeful rudder movement also proves to the tow pilot that there really is a pilot aboard the sailplane; yes, unmanned gliders have been towed aloft.)

Glider drag and weight limit takeoff acceleration and yaw control of the tow plane somewhat, but there still is enough rudder authority to maintain directional control (provided the glider pilot maintains a position directly behind the tow plane). The good news is that the pull of the tow rope makes it almost impossible to lose directional control of the taildragger during takeoff.

Because of its lower stall speed, the sailplane will lift off before the tow plane, and this represents one of the most hazardous moments of an aero tow. If the glider pilot allows his aircraft to begin climbing, the towline will hoist the tail of the tug and could prevent the tow pilot from taking off. (If the tug's tail is raised high enough, the propeller can be made to buzz-saw the runway.) If the tow pilot is unable to become airborne, he has no alternative but to pull the tow-release mechanism in his cockpit and set the glider free. The tow pilot should continue with the takeoff and get out of the glider's way, because the glider pilot will have no option but to land straight ahead.

If the tow pilot encounters a problem with his airplane during takeoff and is forced to abort, he should release the glider and veer left, which gives the glider pilot room on the right side of the runway to roll past the tug and brake to a halt.

If the towline breaks during the takeoff roll, the airplane should continue the takeoff and yield the entire runway to the glider pilot.

After liftoff, the glider pilot should fly no more than five feet above the runway until after the tug is airborne. He must concentrate on staying immediately behind the tug. If the glider drifts to one side, this will pull the tow plane's tail in the same direction and create directional difficulties for the tow pilot.

The tow pilot usually stays in ground effect after liftoff until reaching climb speed. Otherwise, the drag of the glider can make it difficult to accelerate, especially at high density altitudes. (Tow speed varies from 50 knots for a trainer to 70 knots or more for a high-performance sailplane loaded with ballast.)

Should a rope break occur when less than 200 feet AGL, the glider pilot will land straight ahead (on or off the airport). If the break occurs above 200 feet, he probably will turn around and land downwind. If above 400 feet, he has enough altitude to fly an abbreviated traffic pattern and land into the wind.

During climb, the glider pilot flies in either the high-tow position (above the propwash of the tow plane) or the low-tow position (below the propwash). Tow pilots generally prefer that the glider pilot maintain a "high tow," because this makes it easier for them to see the sailplane in the rear view mirror. Glider pilots also prefer a high tow. If the rope breaks, that portion remaining attached to the tug will fall safely below the glider.

Considerate sailplane pilots fly slightly left of the tug's tail to apply a slight right yaw to the tow plane. This relieves the tow pilot of having to hold right rudder throughout climb and is most appreciated. If the glider is flown too far left, however, the tow pilot must apply left rudder during climb to maintain heading, which is opposite to normal rudder application and feels very strange.

Unless arrangements have been made to the contrary, the tow pilot should keep the sailplane within gliding range of the airport throughout the climb. Extended tows usually are made upwind of the airport to facilitate the glider's return for landing. When beyond gliding distance of the airport, the tow pilot should alter course as necessary to keep the glider near an area where a safe forced landing could be made.

Towing in turbulence is a physical workout. The sailplane, especially when flown by a student, yanks the tug's tail every which way. Should the sailplane pilot get so far out of position that he loses sight of the tow plane, he is instructed to immediately release from the tow to reduce the potential for a midair collision. Also, if the glider gets too high while being towed, it can force the tow plane into a dive.

One consequence of turbulence can be a slack rope at which time the glider might begin to catch up with the tow plane. The sailplane pilot corrects this problem by turning slightly toward one side of the formation until the rope begins to straighten. To prevent the rope from jerking both aircraft (or breaking) as it becomes taut, the sailplane pilot simultaneously yaws his aircraft toward the tail of the tow plane and lowers his nose slightly, which softens restoration of tension on the line. (Another way to take up slack is to deploy the spoilers or induce a gentle slip or skid.)

Slack ropes are more of a problem when towing a sailplane in level flight, such as when towing cross-country. The sailplane is much "cleaner" and tends to catch up with the tow plane. Slight deployment of the glider's spoilers at such a time creates the extra drag needed to keep the towline taut.

Sailplane pilots are required to know how to "box the wake" (fly a rectangular pattern in the smooth air outside the tow plane's wake) and occasionally practice this proficiency maneuver during tow. The sailplane pilot transitions into a low tow, slides left, for example, pulls up, slides right, and so forth. After completing the box, the glider pilot returns to the high-tow position. To prevent his tail from being pulled in all directions, the tow pilot must constantly compensate by applying appropriate rudder and elevator pressure throughout the maneuver.

It is helpful if the tow pilot also is a sailplane pilot and knows where to find rising air ("lift"), because this helps the formation to climb more rapidly.

Ultimately, the glider pilot pulls the release knob in his cockpit and leaves the formation. It is natural to assume that the tow pilot would notice the release by a sudden surge in performance, but he might not notice this at all (depending on the amount of towline tension at the instant of release). After visually confirming that the sailplane has released, the tow pilot usually descends to the left, while the sailplane pilot turns right to eliminate the possibility of a midair collision.

In rare instances, a glider pilot might not be able to release from the tow because of a faulty mechanism. In such a case, he will move to the right and rock his wings. This signals the tow pilot to fly toward a safe area and pull his release to give the glider its freedom.

In the rarer instance when neither pilot can release, the glider pilot will move to a low-tow position beneath the tug's wake in preparation for a formation landing. This maneuver is not as difficult as it might seem and is practiced by new glider pilots. The tow pilot, however, must land far enough down the runway to give the sailplane pilot (who is below the tug and will land first) plenty of room to touch down on the runway and not before it.

After landing, the glider pilot applies brake pressure to slow both aircraft. This prevents the glider from catching up with and passing the tow plane, which could force the tug into a ground loop.

Following a normal release at altitude, one of a tow pilot's major concerns is shock-cooling the engine. Slow climbs and rapid, power-off descents are not conducive to powerplant longevity. The key is to reduce power only partially until the cylinder head temperature cools to some established value. Although Soar Hawaii has experienced a few scored and cracked cylinders as a result of shock-cooling, Udd claims that he still gets about 2,000 hours out of each engine. This, he says, probably is because he and his pilots are careful not to reduce power too rapidly at the top of climb, and because the airplanes are flown so frequently.

In some cases, the tow pilot overflies the runway and drops the rope, whereupon it is retrieved by someone on the ground. Although this is the best way to preserve a towline, many operators prefer landing with the towline attached, because this reduces turnaround time on the ground.

When landing with the towline attached, the pilot must approach high enough to prevent the rope (which dangles 50 feet or so below the tow plane) from snagging something in the runway threshold and grabbing the pilot's attention.

Becoming a tow pilot is not a simple matter of hopping in a tug and taking off. The regulations mandate specific training and a logbook endorsement by a glider instructor.

Being a tow pilot means working outdoors ("working" is the operative word here), meeting great people, building flying time, and earning a few (very few) dollars in the process. For some, it can be an enjoyable and challenging way to begin a career as a professional pilot.

Chapter 62 **Flying on Skis**

Flying offers a large array of sensuous, aesthetic experiences. One of the most gratifying is a landing so smooth that the moment of touchdown cannot be detected. It is so elusive that most pilots never experience the smug satisfaction it can bring. The perfect touchdown, however, probably is more a matter of luck than skill.

Seaplane pilots, then, must be a bit luckier than most of us. Sliding a pair of floats onto a mirror-like surface of glassy water does occasionally result in a velvety touchdown.

But those who fly skis may be the luckiest of all. They are rewarded with the exhilaration of a near-perfect landing almost every time they glide onto a powdery blanket of virgin snow.

Skiplanes, of course, are conventional airplanes equipped with skis. The largest is the Lockheed Hercules, and there was a time when DC-3 skiplanes were a common sight in the winter skies at high latitudes. Almost any kind of an airplane can be converted to skis except those without either a steerable tailwheel or nosewheel. (Differential braking obviously is of little value on a skiplane.)

Early skis were made of wood but were relatively heavy. Most modern skis are constructed of aluminum and steel alloy. A small number are made of fiberglass, but these are heavier than aluminum and more susceptible to damage.

There are two basic types of skis: plain and combination units. Plain skis replace all three wheels and are used exclusively for operating from snow or ice. Taildragger operators, however, often do not replace their tailwheels except when planning to operate on soft, deep snow.

An older style of plain ski clamps onto the main tires and takes advantage of the shock-absorbing nature of air-filled tires. Although they can be installed or removed in only a few minutes, clamp-on skis never became popular. This is because they can tear a tire from its rim when landing in a crab or turning sharply with low tire pressure.

Combination wheel-skis are to a skiplane what amphibious floats are to a seaplane. They offer a pilot the option of using skis or wheels, depending on the surface. When using a clean, dry runway, the skis are retracted (or raised) so that the wheels extend beneath the skis, or the skis can be lowered for use on snow.

Another version of the wheel ski is the wheel-through, or penetration wheel-ski. In this configuration, the skis and wheels are fixed in position; the skis cannot be raised or lowered. Instead, the tires always extend slightly below the skis. This compromise provides adequate ground clearance of the skis for landing on dry runways and plenty of ski surface for landing on snow. The disadvantage of penetration skis is that tires extending beneath the skis add drag and increase takeoff distances when operating on snow.

Exchanging wheels for plain skis does not noticeably affect aircraft performance. This is because plain skis do not create more drag or add more weight than the wheels they replace.

Combination wheel-skis, however, do increase empty weight and drag. For example, they add about 120 pounds to a Piper Super Cub and 175 pounds to a Cessna 185. (Wheel-penetration skis weigh about 25 percent less because they lack hydraulic systems.) Wheel-skis typically reduce climb performance, airspeed, and range by 5 to 10 percent.

One of the significant differences between operating on skis and wheels becomes obvious as soon as you start the engine. Skiplanes obviously do not have brakes (when operating on skis), which means that the aircraft should be headed in a safe direction and the pilot should be prepared to taxi as soon as the engine starts.

This explains why some pilots leave their aircraft tied down during engine start and runup. (Otherwise, the before-takeoff checklist is performed "on the go.") A second person unties the aircraft when the pilot is ready to taxi and no traffic is in the way.

Skiplane operations obviously include many problems associated with winter flying. For example, cold-soaked batteries can be too weak to operate the starter. (This explains why bush pilots have been known to take their batteries to bed with them.) If someone volunteers to hand-start the engine, be certain that he is on firm ground and that the aircraft is tied down.

The only braking available to a skiplane pilot is provided by ski drag and wind. This means that taxi speeds should be held in check. Operating on a slick surface can be difficult, especially in a strong crosswind, which can force the aircraft to slide sideways and behave like an overgrown weathervane.

Taxiing turns are wider in skiplanes and should be kept to a minimum (especially on slippery surfaces). There are two tricks of the trade that can be used to tighten turn radius. When the aircraft is equipped with wheel-skis (instead of plain skis), raising one ski lowers its respective wheel into the snow and adds drag on that side. The effect is similar to using a small amount of differential braking.

Another way to reduce turn radius in taildraggers is to approach the turn slowly, almost at a crawl. When the turn must be made, simultaneously apply full forward elevator, kick full rudder, and add a burst of power to blast some prop-wash across the tail. The aircraft will pivot in the direction of applied rudder if enough power is used to lift the tail off the ground.

This technique obviously is only for experienced ski pilots. If the power burst is applied too long, the aircraft might pick up too much speed. Or if the maneuver is performed too aggressively, the tail might get too high and force the propeller into the ground.

When departing from other than a regular runway, a pilot might consider taxiing along the intended takeoff path to check for obstacles such as frozen snow mounds, ice hummocks, cracked ice, and so forth. Be cautious also about slush and deep or wet snow, which can substantially increase takeoff distance.

There is nothing unusual about a normal takeoff on skis except that a soft-field procedure is the rule rather than the exception; skiplanes do not have the benefit of tires to serve as shock absorbers. The tail-low attitude allows the wings to begin supporting aircraft weight early in the roll, which relieves the load on the skis.

Taildraggers usually have the best takeoff performance. This is because a nose ski tends to dig into the snow and hinder acceleration. Also, a ski in front creates more drag in flight than either a tailwheel or the smaller tail ski.

Once airborne over snow-covered terrain, the ski pilot has a seemingly unlimited choice of landing sites. Every carpet of fresh-fallen snow invites the kiss of a ski. And because he is not restricted by runway direction, a skiplane pilot can land in any direction and almost always into the wind.

But there is more to it than finding a clear spot and landing there. It takes experience to gauge landing conditions from the air. For example, a frozen lake frosted with snow may look inviting but instead consist of rough ice camouflaged by a thin layer of snow. Sticky or deep snow can have the consistency of molasses. Ice with a yellow tint might indicate slush; gray patches on white snow might indicate water beneath the snow; and white ice on a lake might be dangerously thin. (The thought of landing on thin ice and sinking into frigid water is one of a skiplane pilot's worst nightmares.)

Here are some additional suggestions:

1. Avoid landing on slush because it cannot support the aircraft;
2. When landing on a frozen lake, the smoothest snow usually is near the lee shore;
3. Avoid landing on areas of a river where the current is strong because this often prevents sufficiently thick ice from forming;
4. When landing on a slick surface, do so directly into the wind (if practical) and as slowly as possible; and
5. Consider that you can land safely in snow so soft and deep that it might not be possible to take off. Although skis usually support the weight of an airplane in soft snow, the pilot might not be so lucky. Some deplaning pilots have sunk from view, which explains why snowshoes often are standard equipment.

When doubtful about surface conditions, consider making a high-speed, touch-and-go landing without allowing the full weight of the aircraft to settle onto the skis. Then return over the area to inspect the tracks. If they have filled with water, land elsewhere.

Skiplane landings are relatively conventional, but slippery surfaces and strong crosswinds may be an unacceptable combination.

Landing without brakes can be exciting, which explains why it is important to select runways with plenty of room for a rollout. One "braking" technique involves holding the stick fully aft (in a taildragger) or forward (in a trike) to create resistance by forcing the steering ski into the snow. A pilot landing an aircraft with wheel-skis can raise the skis slightly to take advantage of the drag created when the tires extend beneath the skis and into the snow.

Conversely, when landing on wet or deep snow, power might be required to keep the aircraft moving after touchdown. Do not allow the aircraft to stop until reaching the tiedown spot. If the aircraft stops too soon, the skis might "lock" in position such that further movement is impossible, even when applying full throttle. Wet snow can be very sticky. (Snow conditions generally improve with lowering temperatures.)

Oh, yes—one further and very important point. When landing uphill on a relatively slick surface, be sure to turn the aircraft sideways before stopping. Otherwise, you can expect it to begin schussing backwards uncontrollably.

The frictional heat created when skis slide along snow or ice can produce a film of slush under the skis. If the slush freezes after the aircraft is parked, the skis can freeze in position and prevent the aircraft from moving.

If this "freeze-down" occurs, rock the wings gently to loosen one ski at a time. If that does not work, you might have to use tools to dig out and free the skis.

Another technique involves shoveling snow from under the front half of the skis. This might allow the aircraft to tip downhill and be taxied away from its parking spot. Or it might be necessary to use substantial engine power and left rudder (in the same direction as p-effect) to help twist the aircraft out of its dilemma. In extreme conditions, full power may be insufficient to move the airplane.

Once the aircraft begins to move, consider that frozen slush under the skis can create so much drag that a subsequent takeoff might be impossible. Contaminated skis should be cleaned before takeoff.

Preventing freeze-down is preferable to coping with it. This can be done by placing boards or small tree branches under the skis before tieing down. Better yet, use skis that have bottoms laminated with high-density polyethylene, which—like Teflon—resists sticking to anything.

At winter's end, skis give way to wheels or floats. Unlike seaplanes, however, a separate class rating is not required to fly skis. A pilot needs only a check-out by a competent instructor.

The versatility of snow skis causes some to wonder if airplanes could be equipped with water skis. Not likely, but this does not prevent some intrepid bush pilots from trying to land a skiplane on water. After literally touching down on a smooth lake, for example, they head for land so that—like water skiers coming ashore—they can beach the aircraft before losing too much speed and sinking.

Those who use skis to land on water probably are the same ones who also believe that they can walk on water.

Section 6

Special Treats

For many pilots, flying is a passion; the reason for soaring aloft is unto itself. Once in a rare while, however, we embark on an adventure that confirms our love of flight in a special and memorable way. I have had three such adventures that I would like to share with you. The first involves my first flight around the world; the second describes a flight of romanticized nostalgia; and the third... well, you'll see for yourself why such a flight can occur but only once in a lifetime.

Chapter 63 **The Ultimate Cross-Country: Around the World**

In the years since Neil Armstrong and Buzz Aldrin set foot on the moon, only 10 men have ever walked on an extraterrestrial surface. Each of these Apollo astronauts has been asked, at one time or another, to describe his most memorable lunar experience. You might expect the answers to include comments about exploring another world. But almost unanimously, their most cherished moments were those spent looking back across the blackness of space to see this world.

The world is smaller for astronauts and pilots than ordinary people make it out to be. I fly airliners for a living and lightplanes for fun. During my stints at work, I have looked down on places that only a few general aviation pilots will ever see and have encountered problems, humorous situations, and experiences that simply do not crop up on a cross-country between Dubuque and South Bend.

The farther afield we go, the more new and interesting countryside slides beneath our wings. So if you are inclined to wander, I invite you to join me as I take notes on a round-robin flight around the world, Los Angeles to Los Angeles.

This is the first leg of our 11-day flight. The course-deviation indicator points an electronic finger toward our first destination. Guam is a dot on the map, a fleck of land floating on the Pacific vastness. Far below, the puffy clouds are like sheep grazing on a boundless blue meadow. But ahead, the cumulus clouds grow tempestuously taller, confirming that our route coincides partially with the equatorial front, a cauldron of thunderstorms brewed by mixing moist tropical trade winds.

Because a mature thunderstorm contains more destructive energy than a nuclear bomb, it must be avoided. It seems inconceivable that more than 50,000 thunderstorms occur daily over the Earth—until you've flown the South Pacific. At times, almost all of them seem to challenge our right to the sky and necessitate the most serpentine flight path imaginable. This inevitably leads to a late arrival and an assortment of complaints from passengers. (One of my pet peeves is that passengers judge an airline crew's performance only by the timeliness of arrival and the smoothness of the landing. Seldom considered is the skill we might have used to sidestep hazards along the way.)

Not long ago, airliners were led across the oceans of the world by navigators who used sextants to "shoot" the stars in the mystical manner of ancient mariners. Today, we depend on inertial navigation and global positioning systems that are similar to those used to guide intercontinental missiles. On this flight, these electronic computers advise that a strong headwind has dramatically slowed our progress, adding to the deceiving effect of slow motion at high altitude. We are suspended in ethereal blackness where nothing seems to move except the fuel gauges.

A patch of turbulence, a change in outside temperature, an increase in groundspeed—these indicate that the jet stream, a meandering river of high-velocity winds, has tired of pushing against us and has veered north to perpetrate its folly elsewhere. And it really is cold outside, dangerously close to the fuel-freeze point of -100°F. A lower, warmer attitude is requested from the air traffic controller in Hawaii, and we discuss with renewed amazement the incongruity that the coldest temperatures in the atmosphere occur above the South Pacific.

Sunday evening suddenly becomes Monday evening. We have crossed the International Date Line, a line on the chart drawn to pacify man's obsession for order and definition. A passenger sends a note to the cockpit, announcing with mock disappointment that he's been cheated out of his birthday. We respond unsympathetically, advising that he should have caught an eastbound flight and celebrated his birthday twice.

Our shadow streaks south of wishbone-shaped Wake Island, a 4.5-mile-long atoll that became a base for Pan American Airways' China Clippers in 1935; they couldn't carry enough fuel to cross the Pacific nonstop. Today, the island is governed by the FAA, and those learning to fly there are not required to make cross-country flights. The closest airport is on Eniwetok, which is 600 miles south.

Below, the cumulus clouds continue to drift behind with metronomic regularity, casting shadows on the water that resemble small islands. This makes us wonder how many flight-weary pilots might have unwittingly descended to a shadow thinking that it was an island.

The Pacific's immensity is monotonous. More clouds, more water, more sky. Because an automatic pilot flies an airplane more efficiently and smoothly than can human hands, it usually is assigned the task of maintaining heading and altitude. When everything functions properly, we have little to do except monitor aircraft systems, make an occasional position report, and stare at the repetitious seascape.

Occasionally, the pilot of a nearby flight breaks the boredom by broadcasting risqué jokes on the air-to-air frequency. Occasionally, someone sings or even plays the harmonica. Although this abuse of the frequency might be illegal, such diversions rarely last more than a few minutes. And then each pilot returns to his personal bout with the "Pacific blues," a fatiguing form of boredom.

Those in the cabin also do strange things to break the monotony of a long flight. Yemenis have been known to start a campfire in an aisle to cook a meal. Other passengers accustomed to train travel have attempted to climb into overhead baggage compartments for a nap. And then there are the inevitable honeymooners who can't wait to consummate their marriage.

Below us, South Pacific islands are encircled in rings of turquoise and green where the water is shallow over the coral reefs. Approaching Guam, however, the water is a single shade of midnight blue. This island rises straight from the water, the tip of a 37,000-foot-tall oceanic mountain.

After a 25-hour layover, we prepare for the next leg of our global odyssey. The dispatcher adds another chart to the maze of preflight paperwork spread before us. It contains the last known position of every large surface vessel steaming in the vicinity of our route to Hong Kong as well as recommended ditch headings to use in the vicinity of each. Apparently, he is concerned about the possibility of a jetliner having to ditch in the Pacific. Although this has never happened, the thought of such a possibility gnaws at the psyche of every command pilot (especially now that twin-engine jetliners are routinely used for oceanic crossings.)

Our flight to Hong Kong will be via "Typhoon Alley," a nickname given to this region when Pacific hurricanes are on the rampage. It can be a severe-weather area, but neither it—nor any other part of the world—can be as vicious as "Tornado Alley" in the midwestern United States. I recall once flying inadvertently through an innocuous-looking Kansas rainshower not large enough to show on radar. It lifted the crew meal from my lap and slammed the tray against the instrument panel, obscuring several gauges with a gooey film of coq au vin.

Flying to Hong Kong, I review the published approach instructions for the Taiwanese capital of Taipei, an enroute stop. Numerous restrictions are imposed on arriving aircraft. According to reports, this is because some cunning aviators from the People's Republic of China once managed to land unnoticed at Taipei late one night and abscond with several aircraft belonging to the Nationalist Chinese Air Force.

Friends occasionally ask for my impressions of Taipei, and for countless other capitals of the world, as well. Although I have been to Taipei many times, I often am forced to admit that I can describe only the airport. For many of these places, I have never been in the country for more than an hour at a time, often in the dead of night.

While we taxi for takeoff at Taipei, a red light warns us to stop so that a military guard can verify that the aircraft registration number on our tail coincides with the one on the flight plan. If the two don't match, we will be escorted back to the terminal. The guard's machine gun—along with several anti-aircraft batteries surrounding the airport—convinces us that this is one red light we can't afford to run. The guard salutes respectfully and shines a green light, and we trundle to the runway.

We are soaring through placid valleys of white cotton candy, banking gently on occasion to follow the contours of an aerial fantasy land. Our wings are like outstretched arms and slice through soft cumulus castles. To a pilot, this exhilarating sense of speed and freedom is what flying is all about.

Still, a glance at the chart abruptly returns us to the stark reality of the world below. We have passed over Makung, a small island in the strait separating Taiwan and China, and are paralleling a buffer zone intended to protect the Chinese mainland against trespass by aircraft that have not been invited there. One notation on the chart informs us to be on the alert for erroneous radio signals from within China that could be hazardous to navigation. Another states that "any aircraft infringing upon the territorial rights of China may be fired upon without notice." We are reminded of Korean Airline's Flight 007 that was shot down by a Soviet fighter and slide somewhat farther away from the mainland.

Nearing Hong Kong, we lower the nose and prepare for the world's most unusual landing approach. At first blush, the approach instructions seem confusingly similar to the diagram of an Aresti aerobatic chart. Upon reaching the Cheung Chau radiobeacon, we descend through globs of nimbostratus cloud while flying a series of graceful figure eights, using the beacon as a pivot point. Inbound to the airport, we slip out of the soggy overcast and peer through an onslaught of heavy rain. We must now fly 15 miles at only 750 feet above the sea. Forward visibility is only a mile, but 12 miles ahead, the Stonecutters radiobeacon urges us to continue. We pass abreast of the tip of Hong Kong Island and enter Victoria Harbor, our screaming turbines seemingly unnoticed by those aboard the hundreds of junks below that plod and heel through windswept waters.

Crossing Kowloon Beach, we begin a gentle right turn, our eyes straining to see the aiming point, a large orange and white checkerboard on the side of a 300-foot-high hill near the approach end of Kai Tak Airport's Runway 13. Tall buildings below stretch for the sky, probing for our belly. The illuminated checkerboard appears like a target at 12 o'clock. We bank the aircraft right to avoid the hill and simultaneously descend toward manmade canyons and through torrents of turbulence. Wings level at 200 feet, we are at last lined up with the 8,000-foot-long concrete ribbon projecting into the harbor from Kowloon's east shore.

Hong Kong: a sweet and sour mixture of Chinese antiquity and modern British colonialism, a place where you can go broke saving money, where the brave can sip bird's-nest soup, a glutinous compound made from the saliva of birds.

On the ground, I take care of an essential chore: the purchase of a "survival kit." Not for an enroute emergency, this survival kit contains instead canned groceries to obviate my having to eat anything cooked or grown in Bombay, our next layover point. I have found that the food in India can incapacitate the delicate Western stomach with something certain to baffle the medical world. The water there makes Mexico's seem like vintage champagne. Anyone who insists on drinking tap water in India should first hold a glassful up to the light to see if anything inside returns the stare.

Now we are high above the South China Sea, listening to the high-frequency receiver on a channel normally used for air traffic control. But instead of traffic controllers, we hear the English edition of Radio Beijing's modern-day version of Tokyo Rose spewing her daily dose of political air pollution.

At times, navigation and communication difficulties occur over Southeast Asia. I recall once trying to communicate with Hong Kong Control, but the frequency was jammed for about 10 minutes with what seemed to be China's answer to Wolfman Jack. These problems seldom last long but are annoying. The Chinese invariably are blamed for them and anything else that goes wrong, even an aft toilet that won't flush.

The 115-mile flight across Vietnam takes only 13 minutes and begins over the coastal town of Qui Nhon, south of Da Nang, north of Ho Chi Minh City. Broad, vacant beaches of white sand characterize the scalloped coast and are most inviting. From our perch, Vietnam seems a paradise. But looking carefully, we still can see bomb craters, pockmarks on the face of the earth, on the face of man.

We sweep across the muddy, swollen Mekong River and then the rice-rich fields of Cambodia and Thailand as we prepare for an enroute stop. While approaching one of Bangkok's two parallel runways, I marvel at what lies between them: a golf course. Like the rabbits that dwell between the runways at Los Angeles, the golfers at Don Muang Airport must be stone deaf.

A few hours later, we are over the southern extremity of Myanmar (nee Burma), gazing at pagodas so large they are visible from 7 miles above. Ahead lies the 1,000-mile-wide Bay of Bengal and, on the other side, India.

We estimate landing in Bombay at 8 p.m. Greenwich Mean Time (GMT), which is 1:30 a.m. local time. Because Bombay is 5.5 hours ahead of Greenwich, we conclude that Indian leaders couldn't decide whether their country should be GMT plus five or six hours, so they compromised. But what form of logic was used by the Guyanese, who decided that their country should be 3 hours 45 minutes behind Greenwich? (Until recently, local time in Saudi Arabia was based on Arabic or solar time, which varied each day according to sunset.)

Forgive this preoccupation with the hour, but when crossing numerous time zones, it becomes a vital issue. Airline pilots live in constant psycho-physiological turmoil, trying to synchronize their body clocks with the sun. Passengers frequently ask what airline pilots do to cope with jet lag. The painful truth is that we can't do anything. Because a layover seldom is more than 24 hours long, our bodies do not have a chance to adapt to local time. I often find myself staring at the ceiling when in bed and falling asleep over lunch. Perhaps the Mongolians had the right idea. Until recently, their People's Republic had no legal time whatever.

Our weather radar screens display water and land in different colors, which enables us to identify uniquely shaped coastal regions. It now shows that we are passing south of the mouths of Burma's Irrawaddy River, and two hours later, we soar over Vishakhapatnam, a fishing village on India's east coast. Fortunately, we are not required to pronounce these strange names. Instead, each checkpoint is assigned a two- or three-letter identifier. In this case, we simply report passing over "Victor Zulu." Even more difficult to pronounce is Inoucdjouac, a beacon on the east coast of Hudson's Bay that is referred to as "Papa Hotel."

The lights of small towns passing below are like jewels scattered on black velvet. We begin our descent toward Bombay's Santa Cruz Airport, where holy cows are free to wander. The landing lights spike the blackness, and we pray that tonight there are no cows on the runway. Animals rarely necessitate our having to pull up and go around, but I recall once having to brake heavily during a landing in East Africa to avoid rolling into a family of wart hogs.

After passing through customs, we are confronted by a group of consummate beggars, pathetic, destitute children ranging in age from two to five. But we are prepared and pass out handfuls of candy to these scantily clad urchins.

Later, the crew bus rattles through unlit streets, weaving once to miss a toddler straying in the night. People are asleep in gutters, on sidewalks, and in doorways. An airline crew normally is a jovial group, but during this ride, we are in silent depression.

The unrelenting monsoon rains have begun their seasonal assault, dampening my spirits and adding fuel to my burning desire to leave. It is raining so heavily that it might be easier to swim from the terminal to the aircraft than to walk; any three raindrops would nearly fill a coffee cup. It is so hot and humid that unfolding the wilted charts in the cockpit requires the care used to unravel cooked spaghetti.

The runway lights have not survived the deluge and have been replaced by flare pots. As the aircraft gathers speed, the flickering candlelights become indistinguishable blurs. Visibility through the wall of rain is almost nil, and we curse the windshield wipers, which are more noisy than effective. Soon the wings flex, and we are airborne in a flying Noah's Ark.

Above the wet, lumpy cumulus, we sail on silken air beneath a canopy dotted with distant diamonds. We are strangers flying over foreign lands, but my celestial companions provide comforting familiarity. Polaris winks from starboard, and the Southern Cross watches from port.

The flight to Tel Aviv will take 6 hours 25 minutes, an hour and a half longer than would be necessary if the Middle East nations could coexist peacefully. Because our destination is in Israel, we must fly 850 miles out of the way to avoid neighbors unfriendly to Israel. In this part of the world, flight planning is determined more by the political climate than by winds and weather.

The flight engineer is balancing the fuel tanks and calculating the amount of fuel remaining while monitoring a special communications frequency, listening for news of any reported disturbances in the Middle East. On another receiver, we overhear an Air France pilot relaying a clearance in English from Tehran air traffic control to a Russian flight enroute from Moscow to Karachi, punctuating the camaraderie that exists between pilots of all nations.

We turn northward and fly an aerial tightrope over the narrow Red Sea. Passing between Egypt and Saudi Arabia, we stare upon a world seemingly uninhabited. It is difficult to appreciate the reality of global overpopulation. From our vantage point, it seems that most of the earth is untouched. Our topographical chart contains a proliferation of "UNSURVEYED" notations.

Approaching Israel from over the Mediterranean, we aim for the Shalom Tower, one of the tallest buildings in the Middle East, and pass over Tel Aviv, a sprawling coastal city that—from aloft—could be mistaken for Miami. Over the nose, however, we can see the Dead Sea and, beyond that, the mountainous spine of western Jordan.

The landing at Tel Aviv is routine, but to some Jewish passengers, the view is like seeing their newborn child for the first time. The touchdown on Israeli soil triggers cheers and applause that echo throughout the cabin, a spontaneous flood of emotion from people who have struggled for years—if not centuries—to make this moment possible. An elderly couple bolts from the aircraft and weeps without inhibition as they fall to their knees to kiss the cold tarmac.

Airline pilots hold that the most dangerous part of a flight is the drive to and from the airport. Nowhere in the world is this truer than in Israel. Israelis drive as if they were in Sherman tanks on the road to Beirut.

Later, our engines etch four contrails above the jagged coast of Greece, which lies fragmented at the base of the Balkan Peninsula like the ruins of an Athenian temple.

Flying in the Mediterranean can put Yankee patience to the supreme test. In Rome, for example, one American pilot, at the end of a long line of aircraft progressing slowly toward the departure runway, finally lost his patience. On the radio, he exhorted the tower controller with, "Can't you move this parade a little faster?" After a pause, the Italian controller announced calmly, "To all aircraft on the ground. Roma Tower going off the air." Traffic came to a halt, and further efforts to contact the tower were fruitless. Half an hour later, the controller keyed his mike and announced with marvelous one-upmanship, "All right, fellahs. Now tell me, who's the boss here?"

In central and northern Europe, the shoe is on the other foot, and controllers lose patience with pilots. It is difficult for a pilot to stay ahead of the game when the rules change every time a border is crossed, which is frequently. And just when you have become accustomed to the heavily accented English of one nationality, it is time to change to another. (Although all traffic controllers must communicate in English, the international language of aviation, most American pilots find the French controllers most difficult to understand.)

But a flight across Europe involves more than conforming to the dictates of regulation. It is sailing above a fairyland of castles, cultures, and contrasts. A glance in any direction finds a scene lifted from the pages of history.

London's Heathrow Airport is the busiest and often the foggiest in Europe. Fog here can be so thick that a pilot taxiing to the gate could get lost for hours. To solve this problem, the British have installed a guidance system. Working like the track switcher at a railroad yard, the Heathrow ground controller leads a pilot to his gate — or wherever else he needs to go — by turning on only the appropriate taxi lights.

We are about to take off on the last leg of our globe-girdling journey. The fuel tanks burgeon with fuel, and the wings sag noticeably under the load. Los Angeles is at the far end of a 6,000-mile-long great circle route across the roof of the world, an aerial Northwest Passage.

The throttles are advanced, and the aircraft accelerates slowly, demonstrating little apparent will to fly.

In the cabin, a veteran flight attendant sits in her jump seat facing the passengers and is accustomed to the necessarily long takeoff roll. Sensing passenger concern, she announces on the public-address system: "Ladies and gentlemen, you can help by lifting your feet." Obediently, hundreds of feet rise, and the aircraft pushes the ground away at nearly 200 mph.

We are over Scotland, heading northwest along the great circle route, leaving behind the spider web of European airways and the unceasing chatter of radio communications. Ahead is peace and quiet, the serenity of watching ice floes of brilliant white drifting in frigid black water. Here in the High Arctic, visibility is so unlimited that it hurts your eyes to look that far.

After crossing the Denmark Strait, we interrupt the cabin movies to point out the spectacle passing below: Greenland, the world's largest island with the most inappropriate name. Jagged peaks cast ragged shadows against the 2-mile-thick icecap. Glacial fingers of ice probe for the sea, grinding mountains that stand in their way, the same awesome, slow-motion process that carved the continents.

From above, the Arctic has a fearsome, almost inviting beauty, yet there is an incongruity here that makes flying above it most pleasant. These polar regions are vast deserts, characterized by light winds, low humidity, infrequent and thin cloudiness, and little rain or snow. Winds aloft seldom exceed 30 knots at any altitude. By contrast, a flight across the United States presents far greater problems: frontal systems, thunderstorms, tornadoes, strong winds, and considerable precipitation in all forms.

We cross the Davis Strait, aiming for Frobisher on Baffin Island in extreme northeastern Canada. As we approach the Magnetic North Pole, the magnetic compasses become unreliable and soon fluctuate wildly or point east when they should point west. Our long-range navigation systems fortunately provide accurate reference to true north.

Our track angles southwest, and Mount Rainier soon pokes its lofty head above the clouds, welcoming us home. Although it will take several days for us to recover from this 23,423-mile odyssey across 24 time zones, our aircraft has no such human frailties. Within a few hours and with a fresh crew, it will begin another flight around the world.

Chapter 64 **My Favorite Airplane**

We were flying low and in formation over the coastal hills east of Livermore, California, maneuvering for a camera in the warm light of a low sun.

Lengthening shadows began to fill the valleys and hide the few flat spots that could be used for an emergency landing. I was not thrilled about having to rely on an antique engine at such a time. My grip on the control stick tightened slightly, and I began to consider my options in case of power loss.

But then a strange thing happened. It was as if the airplane was trying to tell me something. I could almost hear the words. "When I taught you to fly so very long ago, I endured and forgave your ham-fisted blundering. It seemed as though you were trying to break both my back and my spirit. But I never let you down. Not once. I protected you from yourself more times than I can remember. Shame on you for thinking that I might betray you now."

The words were right. I knew that I could trust this airplane without reservation. I felt secure and comfortable as the bond between us renewed. My grip on the stick relaxed, and I needed only the tips of my fingers to lead the Champ through an aerial ballet in the disappearing rays of sunlight.

During the summer of 1992, I realized that in a few months I would complete my fourth decade of flight. I took my first lesson at Clover Field (now called Santa Monica Municipal Airport) at the age of 14 in an Aeronca 7AC Champion on November 7, 1952.

Not only did I receive my aerial baptism in N81881, but it also was the airplane in which I soloed and earned my private, commercial, and flight instructor certificates. But I learned the most about flying when the Champ and I taught others to fly.

I wondered if N81881 was still flying. Or had this number been passed unceremoniously to some other aircraft? Surely, I thought, the old trainer had yielded to the ravages of time. But a search of FAA records showed that the Champ had survived and was registered to James Bottorff of Livermore, California.

I contacted Bottorff to see if I could arrange to once again fly what undoubtedly has been the most meaningful and memorable aircraft of my career. What a wonderful way that would be to celebrate my fortieth anniversary aloft. To my delight, Bottorff agreed to let me fly his Champ. He even seemed to sense and share my excitement.

A hopeless romantic, I suffered some anxiety as I approached the Champ a few weeks later. It was as though I were about to rendezvous with my first love, fearing I would discover that the relationship was not as wondrous as the memories had made it seem.

N81881 was parked in front of Bottorff's hangar. Its door was open, leaning against the aft wing strut, as if inviting me to step in for a nostalgic rendezvous with the past. The Champ has aged more gracefully than I have. It had had four changes of fabric, at least as many paint jobs, and plenty of affectionate care.

The aircraft had undergone a few changes since the last time I flew it. These included removal of the wind-driven generator and the low-frequency radio, which had the broadcast range of a megaphone. These were replaced with a VHF transceiver powered by a rechargeable battery pack. Also added were wheelpants, a larger tailwheel, and an increase from 65 to 75 horsepower.

Bottorff is an architect working at the Lawrence Livermore National Laboratory. He had liked the idea of an affordable, fabric-covered taildragger with a control stick instead of a wheel. "It seems more like real flying," he said. Bottorff bought N81881 in May 1985.

He told me that one of the Champ's previous owners was Doren Bean, who also had kept the aircraft at Livermore. In 1980 and while still owner of the Champ, Bean borrowed a Pitts S-1 from his good friend, Jeff Chambliss. During his second flight in the Pitts, Bean had an accident and was killed.

During the subsequent investigation, the FAA determined that Bean did not have a pilot certificate. The San Joaquin County Sheriff's Department discovered also that Bean had some aliases. One of these was D. B. Cooper. Doren Bean, therefore, might have been the world's first skyjacker (who bailed out of a Northwest Orient Boeing 727 in 1971 with a $200,000 ransom). During a telephone interview, Chambliss told me that Bean had frequently mentioned his exploits as a skydiver, and this explains why many of the locals at Livermore are convinced that the infamous skyjacker played a minor role in the history of N81881.

The squatty, pug-nosed Aeronca Champ is neither glamorous nor distinctive. Its features are almost nondescript and resemble the typical rubber-band-powered model airplane found in hobby shops. Nor does it go very fast. Aeronca pilots must be content to match the pace of freeway traffic. But the Champ's leisurely stride is a refreshing escape from the frenetic pace of modern life.

Climbing aboard a Champ requires the agility of a contortionist, but once inside, the accommodations are comfortable.

But my mother, who was one of my first passengers, did not consider the Champ very comfortable. As I sat in N81881 at Livermore almost 40 years later, I could still hear her scream reverberating throughout the fabric-covered hull. "Stop tilting the airplane," she shrieked. I continued around the traffic pattern using the shallowest possible bank angle, but she would never again fly with me in a light airplane.

The instrument panel is Spartan, and few Champs are equipped with more than is required. The fuel gauge atop the glareshield is the same design used in the Model A Ford and occasionally allows fuel to leak into the cockpit. The solution is to replace the indicator with a floating cork-and-wire gauge.

That fuel gauge almost ended my flying career before it had begun. The smell of leaking fuel from the 13-gallon tank made me so airsick that I almost quit after my third lesson.

The Champ can be flown solo from the front or rear. Instructors, however, prefer the student in front, where he can see the instruments and get the best view of the outside world. The rear perch is the domain of the instructor. From there, he can bop an errant student on the noggin with a rolled-up chart.

I used to take advantage of the rear seat while instructing to sneak short naps on cross-country flights. After all, how far astray could a student get in 15 minutes at 74 knots?

According to a bulletin issued by the Aeronca Owners Club, "Cross-country flight in a Champ is slow but possible." If a Champ pilot becomes impatient when flying into a headwind, he simply turns around and heads the other way. It is understood that where we go is not as important as the fun we have in getting there. Champ pilots also become topographical experts. This is because the terrain beneath our wings moves so slowly that we have time to study what other pilots see only as a blur.

When the 7AC is flown solo from the front, 40 pounds of baggage may be carried in the canvas catch-all behind the rear seat. If the rear seat is occupied, only 20 pounds is allowed.

Starting the 65-hp Continental engine is easy as long as someone is available to hold the brakes while the prop is turned by hand (a device known as an Armstrong starter). The engine has no provision for an electrical starter, which is just as well. Most Champs do not have an electrical system either.

The on/off fuel valve, carburetor heat knob, and magneto switches are in a recessed panel on the left cabin sidewall below the window and between the tandem seats. These controls are easily accessible to the rear pilot, but the front pilot must crane his neck, twist his torso, and manipulate his double-jointed left arm to use them.

Most pilots accustomed only to tricycle landing gear have no difficulty taxiing a Champ. The steerable tailwheel responds nicely to rudder-pedal movement. Over-the-nose visibility is good, so that S-turning to see ahead is unnecessary. The Champ, however, is an outstanding weathervane and tends to turn into the slightest breeze.

I used to win a fair amount of money betting that I could taxi a Champ into a strong wind using only the ailerons for steering. I simply took advantage of the adverse yaw effect of the ailerons, which demonstrates why most airplanes need a rudder.

While taxiing into the wind, I would move the control stick full left. The seemingly contrary little Champ would turn right; full right stick caused it to go left. Using only adverse yaw effect, I could S-turn an Aeronca the full length of a mile-long taxiway.

The Champ's large ailerons also produce considerable adverse yaw in flight and require substantial rudder application. This trainer is intolerant of sloppy flying and demands adroit stick-and-rudder coordination to keep the slip-skid ball under control.

The mechanical brake system obviously was designed by a sadist who disregarded the limited dexterity of the human ankle. Operating the two heel brakes requires resting the balls of the feet on the rudder bars. Next, the heels are brought together until cocked at 45-degree angles. The pilot then jabs at the plywood floor with his heels until they find the tiny brake pedals (which are barely larger than postage stamps). The brakes are not very effective and should be used only at low speed or when out of other ideas.

The parking brake handle is under the right side of the instrument panel but should not be used because it never works. Immediately above that is the cabin-heat control. I learned never to pull this out completely because the heat is so highly concentrated that it would broil my right foot while the rest of me froze.

The takeoff is relatively easy for a taildragger. Cruise altitude, however, is reached in far less time than is required of more powerful aircraft. This is because Aeroncas are not flown very high. The advertised climb rate of 500 fpm is incredibly optimistic (300 fpm is more like it), but the angle of climb is surprisingly steep (because of the low forward speed).

Aloft, the Champ is as docile and forgiving as any pilot of the late 1940s could expect. The ailerons are heavy, though, and, when deflected during a stall, can induce an unexpected spin. Also, the Champ is slightly deficient in nose-up trim when the rear seat is empty. Otherwise, it is a delightful aerial playmate.

Aeronca never published a pilot's operating handbook for the 7AC, but the pertinent number seems to get passed along from one pilot to the next: Climb and glide at 52 knots. If the airspeed indicator seems in error, which it usually is, just fly a comfortable attitude.

Steep turns at Aeronca speeds are remarkable. The Champ can pivot around a pylon in only 10 seconds when in a 60-degree bank, which is impossible in faster machines.

The Champ does not have flaps, but because of large and effective control surfaces, it can be slipped from the sky more dramatically and steeply than modern airplanes being slipped with flaps extended.

Anyone who claims that flying has to be expensive has not been introduced to Aeronca economics. The Champ is inexpensive to buy and fly. A refurbished 7AC with new fabric, new paint, and a low-time engine can be purchased for less than the price of a medium-priced automobile and sips only 3.5 gallons of fuel per hour during cruise. Depreciation? There is none. Aeroncas probably will continue to increase in value as they have for the past 20 years.

When I brought the Champ to rest at the end of our flight together, I turned off the mags and watched the wooden propeller tick to a stop as I had so many times before. Memories continued to rattle around like pennies in a drum. I closed my eyes, leaned my head back, and remembered with fondness many of the students we had taught to fly, and with relief, many of the mistakes I had somehow survived.

No other airplane taught me as much or as well about flying.

No other airplane ever will.

Chapter 65 **My Favorite Flight**

I don't know what time it was, but I will never forget the date: August 27, 1991. We were flying on the back side of the clock over the middle of the North Atlantic at Flight Level 370, enroute from New York to Berlin, Germany.

The radios of our Lockheed 1011 were silent. It was one of those peaceful moments when the mind begins to drift. I recall staring out the left cockpit window, gazing at those friendly pinpoints of light dotting the celestial dome. They are my compatriots of the night sky that accompany me wherever in the world I wander.

It was one of those times when a pilot's eyelids tend to become heavy.

My head might have begun to bob a bit, but only for a few seconds. I was stunned back to reality by the sting of a rolled-up newspaper used by the flight engineer to swat me on the back of the head.

The young man blurted, "Sleeping is not allowed on the flight deck!"

The first officer, Bob McLoskey, was not surprised by such disrespectful and mutinous behavior. That is because the engineer was my son, Brian. This was our first flight as crewmembers on the same TWA flight.

Brian had come a long way since I had taught him to fly in the family Citabria. And no father could have been prouder. It brought a tear to the eye, a tear that I was careful to hide.

Brian's addiction to flying apparently was born before he was. This is because his mother, Sandy, was not content to sit at home knitting booties while pregnant with Brian. Instead, she busied herself learning to fly. I was her instructor.

But Sandy encountered a road block. The doctor was uncertain about approving a woman in her ninth month of pregnancy for a medical certificate. The FAA, however, unexpectedly came to the rescue by declaring that "being pregnant is a normal, healthy condition and not a basis for denial."

Sandy soloed the next day. Or did she? Local "hangar lawyers" asserted that she did not solo because she had carried a passenger. That may be true. After all, Brian did make her flight safer. His "presence" made it impossible for his mother to bring the control wheel far enough aft to stall the Cessna 150 (intentionally or otherwise).

Brian was born a few weeks later, on September 8, 1967, and almost immediately embarked on an aeronautical career. It began with crayon drawings of TWA airplanes. (Thankfully, I still have one.) He couldn't wait for me to come home from my flights so that he could grab my captain's hat and run around the house pretending to be a TWA pilot. He cut out and saved TWA advertisements from newspapers and magazines. He made models of TWA airliners.

But we knew that this passion wouldn't last. We knew that he would grow out of it (or so we believed).

On that flight to Berlin, I occasionally found myself looking back at Brian. He would be hunched over his small engineer's table making fuel calculations or entering engine data in the aircraft log or reading a company bulletin.

He turned around once and caught me looking his way. I pretended to be checking something on his panel, but he knew better. And I knew that he knew. We smiled at each other. Without saying a word, I was telling him, Son, I am proud of who you are, what you have accomplished, and where you are going. Brian's smile said thanks for helping me get here. These were thumbs-up smiles filled with love.

This was the passing of the baton, a highlight of my career, of my life.

I turned away, misty eyed. It was a time to reflect upon my own beginnings.

My first exposure to aviation occurred 13 years after I was born. My parents shipped me from Los Angeles to spend the summer with my grandparents in New Jersey. And so it was that a North American Airlines DC-6 whisked me in the dead of night from Burbank, California, to Wichita, Kansas, to Chicago's Midway Airport to New York's LaGuardia. It was my first flight ever.

During the journey, I kept staring at the left wing. There it was, this huge iron thing that seemed like the outstretched arm of some giant predator. Noisy, too. And blue fire streaked from the engines bolted onto its leading edge. And those iron wings didn't move. They didn't seem to do anything. No flapping, no nothing. I couldn't understand how they managed to keep the beast in the air.

Curiosity drew me to the library in that little New Jersey town (partly because there was little else to do except throw eggs at the chickens running around my grandmother's back yard). There, I encountered those words now so familiar. Bernoulli. Venturi. Airfoil. Camber. It was so beautiful, so elegant. The wing did so much work—without really doing anything.

After returning home, I headed straight for the local airport, a place called Clover Field, now known as Santa Monica Municipal Airport. I desperately wanted a ride in one of those little airplanes. Any one would do. I wanted to look at the wing in flight with the smug awareness of what it was doing. I wanted to visualize the air caressing the curvaceous upper surface.

Not knowing better, I stood at the edge of a taxiway and tried to hitch a ride. Really. Thumb out. A pleading look on my face. A begging look.

I got kicked off the airport three times before I learned how to hitch a ride without getting caught. My first was in a Bonanza, an original one with a small engine. There was a painting of a glass of beer and a shot of whiskey on the side of the fuselage. That was because the owner of the Bonanza, Ed Grant, was in the business of making boilers. The whiskey and the beer together made what bartenders call a boilermaker.

The flight was infectious, addictive. I knew immediately that I would become a pilot. Flying was to become the most passionate and compelling aspiration of my life. It was Ed Grant's passion, too, but it killed him. Boilermaker's engine caught fire one day, and he couldn't get it down in time.

My first aviation job came within months of my Bonanza flight. It involved painting the men's room at Bell Air Service, a local flight school. The toilet there faced a wall that was uncomfortably close to your knees when you sat down. It was almost claustrophobic. But it was the perfect reading distance. So I glued a poster containing airport regulations to that wall so that everyone who sat there—having nothing better to do—would learn the local rules. This was my first attempt at instructing, and it apparently went over pretty well. Somebody did the same thing in the ladies' room.

My TWA career began in 1964 as a first officer flying Lockheed Constellations. Those were exciting times. It was when people went to an airport hoping to witness a Connie or a DC-7 crank up, belch smoke, and come to life. It was when people dressed up for an airline flight. Flying was an adventure, not a bus ride.

TWA hired Brian in 1989, a quarter-century later, as a flight engineer on a Boeing 727. His career will not be the same as mine; times have changed. But it still will be rewarding and gratifying, as mine has been. His first flight as captain of a jetliner will be as memorable as when he first soloed our Citabria on his sixteenth birthday. His first command flight to the other side of the world will be as cherished a memory as his first solo cross-country up the coast to Santa Barbara.

He will continue to be awed by a world of experiences and sensations about which ordinary people only dream and which forms the bond that unites all airmen, especially when they are father and son.

Index

by Robert Sacks

Boldface *page numbers refer to figures.*

The Proficient Pilot, Volume 1
Contents

The Proficient Pilot, Volume 2
Contents

About the Author

Barry Schiff, with more than 25,000 hours in 250 types of aircraft, has received worldwide recognition for his wide-ranging accomplishments. He was a rated Airline Transport Pilot at 21, and has earned every FAA category and class rating (except airship) and every possible instructor's rating. As a 34-year veteran of Trans World Airlines, he currently flies the Lockheed 1011. Captain Schiff holds five world speed records (one captured from the Soviet Union) and has received numerous honors for his many contributions to aviation safety. These include a Congressional Commendation, the Louis Blériot Air Medal (France), Switzerland's Gold Proficiency Medal, an honorary doctorate in aeronautical science, and AOPA's L. P. Sharples Perpetual Award.

An award-winning journalist and author, he is well known to flying audiences for his numerous books and 1,000 articles published in some 90 aviation periodicals, notably *AOPA Pilot*, of which he is a contributing editor. Many of his articles discuss personally developed concepts, procedures, and techniques that have received international acclaim. Schiff also developed and worked to have adopted the concept of providing general aviation pilots with safe VFR routes through high-density airspace.

These credentials have not diminished his passion for flying lightplanes, which he has used to span oceans and continents. He continues to investigate and report to the aviation community various aspects of proficiency and safety, and remains a vigorous and outspoken advocate for general aviation.